Effect of Digital and Climate Changes in the Business Models of Companies

Editors

Adam Jabłoński

Institute of Management and Quality, WSB Merito University in Poznan, Poland

and

Marek Jabłoński

Institute of Management and Quality, WSB Merito University in Poznan, Poland

CRC Press
Taylor & Francis Group
Boca Raton London New York

CRC Press is an imprint of the
Taylor & Francis Group, an **informa** business

A SCIENCE PUBLISHERS BOOK

First edition published 2025
by CRC Press
2385 NW Executive Center Drive, Suite 320, Boca Raton FL 33431

and by CRC Press
4 Park Square, Milton Park, Abingdon, Oxon, OX14 4RN

CRC Press is an imprint of Taylor & Francis Group, LLC

Library of Congress Cataloging-in-Publication Data (applied for)

ISBN: 978-1-032-62876-9 (hbk)
ISBN: 978-1-032-62880-6 (pbk)
ISBN: 978-1-032-62878-3 (ebk)

DOI: 10.1201/9781032628783

Typeset in Times New Roman
by Prime Publishing Services

Preface

The mechanisms of the modern economy and the development of society are strongly dependent on external conditions. On the one hand, these external conditions generate a strong potential for opportunities and chances, but on the other hand, they generate a multidimensional stream of threats and risks embedded in the socio-economic ecosystem of many countries both in Europe and beyond. Both opportunities and emerging risks constitute the basis for decision-making by managers in conditions of permanent pressure from limitations and possibilities. The presented dichotomy between various opposing components is today a key area of decision-making processes at both the political, social and economic levels. Only those countries and only those regions and only those enterprises will survive in a comprehensive and systemic way that understand the adequacy of decision-making processes in their organizations and other entities. This should apply to the dimension of threats, opportunities and prospects shaping the image of the socio-economic ecosystem at both the macroeconomic and mesoeconomic levels. It then becomes a factor opening the way to the management of organizations by wise, climate-sensitive and responsible in various dimensions managers creating the principles of modern market leadership.

The aim of the monograph is to present a modern and original approach to the design and implementation of effective and effective solutions ensuring the induction of positive climate change. The monograph present the application of digital business models and strategies combining solutions of digital and climate transformation. Digital solutions changing the functioning of technical organizations in environment of many crises will be presented. Applied technological management supported by elements of automation and robotics will shape the emergence of new climate services. The described mechanisms for implementing cybersecurity and safety principles will serve to reduce climate threats.

Key topics discussed in the monograph:

- A specific and innovative approach to digital and climate transformation solutions,
- Presentation of unique digital business models and strategies based on new economies,
- The use of technological management of enterprises that change the logic of operation in order to have a positive impact on climate change,
- Linking innovative solutions with the creation of new services for the climate,

- Creating new technical enterprises based on digital solutions to reduce climate risks,
- Presentation of the practical implications of the use of modern solutions of the nature technological and social for inducing positive climate change.

These topics are particularly important from the perspective of today's dynamic changes at both the economic and social levels caused by a number of climate threats manifesting themselves in various dysfunctions of the ecosystem of realized human and economic existence. Issues related to climate change should be solved at the level of logic, methodology and conceptual framework adequate for science. Due to the fact that the problem of climate change is interdisciplinary in nature, the power of the scientific message related to it should be embedded in this interdisciplinarity. The chapters of the smaller monograph are selected and constructed in such a way as to demonstrate this particular interdisciplinarity of the currently key strategic problem, which generates a whole series of crises at both the local, regional and global levels.

We invite you to familiarize yourself with our monograph.

Adam Jabłoński and Marek Jabłoński

Contents

Chapter 1

Digital and Climate Changes on the Business Models of Companies

*Adam Jabłoński** and *Marek Jabłoński*

Introduction

The dynamic climate change observed every day in the reality of the modern world requires appropriate responses from various decision-making groups that affect society, economy and business. The complexity of these changes and the degree of threats they generate strongly affects all aspects of human existence. From this perspective of the perception of the world, management mechanisms adopted in the management of countries and other entities forming the entire socio-economic system of the world are at the forefront. In addition, growing and overlapping streams of various types of crises create strategic behaviours of decision-makers in political, social and economic terms. The environment of numerous crises is currently an ecosystem which is very difficult to manage, determined, for example, by social, health, military, political, migration and economic crises. It is exacerbated by the climate crisis, which is increasingly being understood by the societies of different regions of the world (Swart et al., 2021). The climate crisis is the result of a sequence and series of actions affecting the natural ecosystem directly caused by man (Snihur and Bocken, 2022). It is related to the lack of proper renunciation of factors created by man which also strongly affect the climate. It also results from natural and climatic factors and anomalies that man has no influence on, such as earthquakes, volcanic eruptions, etc. The sum of these effects resulting from the above-mentioned causes is vast and highly visible in various fields of human life around the globe. Hence, the growing awareness and social sensitivity turn into a new dimension of perception of this strategic problem for the whole world. The dynamic management

WSB Merito University in Poznań.
Email: marek.jablonski@ottima-plus.com.pl, OCRID: 0000-0001-7964-6522
* Corresponding author: adam.jablonski@ottima-plus.com.pl, OCRID: 0000-0003-4008-941X

of climate change has become a reality. Entrepreneurs and managers of various types of organisations have a significant impact on this management. At the same time, the COVID-19 health crisis of recent years, which led to a whole range of restrictions, has decisively triggered an accelerated digital transformation of the economy and society in all areas of human activity. As a result, the principles and mechanisms of the climate and digital transformation adopted systematically are of the greatest importance and have the greatest impact on the entire human population. They are implemented systematically by companies by means of the key ontological entities of organisations, which can include business models, strategies, business processes and projects, which create a kind of strategic hybrid of organisations of various types. The key in this strategic hybrid is business models that materialise through the value proposition offered to the customer, which he is ready to pay for, and the appropriate income generation logic, which ensures the ability of the organisation to survive in the difficult conditions of the current market economy. The aim of this chapter of the monograph is to present the impact of digital and climate change on the business models of companies. The subject of the chapter is to present the place and role of digital and climate change in the design and implementation of effective and efficient business models of companies. The scope of the chapter covers different types of organisations and different types of business models used in various sectors of the economy and business. In the chapter, the author attempts to answer the following questions:

1. What is the impact of digital change on business models?
2. What is the impact of climate change on business models?
3. What is the place and role of technological business models in the current socio-economic ecosystem?
4. What is the place and role of climate-changing business models in the current socio-economic ecosystem?

The answers to these questions are not easy. However, an attempt to answer them can give rise to multidimensional research, which is a platform for solving numerous economic and existential problems embedded in contemporary social, economic and business environments.

Negative versus positive impact of the economy and business on the climate in the space of strategic market changes

Both scientists and business practitioners have different approaches to climate change and have different interpretations thereof (Auer et al., 2021). The key to the dispute is the warming of the climate, whether it actually occurs and what the relationship of human activities to this process is. From the economic and business perspective, however, it is primarily about the effects of climate change resulting in dangerous climate events or even climate catastrophes caused by human intervention in the natural environment and those which are completely uncontrollable, such as earthquakes, volcanic eruptions, etc. This has a direct impact on society, the economy and business. To reduce this, different stakeholder groups need to understand these issues, including in particular policy-makers and entrepreneurs who have an impact on different aspects of the functioning of the world in global and local terms; different formulas and ways of climate value creation can be generated by politicians and businesses in an environment of ever-increasing climate crisis (Swim and Nathaniel Geiger, 2021). For climate-conscious and climate-sensitive entrepreneurs, an important market opportunity and space for dynamic development is emerging (Hewitt and Stone, 2021). Hence, understanding this business gap from the perspective of the lack of response of many companies to climate change is undoubtedly a strong factor which stimulates the development and growth of the organisation in both the short and long term. Climate change must therefore now be regarded as a market opportunity rather than as a serious threat to the continued existence of businesses on the market. This can be done using the concept of business models, where different types of business models can create different climate services which are suitable for different business models (Larosaa and Mysiak, 2020). It is also worth noting that this issue concerns both the public and private sectors, which have a strong impact on the creation of business models that affect the climate. This interpretive embedding of the subject opens the way for thought processes that change the logic of the value chain by reversing it. Instead of the classic linear value chain, which generates, in addition to the products and services created, the emission of negative substances into water, soil, air and waste and consumes natural resources, a circular value chain is created, creating a so-called ecological and/or climate loop that closes these emissions in its own circulation. This generates dynamic technological, organisational and management changes towards creating opportunities for a positive impact on the environment and climate change by also creating new climate products and services (Wang, 2021). It is important to search for such tools and solutions, including digital ones, and in industrial conditions additionally built in automation and robotics, that will reverse the logic of technological processes, for example those carried out without the so-called carbon footprint (Cavalcanti Sa de Abreu et al., 2021). What is important here is net zero strategies, which means a state in which the greenhouse gas emissions generated by an entity (e.g., a company, a country) are offset by actions aiming to reduce or remove them, which leads to a net-zero balance of emissions. A factor supporting such a situation in the economy is the development of detailed quality criteria for emerging new climate services implemented by means of newly created business models positively affecting climate change, which contain new components in the canvases of these business models with a consistent configuration. This is when it can strongly strengthen business resilience and provide an incentive for companies to respond quickly and appropriately to climate change.

A strong reinforcement of such activities will certainly be the so-called ESG reporting implemented by various types of organisations, based on the assumptions of social, ecological and climate transformation and the development of rules for standardisation of climate services and their core attributes (Comyns, 2018). In addition, it becomes crucial to emphasise the place and role of public, government and local government administration in creating climate services.

The impact of digital change on the business models of companies

The strength of today's economy, business and society is conditioned by the technological and digital potential. The competitive advantage of the market depends on a great number of aspects and factors, including climate factors which are the attributes of the competitiveness of companies. Most of these attributes are embedded in the logic of technological management. Currently, technology solutions generate decision-making streams, including at the level of corporate governance (Albitar et al., 2023), and are a platform for creating new market services and products (Jiang and Li, 2020). The growing influence of technology on management mechanisms, including climate technologies, leads to the emergence of new paradigms in management. Businesses are now on the edge of two worlds, namely digital and analogue (Baccarani et al., 2021). These worlds are constantly intertwined, creating either a coherent system of market communication or two alternative worlds of doing business. Both of these solutions are dynamically changing the rules of the game and market competition. This applies in principle to all areas of the organisation's operation, resulting in a complete transformation not only of organisational and management principles, but also of the perception of the company and its core components and functions. In such a space of thought, the question of the impact of digital changes on business models of companies, which are the core ontological entity determining the company's victory or failure on the market, arises. While searching for an answer to this question, it is worth noting that currently a digital enterprise can be reduced to an interactive digital platform embedded in the Internet and which offers a new unique, innovative digital value proposition for Internet users, who become Netizens.

It can also be a highly computerised industrial enterprise, most of whose organisational, management, operational and technological processes are conducted by means of adopted digital solutions. They can also be enterprises of various types whose key products and/or services are digital.

Impact of climate change on the business models of companies

Climate change, which is visible everywhere, shapes the dimension of the modern economy and business. In principle, they affect most of the components of the management of various types of organisations. Dynamic but unfortunately negative climate change in a way forced society as a whole to implement new principles of climate transformation, which can be called "climate pupation" of the entire existing ecosystem in which the human population operates. The climate transformation perceived and understood in this way basically becomes a platform for continuous strategic change (Paul et al., 2017). This change involves de facto all actors around the world who understand the seriousness of this very negative phenomenon. Hence, some strategic reflection, some kind of business empathy and understanding of the impact of current economic and social processes on future generations is required of entrepreneurs and business managers. This can only materialise through managerial decisions, which may result in limiting the adverse impact of various types of organisations on the climate in our natural ecosystem. It may also include the creation of such organisational, management and technological solutions that reverse the negative spiral towards the creation of climate-positive products, services and technologies. In such a space of thought, the question of the impact of digital changes on the business models of companies, which are the core ontological entity determining the company's victory or failure on the market, arises. This impact can be direct and indirect. The direct impact may be related to the generation of climate values embedded in the final product or service of the organisation, while the indirect impact may be related to any type of factors supporting the organisation towards the generation of a positive environmental or climate impact.

Innovative sustainable business models as a source of creation of new types of business models

The decision-making processes of managers of various types of organisations in the context of climate change and an understanding thereof always contain a risk of erroneous thought processes (Bleda and Shackley, 2007). Every organisational and management decision can generate both negative and positive effects. Managers are expected to maintain so-called healthy judgement resulting, inter alia, from rationality and the containment of excessive emotionality. It is important that managers maintain the so-called dynamic balance at the level of people and business management (Arslan, 2021). This can be achieved through the systemic design and implementation of sustainable business models supported by innovative solutions at organisation and technology levels (Bashira at al., 2022). Sustainable business models are built on the principle of constructive confrontation of different types of resources, different types of components of this business model and different attributes of this specific business model. At the resource level, this concerns the relationship between tangible and intangible resources. At the level of business model components, this applies, inter alia, to the relationship between cost and sales components of the business model. At the level of the attributes of the business model, this concerns, inter alia, the relationships between business model scalability and consistency. In this thinking space, innovation becomes an important accelerator for managers to achieve high efficiency and reliability of companies which use these business models.

Technological and digital business models in the current socio-economic ecosystem

Business models, in the logic of the concept of strategic management of enterprises, are crucial and currently play a fundamental role therein. This role is expressed in the ability to succeed on the market, the ability to survive in the most difficult socio-economic conditions, to build a sustainable competitive advantage and to create the long-term value of the organisation. This is done by converting payments into profits, which generates a value proposition or stream of value propositions acceptable to customers. This is also achieved by adopting an economically justifiable income generation logic for an organisation with this business model.

In the current business reality, the core components of such business models are technological components, the advantage of which empowers companies to call them technological business models. If technological components are mainly digital solutions, such business models can be called digital business models. Technology, including digital technology, is significantly changing the focus in the decision-making processes of managers, including in the area of so-called micro-decisions and micro-objectives, which consequently affect the total existential state of many types of organisations. Technology embedded in the business model may refer to the cost and sales components of the business model built into its canvas and income generation logic (as well as through the allocation of business in the analogue and virtual space). This also includes a value proposition for the customer in both the areas of products and services created by the company. Technology then takes on a new context and a new interpretation of the organisation focused on the overall shape of the current business and economy.

Climate-changing business models in the current socio-economic ecosystem

The creation of new types of business models is a natural consequence of changes in society and the economy as a match or adjustment to the current status of these changes. Due to the fact that a number of current changes which companies must respond to are climate changes, they create business models suitable to these changes. They can be referred to differently, e.g., climate business models or climate-changing or climate-influencing business models. Regardless of the adopted linguistic semantics, in the case of business models, their effectiveness and efficiency are important.

These business models can therefore also generate climate change in this sense, in addition to effectiveness and economic efficiency supported by social efficiency and effectiveness. Then a new triangle of values is created, specific to today's times and needs. The climate value generated at that time will be the distinguishing and defining factor of the new type of business models that have emerged (Rosenstock et al., 2020). What will then be the core added value for business, the economy and society? This will be climate added value reducing climate risks at global and local levels, mainly by extrapolating the adopted climate solutions in various places and locations of the global existential space (Demertzidis et al., 2015). An example is the use of artificial intelligence in forecasting climate change in different parts of the world by means of secondary historical data on pre-existing threats and climate catastrophes (e.g., the solution of the so-called Climate Digital Twin).

Strategic recommendations for creating business models in the space of digital and climate transformation

While conducting a synthetic analysis of the presented scientific discussion, it is crucial to develop strategic recommendations that are the result of a multidimensional look at the logic, methodology and conceptual framework necessary to understand the new dimension of the economy built in a way adequate to the ongoing climate changes which generate new threats and limitations, but also potential market opportunities opening a new dimension of innovative social and technological space.

The following is a list of strategic recommendations for creating new business models in the dynamic space of digital and climate transformation.

1. A systemic and innovative approach to solutions in the field of digital and climate transformation at the level of companies and the economy guarantees a constructive confrontation of factors generating new climate products and services for society, business and the economy.
2. The creation of unique digital business models and strategies based on a positive impact on climate change is a particular challenge for climate-conscious and climate-sensitive entrepreneurs.
3. The use of artificial intelligence for the technological management of companies which change the logic of action is an important area of current management at the strategic and tactical–operational levels to positively influence climate change (Galaz et al., 2021).
4. Linking the solutions of new economies with the creation of new services for the climate (the Circular Economy (Bocken and Konietzko, 2022), the Sharing Economy, the Big Data Economy (Papadopoulos and Balta, 2022), the Internet of Things Economy (IoT) and the Artificial Intelligence Economy) is a key challenge for modern managers.
5. The creation of new technical enterprises based on digital solutions and innovations in automation and robotics to reduce climate risks is a new goal and challenge for the development of Industry 4.0 and 5.0.
6. Exploiting the potential of digital transformation as a new dimension of shaping the reality of business and the economy is an important challenge for politicians at the state and local government levels and competent entrepreneurs open to change.
7. Exploiting the potential of climate transformation as a new dimension of shaping the reality of business and the economy and a new path to dynamic processes of socio-economic transformation is a challenge for the climate education of society.
8. The use of artificial intelligence for the development of modern business and social ecosystems is a core opportunity which generates a new context and dimension of climate entrepreneurship.
9. The development of virtual reality as an accelerator for creating new business models and strategies is a space for positive climate business.
10. The development of automation and robotics in the processes of shaping the virtual reality of companies is a way to change the strategic thinking of various types of decision-makers on climate and technological change.
11. The development of digital business models and strategies for creating a positive impact on the natural environment is a new perspective for increasing the value of companies.

12. The development of digital platforms based on algorithms and the Big Data environment as tools for creating new climate services may generate new jobs and thus accelerate changes in labour markets.
13. The creation of progressive Rochlin business models (Rochlin, 2021) using regulatory mechanisms in business and the economy is a new approach for building consensus between business, the economy and society.
14. Changing linear business models of companies to circular ones by means of the mechanisms of green scalability of business is a crucial factor in building an inverted spiral in value chains.
15. The creation of new climate services through different types of digital and technological innovation is a way to reverse the negative polarisation in the area of climate change.
16. Ensuring technological and energy security and cybersecurity of various types of organisations by means of digital business models to achieve regional energy independence, including by means of artificial intelligence (Entezari et al., 2023), is a tool to enhance the security of individual countries.
17. The development of renewable energy sources (Zhang et al., 2022) as an untapped form of potential in business and the economy may constitute a new system for the development of market competences in the modern labour market.
18. The development of energy innovation clusters and their network effect on the development of business and the economy that positively influences climate change is the way to energy independence for various regions of the world.
19. The creation of new values based on assumptions resulting from the climate responsibility of business and society provides a platform for creating a new stream of technologies positively affecting the climate.
20. The creation of practical implications of the use of modern technological and social solutions to induce positive climate change is a key challenge for various areas of management, at the level of both countries and various types of organisations.

Conclusion

The permanent verification and undermining of the existing status of business reality is an important role of every conscious and competent manager. Understanding the state of the economy, business and society in a way appropriate to its functioning requires good market and human observation and intrinsic climate threats. Hence, climate-changing business models supported by digital and technological solutions, which often result in new climate products and services, are today a strategic challenge for modern entrepreneurs and policy makers at the level of individual countries as well as specific regions with individual industrial, landscape and natural characteristics. From this perspective, the proper analysis and synthesis of these phenomena by managers can become a platform for the market success of many organisations and the economic, social and climatic value created in this process can be a core potential for the development of countries and regions and their communities.

This understanding is also related to understanding the place and role of climate change in the context of its impact on the economic, social, technological, organisational and management mechanisms of wisely managed organisations. From this perspective and in this space of the market game, a new dimension of the impact of digital and climate change on the business models of companies as a key attribute of strategic management is being created. Such an understanding of the contemporary economic and social times becomes a generator of innovative decision-making processes that create business opportunities. It also creates a set of positive actions to protect society from the adverse impact on various aspects of human life.

References

Albitar, K., Al-Shaer, H. and Liu, J. L. 2023. *Corporate commitment to climate change: The effect of eco-innovation and climate governance*. Research Policy 52: 104697, https://doi.org/10.1016/j.respol.2022.104697 (accessed 01.07.2024).

Arslan, A., Haapanen, L., Hurmelinna-Laukkanen, P., Tarba, S. Y., and Alon, I. 2021. *Climate change, consumer lifestyles and legitimation strategies of sustainability-oriented firms*. European Management Journal 39: 720–730, https://doi.org/10.1016/j.emj.2021.03.005 (accessed 01.07.2024).

Auer, C., Kriegler, E., Carlsen, H., Kok, K., Pedde, S., Krey, V. et al. 2021. *Climate change scenario services: From science to facilitating action*. One Earth 4, August 20, https://doi.org/10.1016/j.oneear.2021.07.015 (accessed 01.07.2024).

Baccarani, C., Brunetti, F. and Martin, J. 2021. *Climate change and organizational management: Toward a new paradigm*. The TQM Journal 33(3): 640–661, DOI 10.1108/TQM-05-2020-0094.

Bashira, M., Alfalih, A. and Pradhan, S. 2022. *Sustainable business model innovation: Scale development, validation and proof of performance*. Journal of Innovation & Knowledge 7: 100243, https://doi.org/10.1016/j.jik.2022.100243 (accessed 01.07.2024).

Bleda, M. and Shackley, S. 2008. *The dynamics of belief in climate change and its risks in business organisations*. Ecological Economics 517–532, doi:10.1016/j.ecolecon.2007.10.021.

Bocken, N. and Konietzko, J. 2022. *Circular business model innovation in consumer-facing corporations*. Technological Forecasting & Social Change 185: 122076, https://doi.org/10.1016/j.techfore.2022.122076 (accessed 02.07.2024).

Comyns, B. 2018. *Climate change reporting and multinational companies: Insights from institutional theory and international business*. Accounting Forum 42: 65–77, http://dx.doi.org/10.1016/j.accfor.2017.07.003 (accessed 01.07.2024).

De Abreu, M., Webb, K., Araújo, F. S. and Cavalcante, J. P. L. 2021. *From "business as usual" to tackling climate change: Exploring factors affecting low-carbon decision-making in the canadian oil and gas sector*. Energy Policy 148: 111932, https://doi.org/10.1016/j.enpol.2020.111932 (accessed 01.07.2024).

Demertzidis, N., Tsalis, T. A., Loupa, G. and Nikolaou, I. E. 2015. *A benchmarking framework to evaluate business climate change risks: A practical tool suitable for investors decision-making process*. Climate Risk Management 10(2015): 95–105, http://dx.doi.org/10.1016/j.crm.2015.09.002 (accessed 01.07.2024).

Entezari, A., Aslani, A., Zahedi, R. and Noorollahi, Y. 2023. *Artificial intelligence and machine learning in energy systems: A bibliographic perspective*. Energy Strategy Reviews 45: 101017, https://doi.org/10.1016/j.esr.2022.101017 (accessed 02.07.2024).

Galaz, V., Centeno, M. A., Callahan, P. W., Causevic, A., Patterson, T., Brass, I. et al. 2021. *Artificial intelligence, systemic risks, and sustainability*. Technology in Society 67: 101741, https://doi.org/10.1016/j.techsoc.2021.101741 (accessed 01.07.2024).

Hewitt, C. D. and Stone, R. 2021. *Climate services for managing societal risks and opportunities*. Climate Services 23: 100240, https://doi.org/10.1016/j.cliser.2021.100240 (accessed 01.07.2024).

Jiang, S. and Li, J. 2020. *Global climate governance in the new era: Potential of business actors and technological innovation*. Chinese Journal of Population, Resources and Environment 18: 165–171, https://doi.org/10.1016/j.cjpre.2021.04.023 (accessed 01.07.2024).

Larosaa, F. and Mysiak, J. 2020. *Business models for climate services: An analysis*. Climate Services 17: 100111, https://doi.org/10.1016/j.cliser.2019.100111(accessed 01.07.2024).

Papadopoulos, T. and Balta, M. E. 2022. *Climate Change and big data analytics: Challenges and opportunities*. International Journal of Information Management 63: 102448, https://doi.org/10.1016/j.ijinfomgt.2021.102448 (accessed 02.07.2024).

Paul, A., Lang, J. W. B. and Baumgartner, R. J. 2017. *A multilevel approach for assessing business strategies on climate change*. Journal of Cleaner Production 160(2017): 50–70, http://dx.doi.org/10.1016/j.jclepro.2017.04.030 (accessed 01.07.2024).

Rochlin, C. 2021. *Climate change and the progressive business model*. The Electricity Journal 34(2021): 106927, https://doi.org/10.1016/j.tej.2021.106927 (accessed 02.07.2024).

Rosenstock, T. S., Lubberink, R., Gondwe, S., Manyise, T. and Dentoni, D. 2020. *Inclusive and adaptive business models for climatesmart value creation*. Current Opinion in Environmental Sustainability 42: 76–81, https://doi.org/10.1016/j.cosust.2019.12.005 (accessed 01.07.2024).

Snihur, Y. and Bocken, N. 2022. *A call for action: The impact of business model innovation on business ecosystems, society and planet*. Long Range Planning 55: 102182, https://doi.org/10.1016/j.lrp.2022.102182 (accessed 01.07.2024).

Swart, R., Celliers, L., Collard, M., Garcia Prats, A., Huang-Lachman, J., Llario Sempere, F. et al. 2021. *Reframing climate services to support municipal and regional planning*. Climate Services 22: 100227, https://doi.org/10.1016/j.cliser.2021.100227 (accessed 01.07.2024).

Swim, J. K. and Geiger, N. 2021. *Policy attributes, perceived impacts, and climate change policy preferences*. Journal of Environmental Psychology 77: 101673, https://doi.org/10.1016/j.jenvp.2021.101673 (accessed 01.07.2024).

Wang, C. 2021. *The role of technological innovation in global climate policy*. Research in Globalization 3: 100066, https://doi.org/10.1016/j.resglo.2021.100066 (accessed 01.07.2024).

Zhang, L., Ling, J. and Lin, M. 2022. *Artificial intelligence in renewable energy: A comprehensive bibliometric analysis*. Energy Reports 8: 14072–14088, https://doi.org/10.1016/j.egyr.2022.10.347 (accessed 02.07.2024).

Chapter 2

Socio-technical Systems in the Design of Dynamic and Community-based Business Models

Marek Jabłoński

Introduction

The modern economy is based on digital transformation solutions. Business models based on digital platform solutions are being developed and improved. The technological structure and organisation of these models in terms of a process is based on the assumptions of socio-technical systems, such as those where core elements such as technology, i.e., equipment, machines, devices and buildings, as well as social elements, i.e., people, interpersonal relations and their actions (such as goals, values, formal rules and structures), create a coherent dynamic organism, which, supported by mobile communication tools, creates new added value for customers–users. This new space for business creation provides opportunities to connect people focused on similar needs, desires and values. Communities are being built that can communicate with each other, suppliers, intermediaries and service recipients, creating an exchange of goods and services to the mutual satisfaction of all contracting parties. From a technical point of view, it is crucial to combine human relations with device interfaces, ensuring dynamic contact between machines and humans to create added value for the latter. Elements of socio-technical systems and their interfaces ensure the possibility of grouping communities of users. Then business success is measured not only by the profit achieved, but in particular by the number of communities focused around the business solution. These communities guarantee the monetisation of business and the sustainability and stability of business models designed and focused on the needs of these communities. Such a digital business, supported by the number of supporters of such solutions, creates conditions

WSB Merito University in Poznań.
Email: marek.jablonski@ottima-plus.com.pl, OCRID: 0000-0001-7964-6522

for capturing value from the market and building competitive advantages against competitors. The advantage is the number of users and the investment attractiveness of the business model. The more it attracts stakeholders willing to spend money to get the value it proposes to them, the more effective and efficient the business model is. The condition for such a complete success of the solution is the high technical reliability of technical systems using complex algorithms and software, and the ability of the business model to satisfactorily service all people interested in the use of a given business solution.

The aim of this chapter of the monograph is to identify core determinants responsible for shaping dynamic and community-based business models of companies through socio-technical systems.

The subject of the chapter concerns the presentation of the place and role of socio-technical systems as elements that build dynamic social business models.

In the chapter, the author makes an attempt to answer the following questions:

1. What theoretical aspects of socio-technical systems are crucial to designing digital business models based on social platforms?
2. How can one manage large groups of users in technical and organisational terms to ensure the success of companies?
3. How can one create strategies to dynamise and strengthen business models through the effective and efficient management of relationships with business communities?
4. What aspects of technical systems are relevant to the development of business models based on social platforms?

Theoretical aspects of defining socio-technical systems

Socio-technical systems play a crucial role in understanding the assumptions of modern business based on digital transformation processes. They are dynamic and adaptive systems that resist human interaction with other tools, techniques and knowledge necessary to produce innovative and valuable products and services. They are based on interdisciplinarity, including management processes, social sciences, and social behaviour in these processes of organisation development, and all this in relation to complex and complicated systems. The key is interactions between people and technologies, especially the application of science using IT and engineering solutions. The socio-technical system unambiguously describes complex systems based on technological platforms, where simple and dynamic cybernetic feedback occurs that creates dynamic relationships between all sides of the value chain or value loop (Di Maio, 2014, p. 275).

As regards a full understanding of the relationships between technical and social systems from a comparative perspective, the following attributes of these systems can be demonstrated on the basis of research by G. Fisher and his team. The core features of technical systems include the following: in technical systems, products are produced with the participation of a controlling human role. They are designed by means of control systems, taking into account the expected outcome parameters. In addition, these systems rely on the learning of programmes through integration into the environment where they work. In terms of change management, simulation systems are used to improve and change technical systems, which as a result may affect new revisions and modernisation of the configuration and functionality of these systems. These systems should be characterised by avoiding hazard errors, risks and unexpected events that may affect the reliability of these systems, also taking into account their ageing. They should be subject to a periodic assessment of the maturity of suitability for current technical solutions in terms of progress in the development of modern IT solutions. They should be programmed from the perspective of customer expectations and create conditions for achieving the maximum possible solutions in terms of knowledge and technology that meet the highest standards and trends in technical progress. In the case of social systems and taking into account their connection with technical systems, the following attributes can be distinguished. They are the result of an evolution that is crucial to the impact on the social environment. It is essential to build the potential of social impact on the internal and external business environment. It is based on the analysis of human behaviour in normal and critical situations. The key to understanding social systems is to understand small emerging changes, often based on anticipating community behaviour. For this, systems of simulation and identification of changes of large social groups are necessary. Often, a great number of scenarios that occur are based on the randomness and irrationality of societies; therefore, great uncertainty and risk occur in social systems that should be analysed. Individual interests can lead to the goals of large social groups, which may not be achieved or, in a sense, minimised, so it is necessary to constantly monitor social behaviour and adapt it to the proposed business solutions. The development of evolution in this situation will take place through the improvement of communication between people and technical systems as well as the creation of effective and efficient interfaces (Fisher and Herrmann, 2011, p. 5). The complexity of socio-technical systems is characterised by the following elements: uncertainty, access to information, diversity, connection with other elements, the number of elements included in the system, dynamics, and disorder. The elements prove the full complexity of technical systems, taking into account the assumptions of systems theory. In the case of social systems, psychological aspects such as subjectivity, the attributes of the social system, specific ordinary and extraordinary situations, social connections, interpersonal relations, attitude and an understanding of the system are also significant (Schöttl and Lindemann, 2015, p. 3). Such links between technical, social and psychological aspects create a completely new understanding of business, of creating new solutions and designing business models. It is essential to understand these conditions to create business solutions characterised by novelty, freshness and attractiveness.

Principles for designing dynamic, community-based business models

The design of complex technical systems requires shaping the creation processes oriented towards creating such a business model that will have the ability to gather large communities of people around them as a basic functionality. Internet communities shape the knowledge of the crowd that in today's world allows for the detection of the new needs of large social groups which ensure the monetisation of digital business models. The dynamics of such a solution are based on the designers' awareness of the fact that the management of large social groups requires a different approach to the relationship between the capabilities of machines and the behaviour of people who are customers and users of the designed systems. The key in this respect is to build the knowledge of the crowd, which behaves as a single customer, but the scale of the effects of these behaviours is crucial to creating the effect of business scale. The interfaces between machines and people implemented by means of complex technological solutions using mobile devices are essential. In this way, links are built between users and the solution of the digital platform. If the new platform, in addition to its basic functionalities, ensures the ideological character of the delivered value for the customer (focus on climate protection, civil rights, human rights, respect, waste reduction, building good interpersonal relationships, environmental protection, awareness of social impact and building trust), the design of digital business models based on social platforms aims not only to make money, but in particular to use the socio-technical system to carry out a mission acceptable to the general conscious society. Social capital built through appropriately designed algorithms which fulfil the need to create and deliver a new value proposition for the user community therefore plays a crucial role. Such design of digital business models is therefore different from the previous approach, where the key goal was to create a solution that maximised profit for the company. In this situation, profit is also essential, but the condition for achieving it is to create social value and social impact expected by a wide range of stakeholders. In this way, managers who design business systems should use the paradigms of sociology because they explain the behaviour of large social groups who are recipients of the delivered business value. One of the solutions used in the process of designing products based on large communities is projects based on open-source software. This approach is based on the creation of solutions by volunteers who together want to achieve a common goal. In this way, unconventional solutions are based on the interdisciplinarity and knowledge of people with very different points of view, and a model of designing business models and IT software that fulfils unique functions is created, because their ingenuity is based on the work of large teams of people. Thus, community building can refer to project teams who are on one side and large social groups who are users and customers. The exchange of knowledge between them creates economies of scale and mutual exchanges of experience that enable solutions to better meet the expectations of the markets. The business model, as a set of tangible and intangible factors put into motion by means of strategies aimed at building complex relationships between communities, is of a large-scale nature, allowing for the achievement of a critical mass of supporters of the offered value proposition, which is interesting not only for individual customers, but for the masses as well. This approach requires the use of modern forms of designing business models of the potential of the network of interface relationships between devices as part of a coherent uniform idea that is clear and understandable to the recipient. Socio-technical systems based on the role of people and the machines cooperating with them, by creating uniform organisational and technical systems, offer vast potential for creating innovative solutions in the business sphere.

The conceptualisation and operationalisation of the use of socio-technical systems to build a community of users of digital platforms

The conceptualisation and operationalisation of the use of the socio-technical system to build a community of users of digital platforms is not an easy task. It covers both the technological aspects, as the selection of technology and an IT solution which supports the design process are crucial in this area, as well as an understanding of the sociological aspects of human behaviour, especially in the era of digital economy processes of digital transformation and predicted public perception. Not all proposed business solutions become a success; quite the contrary, most of them fail. Therefore, an understanding of the consistency between technical and social aspects is crucial, especially in terms of the rules of operation of digital platforms, where we usually deal with the platform organiser (intermediary) and recipients who use the application. The service provider can be, for example, drivers (Uber) or flat owners (Airbnb) or any other service provider. By creating applications, the intermediary connects both parties to the contract by means of a digital platform, ensuring the ability to settle the service, as well as regulating the rules of service delivery and monitoring the quality and compliance of settlements. Therefore, the business model includes not only a simple value chain, but ensures contact between the parties, associating them and creating new forms of value delivery. The increasing complexity of socio-technical systems makes ensuring their long-term success dependent on the developed model of ensuring business but also technical resilience related, for example, to cybersecurity, technical security and personal protection. Socio-technical systems are crucial in decision-making and support processes. This is because the complexity and completeness of the information provided online allows managers to react quickly in the event of disruptions which affect irregularities in the service provision process. Socio-technical systems are characterised by key parameters that can relate to the security of systems as well as the ability to change them. System parameters as part of security include the number of system-building elements (processes and resources), the variety of elements shaping the system, the level of links between elements, the number of interfaces with neighbouring systems which systems interact with, and the types and variety of interfaces between neighbouring systems. Changes in the number of elements, their diversity, the level of links, the number of interfaces, the diversity of interfaces, as well as the number of elements (processes and resources) will be crucial for socio-technical system changes (Schöttl and Lindemann, 2015, p. 3). It should be noted that the concept of a socio-technical system was established in order to highlight the interrelationships between humans and machines and to ensure that programmes for the development of both technical and social working conditions are supported. The concept of the system was used very consciously using the general systems theory. The idea of socio-technical systems was designed to deal with theoretical and application problems (Ropohl, 1999, p. 59). Therefore, the best solution for providing an effective and efficient solution based on social platforms was to use the assumptions of systems theory as well as socio-technical systems. Both of these areas of science fully satisfy the ability to design such complex systems. It is impossible not to mention that an important concept that links these two concepts is the network theory due to the distributed nature of the resources of places of service provision and the multidimensional system of links of remote locations. It should be noted that in the era of the Internet and universal access to mobile devices, the network nature of connections fits into the assumptions of general systems theory. A network, as a system which combines technical devices with the support of communication systems, makes the distances between objects, resources and the places of process implementation and where people are unimportant. Therefore, socio-technical systems have found widespread use in the design and construction of community-oriented digital platforms. In this way, a new formula for designing digital business models based on the solution of digital platforms was created.

Innovative models of digital platforms as a source of the creation of new types of technological business models—complex human–machine interactions

Business models of digital platforms operate in business ecosystems, which are based on the assumptions of socio-technical systems. They connect parties to the contract through a technological solution and the widespread availability of mobile devices. Digital solution manufacturers ensure that the two parties to a contract can connect and use each other's potential. The key is to create conditions for financial settlements and rules for providing logistics services, ensuring the quality of services provided, as well as providing insurance. The final consumer receives the expected service and support from the service organiser. At the same time, the digital platform provides the operation of management processes that support the development of the business environment, data analysis and data management. Support for these processes is found in various technological solutions such as the Internet of Things, sensors, external websites and financial services (Zutshi et al., 2019). Figure 1 shows the detailed scope of the ecosystem of digital platforms on the basis of which innovative business models are shaped.

In business practice, numerous examples of the practical application of business models based on communities that use the assumptions of systems theory, such as socio-technical systems, which also fit into the network paradigm, can be found. These include solutions such as digital platforms described in the context of digital maturity, namely:

1. In the area of music—CD/Audi cassettes, iTunes for buying music online, Spotify subscription model.
2. Movies—VCT/DVD, Netflix subscription model.
3. Advertisements—New Papers, Yellow Pages, online classifieds.
4. Finance—Cash, Visa/Mastercard, PayPal, Cryptocurrencies.
5. Shopping for products—physical stores, online shopping—e.g., Amazon, Astroprint 3D printing (Zutshi et al., 2019, p. 4).

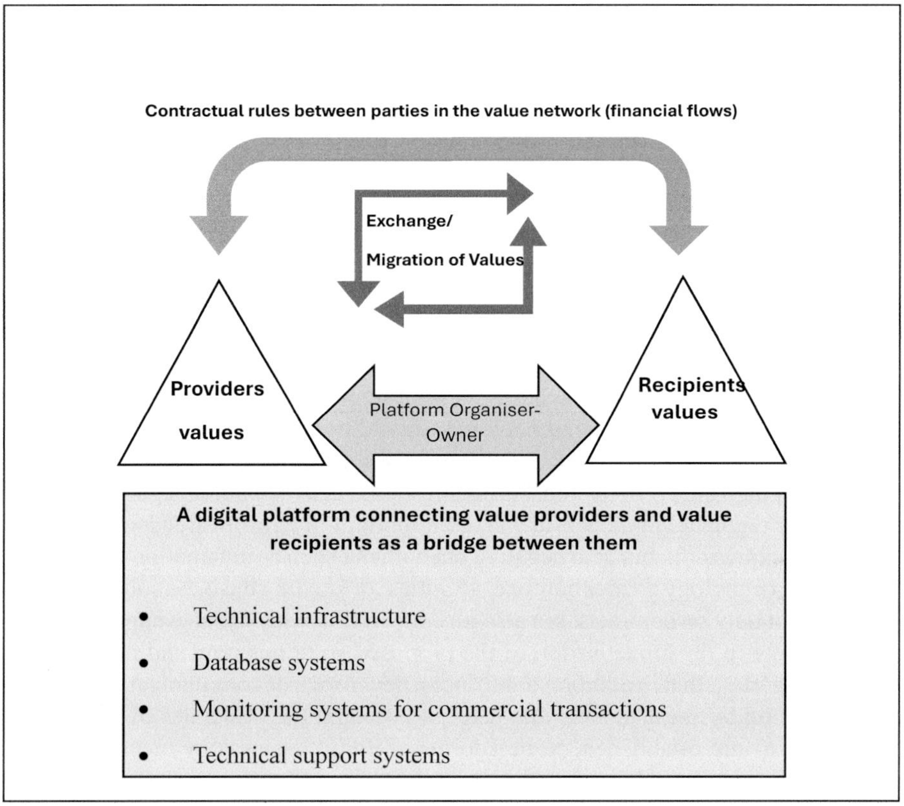

Fig. 1. Core parties of a digital business model based on large human communities. Source: own study.

The presented examples are only a fragment of big business and concern the development of digital platforms gathering large volumes of users. The creation of such solutions along with the growth of technology is based on the assumptions of the socio-technical system, where these solutions have found fertile ground related to the functionality of this solution. Socio-technical systems continue to grow strongly and include not only digital platforms but, in particular, complex systems derived from industry. An example of such an industry is the rail transport sector, the industrial ecosystem of which fully meets the definitions of a socio-technical system. Railway workers operate a highly complex technical system and aim to ensure its operational readiness, reliability and safety. There are many human–machine, human–human, and machine–machine interfaces and services involving passengers take place set against this background. The purpose of the system is to ensure that all links of this complex system are supervised and that no link is disturbed. From a theoretical perspective, there is a crucial need to develop knowledge in this area and to search for new forms of identification of features, attributes, advantages, and disadvantages of core problems that require explanation.

Building knowledge—building communities as the competitive potential of business models

A key aspect for identifying and explaining social groups interested in the participation of digital economy communities is understanding their identities as well as identifying specific demographic groups. This applies not only to age, so-called generations, but also to specific features that can be considered important in terms of marketing activities aimed at presenting the expected value propositions for customers. Such criteria for identifying a community can therefore be age, race, social affiliation, religious affiliation, place of residence, social status and the like. Marketing specialists have a crucial task in this respect to select value propositions for customers so that they reach the right social groups. At the same time, they build communities of supporters of the business solution who will be loyal ambassadors of these solutions. Therefore, social networks should be differently perceived through the prism of identity in the network, creating groups tailored to the specific needs arising from the value proposition. Attention should also be paid to legal aspects that are not fully regulated in the world and are important in terms of freedom of speech, the right of expression, but also negative phenomena such as defamation and slander. In this way, technology creates new opportunities for creating business solutions. They are based not only on contracts, but also on cooperation with social groups-users who can contribute to the monetisation of the proposed solutions now and in the future. It is also important that in addition to business, new forms of communicating business value based on business models that take into account the principles of shaping the content policy are established. Not all forms of doing business by means of digital platforms have yet been invented; therefore, it is important to support the creation of business models and encourage entrepreneurs to develop such platforms to improve the quality of life, optimise costs, improve accessibility and services and develop a democratic society. It is important to create such business models that contribute to improving the quality of life of people, creating positive climate change, improving the welfare of people and animals, eliminating hunger and enhancing the efficiency and effectiveness of doing business.

Strategic recommendations for the creation of community-based digital platforms in the context of the application of socio-technical systems

The concept of socio-technical systems continues to develop very dynamically. It is particularly important today in the context of the development of artificial intelligence. In this sense, socio-technical systems consist of a combination of three core components, namely technical artifacts, human agents and institutions (rules to be followed by agents) (van de Poel, 2020, p. 391). The perspectives of the concept of risk management are also being developed. Socio-technical systems have enabled the identification of attributes to create a risk management framework that is effective for complex socio-technical systems. These attributes may include elements such as systemic thinking, a top-down perspective, the application of non-Bayesian approaches, recursive approaches and storytelling (Luther et al., 2023, p. 4).

The socio-technical system is therefore based on an open systems theory, which assumes that an organisation is a human system in a dynamic relationship with it in a specific environment. Organisations can achieve much, including higher performance, by providing internal structures to control discrepancies in technical systems through the principles of sociology (Botla and Kondur, 2018, p.27). Several key conclusions and recommendations can be indicated after the discussion of the topic related to the creation of business models of companies oriented towards large sets of users based on the assumptions of socio-technical systems. They are as follows:

1. Algorithms and software of socio-technical systems are currently shaping modern forms of business models based on digital platforms.
2. The theory of socio-technical systems meets the challenges of modern needs in the field of electronic business.
3. Human–machine interfaces using mobile devices seem to be the standard in the creation of new business models that change the rules of the market game.
4. The design of socio-technical systems should be based not only on contemporary experience, but in particular on artificial intelligence solutions, digital twins, forecasting, predicting and monitoring new spaces of value creation for users.
5. Technical aspects in management are currently playing a leading role, and what is surprisingly important is the role played by the knowledge of paradigms and sociology.
6. Knowledge of this topic significantly supports current paradigms in the field of quality management science, which at this time seem insufficient and need to be redefined.
7. The combined implementation of technical and sociological knowledge makes it possible to study the phenomena of modern business through the prism of searching for new formulas of business monetisation.
8. Big data sets which monitor large volumes of users and their behaviour are the basis for setting new directions of marketing activities.
9. The full and comprehensive use of technical, managerial and sociological knowledge, including the sociology of the crowd, may result in the creation of space for seeking and finding completely new, innovative and ground-breaking business solutions.

Conclusion

The discussion, analyses and conclusions presented in the chapter highlight the complex nature of the issue of the use of socio-technical systems in the design of business models of digital platforms that use big data sets and are based on large volumes of users. The design of such business models is quite different from the solutions that have been presented so far in the relevant literature. The emphasis on the theoretical aspects of socio-technical systems means that the potential for creating new technological and business solutions should be sought therein. The development of artificial intelligence, building solutions based on big data, paradigms of sociology science and the use of engineering means that contemporary management must be interdisciplinary and draw not only on its subject area, but in particular on technical sciences and sociology. If the creation of economies of scale is a condition for success, the use of sociological methods to study human behaviour, their needs and forecasts of their potential future and current intentions in the field of the use of digital products is a condition for this goal. Most modern startups are not currently focused on searching for individual transactions, but on the scalability effect of the business, and it is only possible if the volume of users exceeds the critical mass value. This is the case when the profitability threshold of a business is based on the assumptions of scalability, i.e. the possibility of expanding (increasing the scale of operation) the system or undertaking. Then, the result of scaling should be development and success consisting of expanding the influence of the organisation. The condition for such a solution is to use the full potential of the theoretical and application aspects of socio-technical systems.

Summary

The chapter addresses key aspects of designing dynamic and community-based business models of companies based on socio-technical systems. Socio-technical systems are crucial in the context of building and creating digital platforms. Digital platforms are based on building large communities of users who expect value propositions that are attractive to them. Designing digital business models is therefore based on the selection of IT technology solutions that will facilitate the exchange of communication and knowledge between all business parties. Large data sets that shape the provision of added value to large groups of users allow for the creation of new business formulas. The chapter presents the determinants of designing digital business models, including explaining the assumptions of the functioning of socio-technical systems. The features of technical elements were demonstrated, but how to approach the creation of a business effect based on large human communities was also indicated. It was pointed out that in management and quality sciences, we should look for paradigms not only in this discipline but also in technical sciences and sociology.

References

Botla, L. and Kondur, H. 2018. *Socio technical systems of a company: The dimensionality of socio technical systems*. Purshartha 11(1); March - August, pp. 27.

Di Maio, P. 2014. *Towards a metamodel to support the joint optimization of socio technical systems*. Systems. 2(3): 273–296; doi:10.3390/systems2030273, p. 275.

Fischer, G. and Herrmann, T. 2011. *Socio-technical systems: A meta-design perspective*. International Journal of Sociotechnology and Knowledge Development 3(1): 1–33, January–March, p. 5.

Luther, B., Gunawan, I. and Nguyen, N. 2023. *Identifying effective risk management frameworks for complex socio-technical systems*. Safety Science 158, Art. 105989, pp. 4.

Ropohl, G. 1999. *Philosophy of socio-technical systems*, PHIL & TECH Vol. 4 Issue 3. Philosophy of Socio-Technical Systems, pp. 59.

Schöttl, F. and Lindemann, U. 2015. *Quantifying the complexity of socio-technical systems – A generic, interdisciplinary approach*. Procedia Computer Science 44: 3.

van de Poel, I. 2020. *Embedding values in Artificial Intelligence (AI) systems*. Minds and Machines 30: 391.

Zutshi, A., Rizvanović, B. and Nodehi, T. 2019. *The evolution of digital platforms*. Computers & Industrial Engineering 136: 4.

Chapter 3

The Concept of the Business Model in Industry 5.0

Analysis Based on the Literature Review

Bożena Gajdzik

Introduction

As technology has progressed, industries around the world have moved between successive stages of industrialisation, which have resulted from the implementation of the technologies of successive industrial revolutions. Technological progress has accelerated significantly in recent decades. A century has passed between Industry 2.0 and Industry 3.0, and only 42 years between Industry 3.0 and Industry 4.0 (calculations based on key inventions of the industrial revolutions). In 2011, as part of the High Tech Strategy, German government policy adopted a development direction called, in German, Industrie 4.0, and in English: Industry 4.0 (abbreviation: I4.0). Technologies such as the Industry Internet of Things (IoT), smart sensors, industrial robots, 3D printers, cloud computing, augmented reality are all part of the current transformation (Kagermann, 2015; Kagermann et al., 2011), even though many of them were embryos in the Third Industrial Revolution, but are now undergoing their boom. Their impact on business development is by no means disputed.

In the ongoing Fourth Industrial Revolution, when it comes to non-hardware technologies such as big data, machine learning or artificial intelligence, factories, each year, are discovering new possibilities for their application in business. Artificial intelligence, supported by autonomous computing systems, is a key industrial innovation. A strong connection between the virtual (IT) and operational (physical) worlds is the key to building cyber-physical systems (CPSs) (Lee, 2015; Lee et al., 2015).

Silesian University of Technology, Gliwice, Poland, Faculty of Materials Engineering, Department of Industrial Informatics.
Email: bozena.gajdzik@polsl.pl, ORCID: 0000-0002-0408-1691

Embedded in cyber-physical systems is the human being, who is not only the operator of the new technologies, but also the user, the teacher and perhaps even the 'buddy'. In each of these situations, man must use the technologies wisely. The human being in the digital transformation taking place remains at the centre of it, and this should not be forgotten (Lorenz et al., 2015; Romero et al., 2016a,b; Romero et al., 2015).

Cooperative cyber-physical systems are changing value chains. M.E. Poter's (1990) previous chain is being transformed into a smart chain, value-oriented, and the value is contained in personalised products, but not only because, according to the concept of socially responsible business, a shared value is pursued, which in global terms is sustainability (Porter and Heppelmann, 2014).

In the net zero strategy, politicians have set the direction of zero carbon emissions by 2050 (COM, 2023). This strategy leaves no white spots on the map of the economies of highly developed countries, so industry, energy, heating, transport, cities, households, etc., must introduce and use zero-emission technologies and participate in energy sharing (grids). In addition to global warming, there are other problems that are enshrined in the 17 Sustainable Development Goals (The 2030 Agenda for Sustainable Development, UN, 2015).

In 2021, the European policy introduced, another level of industrialisation called Industry 5.0 (The document: Industry 5.0, EC, Brussels, 2021). Three key developments are included in the European Commission document, enshrining them in the document's title: "Industry 5.0: Towards a sustainable, human centric and resilient European industry". The first is about strengthening and radicalising industry (and non-industry) towards sustainability. The second is about placing humans at the centre of cyber-physical production systems and orienting technology development towards improving quality of life (e.g., the smart city concept). The third concerns building business resilience to the lability. This third direction emerged after the COVID-19 pandemic, when supply chains were disrupted and business, for the first time in the modern century, felt powerless to 'control' its environment. Previous predictions about where the industry would go had to be revised, taking into account the post-pandemic realities, which were compounded by the effects of the energy crisis and the aftermath of the war in Ukraine.

The totality of contemporary business problems, as well as industrial challenges, outlines (determines) new business models. Contemporary business models attempt to map the many area-based changes in business activity. The research question arises: What elements of the model are important in the industrial transformation towards Industry 5.0? The search for an answer to this question formed the basis for writing this chapter. The content presented in the chapter is the result of a literature review performed in accordance with the SLR (Systematic Literature Review) methodology (Czakon, 2011; De Bellis, 2009). The result of the analysis is the structure of a business model for Industry 5.0. The model prepared is illustrative and incomplete, due to the broad scope of the research issue.

Business models are currently a very important area of research exploration, related to the search for ways to better understand business, as well as the ecosystems that are shaped by it. Ongoing academic research on business models focuses on perspectives on the development of their contemporary forms (Jablonski and Jablonski, 2018). A great deal of emphasis is placed on their dynamisation due to the rapid development of Fourth Industrial Revolution technologies and the creation of shared value in circular economy (Nayeri, 2023).

This chapter focuses on the challenges for manufacturing companies in an Industry 5.0 environment. The last three years have seen a profound revision of the principals associated with the need to deal effectively with potential challenges to industrial development. So far, the concept of Industry 4.0, which was launched in Germany in 2011, is evolving towards Industry 5.0. The fundamental difference between Industry 4.0 and Industry 5.0 is that in Industry 4.0 technologies are exposed, while in Industry 5.0 the focus is on values (Xu et al., 2021).

Methodological stages and research questions

In this paper, a structured literature analysis has been carried out, based on scientific publications registered in the Web of Science (WoS) database, on the topic of the study on Industry 5.0 (the keyword Industry 5.0 was used to search for publications). This paper presents the results of the bibliometric analysis performed, focusing on a discussion of the ten highest-cited scientific publications about Industry 5.0 registered in the aforementioned database and a keyword analysis of all searched publications for the keyword Industry 5.0 as at 26 December 2022.

The analysis enabled:

- to determine the dynamics of scientific publications on Industry 5.0 in the Web of Science database in the period from 2016 to 2022,
- to present the key area of research in the topic of Industry 5.0 in the period from 2016 to 2022 on the basis of scientific publications registered in the Web of Science (abbreviation: WoS) database,
- to show the research scopes of the researchers of the ten most cited scientific publications on Industry 5.0 in the Web of Science database,
- to present the keyword clouds about Industry 5.0 on the basis of the analysed publications (the small cloud was created from the keywords used in the 10 most cited publications, the large clouds from all publications obtained from the WoS database for the keyword: Industry 5.0),
- to prepare the concept of business model around the main research areas of Industry 5.0.

The aim of the study was to present, on the basis of a structured literature review, the areas of scientific research focused on Industry 5.0, which are written in the concept of business model in Industry 5.0. The year in which the first publication on Industry 5.0 was registered in the WoS scientific database was taken as the beginning of the analysis. The analysis was finished on 26 December 2022. The analysis was realized to build a concept of business model.

The following Research Questions (RQ) were formulated:

RQ1: What is the essence of Industry 5.0?

RQ2: What is the structure of the concept of Industry 5.0?

RQ3: What is the architecture of the business models in Industry 5.0.

The research strategy, to understand the importance of Industry 5.0 in industrial evolution, was the search for scientific articles on Web of Science, to provide an overview of existing research and contributions. The selected papers to address the change areas of evolving from Industry 4.0 to the Industry 5.0 perspective. A search was conducted using the term 'Industry 5.0', where 136 articles relating to the topic were returned. The articles revealed were filtered according to the PRISMA methodology (Moher et al., 2009). Search ranges included: topic, abstract and key words. The search was conducted in WoS, for articles published in indexed journals. The search limited the results to the period 2015–2022. The focus at this stage was on performing publication dynamics, with identification of key areas of research, especially in the first publications listed in the database.

In the second stage, publications were ordered by citation frequency, focusing on the most cited (Top 10). This step was used to better define the search, returning 10 articles. The top 10 list (as at 26 December 2022) was analysed by key study areas. Two research area segments are analysed. The first relates to the ordering of scientific publications by base category and the second by research areas of researchers. This stage of research was related to the analysis of Industry 4.0. Such an analysis was presented by Gajdzik (2022). This stage of the research served to confirm the thesis of the lack of variability of the key research areas and, at the same time, the continuation of the key research areas of Industry 4.0 into Industry 5.0.

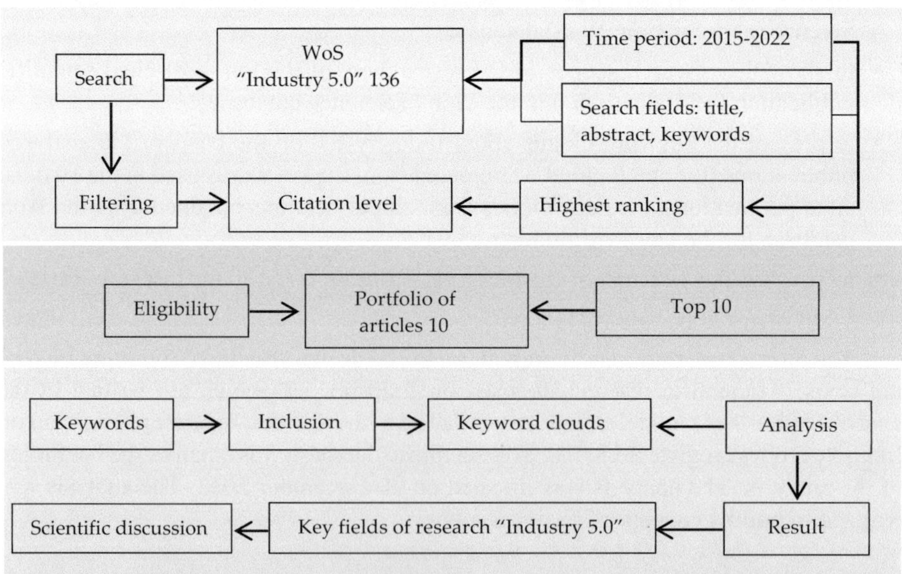

Fig. 1. Study search and methodological stages. Source: own concept.

Having obtained confirmation of the evolution of Industry 4.0 into Industry 5.0, the focus, in the next stage of the research, was on identifying the specific research areas of researchers who used the keyword 'Industry 5.0' in their articles (title, abstract, keywords). This stage was the final stage of the analysis. It was performed on the basis of the 10 most cited publications about Industry 5.0 in the WoS scientific database. A list of the analysed publications is provided in Table 1. Figure 1 illustrates a search strategy using the flow of the PRISMA diagram. The graphical form of the presentation of the areas studied were keyword clouds. The research concludes with the concept of business model that focuses on the main areas of business changes in Industry 5.0.

Additional information: the author informs that has already performed a similar bibliometric analysis on Industry 5.0 (Grabowska et al., 2020), but then the number of publications analysed was smaller than now, and the scope of the analysis, then concerned the frameworks of the new concept, and this time the research areas that fit into the concept of business model in Industry 5.0.

Bibliometric analysis of scientific papers on Industry 5.0

1. The dynamics of scientific publications on Industry 5.0

A decade after the concept of Industry 4.0, that was introduced by German practitioners and politicians (the concept was announced at the Hannover Fair in 2011), the new vision, called Industry 5.0, was presented by European Comission. In 2017, first time, the term Industry 5.0 was used by Esben H. Østergaard, CEO at REInvest Robotics. Two years later, Industry 5.0 was discussed by Aroop Zutshi, CEO of Frost & Sullivan (https://przemyslprzyszlosci.gov.pl/future-industry-platform-the-mission-and-contact/). And in January 2021, the first comprehensive vision of the next concept for the development of industries was created in the form of the European document entitled: "Industry 5.0" (Brussels, 2021). The document states that Industry 5.0 is based on 3 pillars or 3 strategic values: (i) human-centricity, (ii) sustainability and (iii) resiliency. However, this was not the first publication on Industry 5.0. It was preceded by a European Commission study from September 2020, a document by Julian Müller entitled: 'Enabling Technologies for Industry 5.0. Results of a workshop with Europe's technology leaders'. The study describes the technologies relevant to this phase and identifies social, governmental, political and economic challenges. Assumptions for Industry 5.0 were developed before 2020 and written in other documents but without explicitly defining the novelty of industrial development.

Based on an analysis of scientific papers performed using the Industry 5.0 key for the titles of papers included in the WoS scientific database, it was determined that the first publication that had the notation 'Industry 5.0' in its title was registered in 2016. This was a publication by Sachsenmeier (2016). The author pointed out the potential for applications of bionics and synthetic biology solutions in industrial engineering and socio-economic development. The publication was the first to have 'Industry 5.0' in its title and received 37 citations on 26 December 2022, closing Top 10 the most-cited publications on Industry 5.0 in the WoS database. The topics covered by the author of the publication were related to the relatively new science (last 50 years) of synthetic biology, which combines the achievements of molecular biology and engineering. Modern synthetic biology benefits from Industry 4.0 technology solutions, such as artificial intelligence (AI) and accompanying machine learning (ML), which are supported by Big Data and powerful computing powers. Initially, the essence of synthetic biology was based on accelerating medical discoveries and creating new technical solutions used by humans to protect their health, and over time it has been adapted by companies in a variety of sectors, e.g., food, agriculture, environment, materials industry (Hain et al., 2023; Kong et al., 2020).

After 2016, no scientific publication with the term Industry 5.0 in the title was registered in 2017. In the following year, two publications were registered. In one publication, the term 'Society 5.0' (Kang, 2018) and in the other (Ozdemir and Hekim, 2018), the term 'Industry 5.0' appears. The authors of the second publication even use the term 'birth' of Industry 5.0 (Ozdemir and Hekim, 2018) to emphasise the importance of the new concept. The publication by authors Ozdemir, V. and Hekim, N. (2018) can be considered, as the beginning of research in the area of a new development concept such as Industry 5.0. The mentioned publication in the WoS database received 130 citations (26 Dec. 2022), ranking second in terms of citation frequency (the first belonged to Nahavandi 2019).

Authors Ozdemir, V. and Hekim, N. (2018) proposed that the new concept of Industry 5.0 is based on strong (full) automation, on IoT and Big Data but integrates these solutions with security, innovative technology policy and responsible implementation science. The authors proposed a 3D symmetry model for designing an innovation ecosystem with: (i) an embedded strategy for secure digital knowledge networks, (ii) an equal emphasis on both accelerating and decelerating innovation, for diminishing returns and prolonging returns on investment (ROI) (iii) social science and humanities (SSH) research, taking into account technology alternative costs, ethics, frameworks (epistemology) and the independence of SSH research in technology policy making.

In the following year (2019), further scientific publications on Industry 5.0 were included in the WoS database. In 2019, four publications on Industry 5.0 were identified. Among the four scientific publications, three publications referred to the development of Society 5.0 and one (Nahavandi, 2019) dealt with placing humans at the centre of technological development. Nahavandi, S. included the essence of the development of Industry 5.0 in the title of his publication (2019), which in the original reads "Industry 5.0 A Human-Centric Solution". In Industry 5.0, robots are collaborate with the human. The said publication received the highest citation frequency index (Times Cited, WoS Core) of 184.

Human centricity towards technologies also appeared in the European Commission's document entitled: 'Industry 5.0 Towards a sustainable, human centric and resilient European Industry' (2021). The cited document is not only about human collaboration with advanced technologies, but moreover about matching technologies to human capabilities and expectations. In order for a human being (employee or operator) to interact with industry-dedicated technologies, he or she should have IT (digital) skills, which he or she must augment with soft skills. In 2017, a European Parliament document entitled: 'Digital Skills in the EU Labour Market', digital competences were considered to be a range (set) of digital knowledge from basic up to and including advanced knowledge, as well as a set of skills necessary to handle and use digital technologies. This set of digital or technical competences is extended by the cognitive, emotional and social competences that every person working with industrial technologies should have.

Technological advances in themselves trigger the need to be skilled in the use of modern computer equipment and other devices, as well as in the use of the Internet, computer applications and software. People with digital competence should make informed and critical use of the entire spectrum of ICT. This also applies to the operation of intelligent machines (e.g., industrial robots). The ability to interact with intelligent robots is a challenge for Industry 5.0. A human (an operator) should understand the principles of machine-to-machine communication as well as data protection and cyber security. As machines work in specific processes, it is also important to be able to understand processes, including visual input, and to know the algorithms and decision-making capabilities of the systems. In addition to the technical know-how about smart machines needed to operate advanced technologies, teamwork skills, communication competence, the ability to adapt quickly in the workplace and to change one's mind-set as technology advances are needed (Albur et al., 2016; Gajdzik and Wolniak, 2022). Technology needs leaders of change, and these leaders in the company are managers who must be good organisers of change (Kwiotkowska et al., 2022). In Industry 5.0, the discussion about the role of humans in technological development has returned. In a situation where the labour market lacks employees for IT and other departments related to the handling of Industry 4.0 technologies, it has been pointed out, on the one hand, to accelerate actions towards the development of employees' digital competences (Broo et al., 2022) and, on the other hand, to provide technological support towards employees who do not have, for the moment, the appropriate competences. The handling of advanced technologies should be simple and not burdened by human factor errors.

Analysing the scientific papers on Industry 5.0, it is important to highlight the importance, the first publications on Society 5.0, i.e., a society in which technological advances help to solve social issues. Technologies are creating systems that offer a high integration of digital and real space, i.e., a "super smart society" (Encyclopedia MDPI; https:encyclopedia.pub based on Hayashi et al., 2017, p. 264). The concept of developing such a society was initiated in Japan. Publications on 'Society 5.0' (Kang, 2018; Salimova et al., 2019; Hamdani et al., 2019) are naturally associated with Industry 5.0. Socio-economic trends are strongly involved in industrial transformation (Gajdzik et al. 2021).

There is a strong connectivity between the 'human-centred' and the 'technology-based society' in Industry 5.0 (Hamdani et al., 2019). In addition to the cited publications on Industry 5.0, in which the authors attempt to link Industry 5.0 with Society 5.0, this topic was also presented in the scientific forum in the following years. In total, among the 136 analysed publications, searched from the WoS database for the keyword: Industry 5.0 (keyword: 'Industry 5.0' used in the title of the publication), the keyword: 'Society 5.0' appeared 25 times, which accounted for 18.28% of the total number of publications.

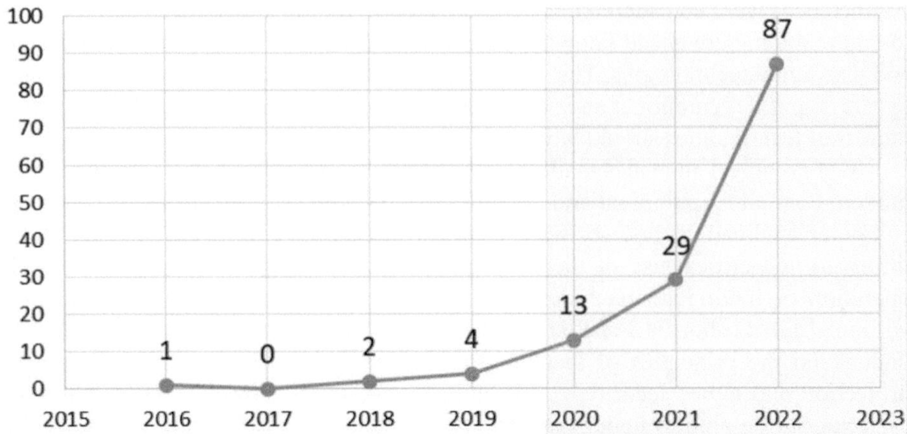

Fig. 2. Dynamics of scientific publications on Industry 5.0 in the WoS database.Source: own analysis based on data base: Web of Science (WoS).

Over time, the dynamics of scientific publications about Industry 5.0 in scientific databases has increased. In 2020, 13 publications were registered in the WoS database, 29 publications in the following year, and 87 publications on Industry 5.0 in 2022. Figure 2 presents the dynamics of the publication on Industry 5.0 (WoS). The increase in scientific publications on Industry 5.0 starting from 2020 was caused by strong changes in the business environment, including the COVID-19 pandemic and its effects. The increase in publications was also influenced by the policy of the European Union and the document on Industry 5.0 published by the European Commission (European Commission, Brussels 2021). The effects of the COVID-19 pandemic have changed the values of companies. According to Glenszczyk, M. (2022), the industry clashed with the "black swan" effect (a term used for the lability of the environment) and began to work towards anti-fragility and resilience of the business model.

The conclusion from the analysis of the dynamics of publications is as follows: strong volatility of the business environment, defined as lability or even unpredictability, rapidly accelerated the number of publications about Industry 5.0 in scientific databases. The events that influenced the development of Industry 5.0 were: the COVID-19 pandemic (2020) and related interrupted supply chains, aggression against Ukraine and the ongoing war (2022), which also limited supplies and trade, as well as the energy, economic, cultural and health crisis.

2. *Areas of research by scientists in the topic of Industry 5.0*

A systematic analysis of the literature carried out through the analysis of scientific publications available in the WoS database made it possible, apart from the already performed publication dynamics, also to identify key areas of research. In the WoS database, two research segments are analyzed. The first concerns the ordering of scientific publications by database category, and the second by areas of research of scientists. The results of the analysis within the fields (categories) of the WoS base

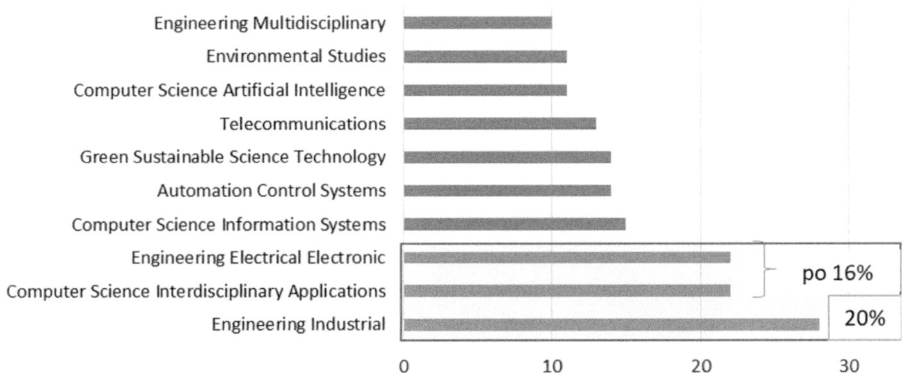

Fig. 3. WoS database fields by Industry 5.0 research area category on the list Top 10. Source: own analysis based on data base: Web of Science (WoS).

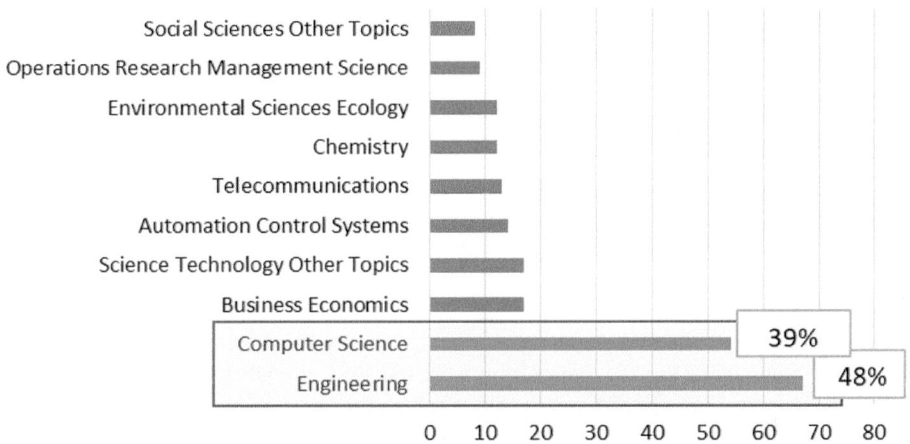

Fig. 4. Research areas of Industry 5.0 in scientific publications of the WoS database on the list Top 10. Source: own analysis based on data base: Web of Science (WoS).

areas are shown in Figs. 3 and 4. In order to maintain the readability of the drawings, the Top 10 list (the top ten highest ranked indications) was used.

Based on the fields (categories) of publications adopted for organizing studies available in the WoS scientific database, the first place was occupied by industrial engineering, the share of publications registered in this category was 20%. The second and third places belonged to the categories: computer sciences in the area of interdisciplinary application of computer technology (16% of the total number of publications) and engineering, electronics and electricity (16%). Detailed areas of research of publications on Industry 5.0 in the WoS database were: engineering and computer science (Fig. 3). The area of research, which is Industry 5.0 engineering, appeared in almost every second publication (exactly 48% of N=136). On the other hand, computer science as a research area accounted for nearly 40% of all

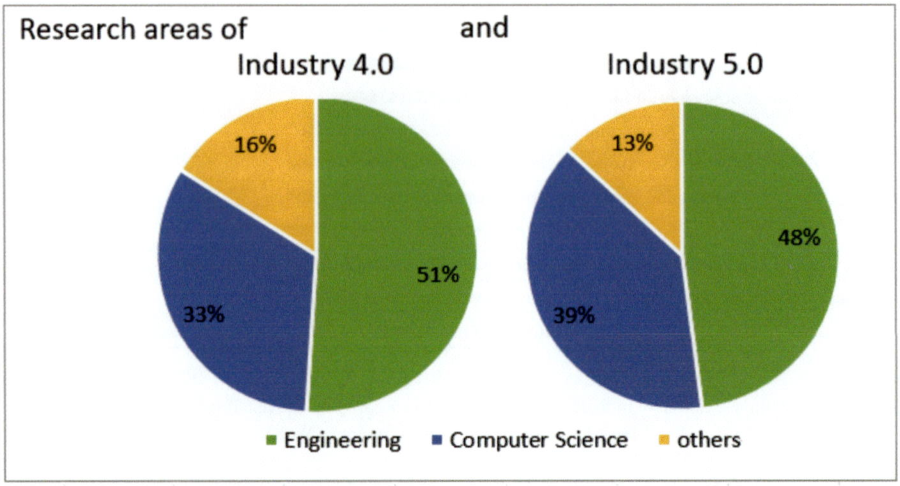

Fig. 5. Comparison of research areas of Industry 5.0 and Industry 4.0 in scientific publications in the WoS database. Source: own analysis based on data base: Web of Science (WoS).

publications. These two areas can therefore be considered as leading in the works that referred to Industry 5.0 in the title.

The conclusion from the scope of the analysis: the popularized concept of Industry 5.0 in the scientific community is located in the areas belonging to industrial engineering and in areas related to the application of IT solutions in industry. On the basis of the previous knowledge about Industry 4.0 and previous bibliometric analyses of Industry 4.0 (Gajdzik, 2022), the author states the existence of identical areas of Industry 5.0 and Industry 4.0 research on the basis of publications in scientific databases (Fig. 5). The authors, based on the analysis of research areas, conclude that the concept of Industry 5.0 refers to the concept of Industry 4.0 when it comes to ordering technologies according to the categories of sciences.

Concluding this stage of the general analysis, the authors formulate a research question: RQ1: What is the essence of Industry 5.0? To answer this question, the authors perform another detailed analysis (point 3), in which they look for new research principles.

3. *Scientific areas of Industry 5.0 in literature review—the list Top 10*

The analysis was based on the ten most cited publications on Industry 5.0 in the WoS scientific database. The list of analysed publications is presented in Table 1.

The thematic scope of the ten most frequently cited publications included a set of values of Industry 5.0. The new values were born on the conditions of the industry, especially the popularized technologies, or pillars of Industry 4.0.

Authors Longo, Padovano, Umbrello (2020) pointed out the ethical problems of applying an uncontrolled form of smart technology application and made a recommendation about the need to build knowledge based on ethical technology engineering. The authors presented an approach based on value design in the

Table 1. Scientific publications about Industry 5.0 from the WoS database with the highest citation rate—the list Top 10.

No.	Citation		Author (year)	Title, source, volume (number), pages, doi.
	WoS	Total		
1	184	185	Nahavandi (2019)	Industry 5.0-A Human-Centric Solution. *Sustainability*, 11(16), doi: 10.3390/su11164371
2	130	134	Ozdemir et al. (2018)	Birth of Industry 5.0: Making Sense of Big Data with Artificial Intelligence, The Internet of Things and Next-Generation Technology Policy. *OMICS-A Journal of Integrative Biology*, 22(1): 65–76, doi: 10.1089/omi.2017.0194
3	122	122	Maddikunta et al. (2022)	Industry 5.0: A survey on enabling technologies and potential applications. *Journal of Industrial Information Integration*, 26, doi: 10.1016/j.jii.2021.100257
4	93	93	Xu et al. (2021)	Industry 4.0 and Industry 5.0- Inception, conception and perception. *Journal of Manufacturing Systems*, 61: 530–535, doi: 10.1016/j.jmsy.2021.10.006
5	70	70	Longo et al. (2020)	Value-Oriented and Ethical Technology Engineering in Industry 5.0: A Human-Centric Perspective for the Design of the Factory of the Future. *Applied Sciences-BASEL*, 10(12): doi: 10.3390/app10124182
6	50	50	Javaid et al. (2020)	Industry 5.0: Potential Applications in COVID-19. *Journal of Industrial Integration and Management-Innovation and Entrepreneurship*, 5(4): 507–530, doi: 10.1142/S2424862220500220
7	45	45	Aslam et al. (2020)	Innovation in the Era of IoT and Industry 5.0: Absolute Innovation Management (AIM) Framework. *Information*, 11(2), doi:10.3390/info11020124
8	43	43	Potocan et al. (2021)	Society 5.0: balancing of Industry 4.0, economic advancement and social problems. *KYBERNETES*, 50(3): 794-811, doi: 10.1108/K-12-2019-0858
9	38	38	Javaid et al. (2020)	Critical Components of Industry 5.0 Towards a Successful Adoption in the Field of Manufacturing. *Journal of Industrial Integration and Management-Innovation and Entrepreneurship*, 5(2): 327–348, doi: 10.1142/S2424862220500141
10	37	38	Sachsenmeier (2016)	Industry 5.0-The Relevance and Implications of Bionics and Synthetic Biology. *Engineering*, 2(2): 25–229, doi: 10.1016/J.ENG.2016.02.015

Source: own analysis based on data from WoS (26-th Dec.2022).

implementation of technological solutions. The migration from value to technology has been represented as the Symbiotic Factory of the Future. In this approach, the highest value is the human being and the "human-centric" orientation, which the authors deliberately call, at this stage of transition, "perspective". Longo, along with co-authors (2020), considers Industry 5.0 as a new revolutionary wave that is emerging as the "Age of Augmentation", when man and machine will reconcile and work in perfect symbiosis with each other.

Also, Nahavandi, S. (2019) uses the term "human-centric", emphasizing that if economies want to avoid dismissing humans from industry they must introduce solutions in which robots will be intertwined with humans and will cooperate with them, not compete. The author relates the connectivity issues to the brain-machine interface and advances in artificial intelligence.

On the other hand, the authors of a publication on the birth of Industry 5.0 (Ozdemir and Hekim 2018) point out the reasons for uncontrolled technological advances under the concept of Industry 4.0, which has been popularized for a decade. In Industry 4.0, "everything is supposed to be connected to everything", which can result in: an increase in the systemic risk of integrated systems in the event of failures or Internet viruses or deliberate actions by hackers, as well as the consolidation of new power centers that will be able to exercise control over all networked devices. For at least these two important reasons, it is important to focus on the concept of Industry 5.0, in which a turn towards the ethics of the technological transformations taking place is needed.

According to Maddikunt with co-authors (2022), Industry 5.0 is not a revolution, contrary to Longo et al. (2020) but an evolution aimed at harnessing the creativity of human experts in collaboration with efficient, intelligent and accurate machines to achieve resource-efficient and user-preferred manufacturing solutions with higher added value than in Industry 4.0. The source of new value is the conscious application of Industry 4.0 technologies to solve socio-economic problems. As examples, the authors cite smart healthcare, cloud storage as a cheaper form than traditional disks, making supply chain management and manufacturing more flexible. Among the technologies supporting Industry 5.0, the authors include edge computing/ computing, digital twins, collaborative robots, the Internet of everything, blockchain and 6G networks.

Very interesting deliberations were conducted by a team of authors headed by Xu, X. (2021), seeking to establish the difference between Industry 4.0 and Industry 5.0. The authors compared the essence of the two concepts, sought to establish a chronology of industrial development and answer the question of whether the concepts under study are two industrial revolutions or one techno-social revolution, as well as what distinguishes the "journey" to Industry 4.0 and Industry 5.0. The final conclusion is that Industry 5.0 focuses on core values (sustainability), human-centricity and resilience, while Industry 4.0 provides technology. Whether companies in their journey to the new industry are at the stage of Industry 4.0, or Industry 4.0+, Industry 4.5, etc., the physical world and the virtual world must be oriented toward human-machine integration (HMMI), and in macroeconomic terms toward global goals with the principles of economics, ecology and development of societies.

Javaid, M. and co-authors (2020a,b) pointed out the necessity of popularizing the concept of Industry 5.0 in connection with the COVID-19 pandemic. The publication was written in 2020, the year in which the world (especially in the first half of the year) undertook a fierce fight against the effects of the pandemic. For the authors, Industry 5.0 can be considered the next revolution worth leveraging to improve healthcare. Technology solutions can provide personalized therapy and treatment processes for COVID-19 patients if detailed patient information is available. The goal of Industry 5.0 technology is to create an intelligent healthcare environment with real-time capabilities. During the COVID-19 pandemic, these technologies can provide a remote monitoring system in healthcare. In addition to the application of Industry 5.0 technology to healthcare, the authors also pointed out the usefulness of the technology in training during the COVID-19 pandemic (training doctors and medical students).

An analysis of Industry 5.0 components in terms of COVID-19 was undertaken by Javaid, M. and Haleem, A. (2020). The article identifies 17 critical components of Industry 5.0, which the authors briefly discuss. These components are the Internet of everything (Internet of everything), 4D CT (Computed Tomography) and 4D MRI (Magnetic Resources Imaging), smart sensors (smart sensors), holography and virtual reality (holography and virtual reality), Internet of medical things (Internet of medical things), artificial intelligence (AI), humanoid robots (humanoid robots), smart inhalers (smart inhalers), 3D printing (and 3D printing), 3D scanning (3D scanning), machine learning and computing (machine learning and computing), 4D printing (4D printing), drones, 5G technology and telemedicine.

In the period of popularization of Industry 4.0, the framework of the enterprise innovation model has not been forgotten, as pointed out by authors Aslam, F., Wang, A.M., Li, M.Z. and Rehman, K.U. (2020), which is established by "Absolute Innovation Management (AIM)". The proposed AIM model is to make innovation more understandable and implementable. The AIM model is part of the organization, and its essence is embedded in the synergy of the innovation ecosystem, design thinking and corporate strategy. AIM is oriented to the human, the consumer, the user, the operator of Industry 4.0 technologies. The centrality of the human will make Industry 4.0 technologies useful and responsible, and such features of the technology will translate into business development.

Also in the top ten citations was a publication on Society 5.0, by the authors Potocan, V., Mulej, M., Nedelko, Z. (2021). The aforementioned authors already put the essence of the study in the title of the publication, and this is the constant balancing of Industry 4.0 around the challenges posed by this concept to the economy, as well as society. The concept of Industry 4.0 is not only an orientation to technological progress and the associated increase in productivity, providing companies with higher revenues from their operations, but above all the usefulness of technology in solving social problems. The authors even state that Society 5.0 should balance the concept of Industry 4.0. Drawing on organization theory, sustainability and social functionalism, the authors proposed a CSR model in line with the goals of a forward-looking and socially responsible society. In this model, the technology of Industry 4.0 is integrated into the environmental, social and economic dimensions of Society 5.0.

The technologies used by Industry 5.0 include artificial intelligence (AI), big data, supply chain, digital transformation, machine learning, and the Internet of Things (IoT). The aforementioned technologies are the most commonly used and among several "enablers" (dedicated technologies) that have been identified by researchers to drive Industry 5.0.

The published literature classifies five major themes for Industry 5.0: supply chain assessment and optimization, enterprise innovation and digitization, smart and sustainable manufacturing, IoT-driven transformation, AI and Big Data, and human-machine connectivity. It has been observed that the topic of Industry 5.0 as a gateway to human-machine connectivity and coexistence has been gaining more interest among the research community in recent years. Dedicated technology is expected to provide better interaction between humans and machines to achieve efficient and faster results. Industry 5.0 is creating a new era of personalization and solving complex problems (Saniuk et al. 2020). Digital technologies are providing a new paradigm in manufacturing and eliminating repetitive work. It applies human intelligence to understand the requirements of the human operator. Data in manufacturing can be analyzed using machine learning and artificial intelligence (AI). The streamlined technology of Industry 5.0 will result in higher value added to the customer (consumer) by using intelligent machines in symbiosis with humans to efficiently solve real-world problems. Industry 5.0 is expected to provide higher accuracy in the execution of activities and accelerate industrial automation with critical thinking human resources. High computing power facilitates digital manufacturing systems that are built to communicate with other systems in a secure manner. It is assumed that Industry 4.0 has not been able to meet the growing demand for personalization and effectively solve complex social, economic and environmental problems, so the term Industry 5.0 was coined, which refers to personalized production and the empowerment of humans in production processes, as well as the stature of using technology to solve the problems of economies and societies around the world.

In the publication (Akundi et al., 2022) was performed a structured analysis of publications on Industry 5.0, extracting abstracts of 196 published papers based on the keyword "Industry 5.0" in the IEEE, Science Direct and MDPI databases. There are several main themes of Industry 5.0, and they are supply chain evaluation and optimization, enterprise innovation and digitization, smart and sustainable manufacturing, transformation driven by IoT, AI and Big Data, and human-machine connectivity. It has been observed that Industry 5.0 is the "gateway" to human-machine connectivity and coexistence. The topic of Industry 5.0 has been gaining more and more attention among the research community in recent years.

The latest in the list of Top 10 publications with a high citation frequency is Sachsenmeier, P. (2016), already discussed above, about the potential applications of bionics (imitation or abstraction of nature's "inventions") and, to an even greater extent, synthetic biology in Industry 5.0. The chemical industry is already using so-called "white biotechnology" for new processes, new raw materials and more sustainable use of resources. Synthetic biology is also being used to develop second-generation biofuels and to harvest solar energy using tailored microorganisms or biometrically designed catalysts. The market potential for bionics in medicine, engineering processes and DNA storage is enormous. The authors have presented the development of bionics and synthetic biology on a timeline.

Many authors in their publications emphasized that Industry 5.0 is taking human-machine communication to the next level. In market terms, the authors focused on new opportunities for personalization using dedicated technologies. Globally, it's about applying technology to solve social problems.

In 2022, the European Commission published a study titled: "Industry 5.0, a transformative vision for Europe. Governing Systemic Transformations towards a Sustainable Industry". The document, created by 15 authors led by Sandrine Dixson-Decleve, is a step between a comprehensive definition of "Industry 5.0" and a developed roadmap for realizing the concept. The cited document was not analyzed in this chapter, but the author points it out so that the reader can complete his knowledge of Industry 5.0. The document upholds the values of Industry 5.0, which are sustainability, the centrality of humans to technology and resilience vs. stability.

"Sustainability" or "Sustainable" are strongly focused on Industry 5.0, there were 10 such publications in the total number of publications surveyed (136 extracted publications for the keyword "Industry 5.0"), and expanding the analysis to include green transformation, closed loop economics, end to end engineering, LCA and others, yielded 30 records, or more than 20% of the total number of publications. Gajdzik, B. and her team (Gajdzik et al., 2020) also performed a detailed bibliometric analysis of areas of sustainability for the use of Industry 4.0, pointing to the need to reinforce the value of sustainability in the technological advances taking place. The authors would also like to emphasize that when referring to the new concept of industrial development, which is Industry 5.0, and cited in this chapter, the authors use alternately the statement industrial evolution and industrial revolution. Since the conclusiveness of using the terms: "evolution", "revolution" was not the subject of the study, the author does not resolve this issue. The period of transition is too short to assess the extent of change in Industry 5.0 and attribute it to evolution or industrial revolution. In the title of the chapter, however, the author uses the statement evolution to depict the significant transformation of Industry 4.0 towards Industry 5.0. The concept of Industry 5.0 is commented on in an interesting way by the I-scoop service founded by De Clerck in the article titled: "Industry 5.0—the essence and reasons why it gets more attention" (Retrieved from: https://www.i-scoop.eu/industry-4-0/industry-5-0/). In the article we read: Industry 5.0 should not be combined with the next industrial revolution, that would be completely wrong. The author goes on to remind that, for example, in the United States, instead of the term Industry 4.0, the term IIoT is often used in the sense of the industrial Internet, while in Japan we have the concept of Society 5.0. Everything is relative, and industrial revolutions today are a matter of vision. In other words, Industry 4.0 is sometimes perceived as something, let's say, "cool", so Industry 5.0 is emerging, which has a more "human" face (cited from https://www.i-scoop.eu/industry-4-0/industry-5-0/, accessed on 28, Dec. 2022).

4. Keyword clouds of research areas of Industry 5.0

Based on the bibliometric analysis performed, the authors developed Industry 5.0 keyword clouds using the word art tool (Rprogram). The presented clouds are answer to the research question RQ2: What is the structure of the concept of Industry 5.0. The methodology for building the clouds included:

- development of clouds large based on keywords used by authors of all publications (N=136, where N - number of scientific publications).

- development of the small cloud based on the keywords used by the authors of the 10 highest cited publications (N=10),
- development of additional clouds organizing keywords (N=136).

The keyword clouds can be considered as the resultant of the impact at a given point in time of all the keywords defined by the authors on the development of Industry 5.0, or more precisely on the evolution of Industry 4.0 to Industry 5.0 In the presented Industry 5.0 keyword cloud, the central area of analysis was also Industry 4.0 (the second largest in Fig. 6).

The first cloud presented is a large cloud (Fig. 6), formed from all retrieved records, with keywords occurring more than 5 times in all publications combined being included in the analysis. Based on this cloud, it is possible to determine the key technology areas that link Industry 5.0 to Industry 4.0, which are AI and IoT.

Artificial intelligence (AI) is typically used in Industry 4.0 to analyse large amounts of data. Combined with IoT and automation, AI acts as a multi-level manufacturing (process) system that relieves the burden on workers. Systems that monitor the operation of machines, if they think a situation threatens to break down, they notify the worker and an automatic repair is initiated or the process is stopped. Artificial intelligence alerts the worker and at the same time provides him with all the important data. Through IoT, the employee can connect to the machine's software to investigate the cause of the malfunction, analyse logs and evaluate the data directly in the system. If the cause of the malfunction is software, it is updated. If the cause of the malfunction is hardware, the worker can receive digital assistance via augmented reality (AR). Both Industry 4.0 and Industry 5.0 in the researchers' research areas are presented in the process of applying technological innovations to satisfy customer needs. The research area of personalization, was evident in the studies of the general scientists selected by their publications in the WoS scientific database for the keyword: Industry 5.0—a large cloud of keywords (Fig. 6) as well as

Fig. 6. Large cloud of keywords in Industry 5.0. Source: own analysis based on scientific publications retrieved from the WoS database for the keyword: Industry 5.0 (26, Dec. 2022).

in the small cloud (Fig. 7), which was based on the keywords used in the publications of the list Top 10 with the highest citation rates (Table 1).

When the two main keywords, which are: Industry 4.0 and Industry 5.0, were used in own analysis, the Fig. 8 was obtained.

In this keyword cloud (Fig. 8), a human being emerges, linked to machine learning and robotization technologies that create, together with IoT, cyber-physical systems, which in Industry 5.0 are becoming more and more social systems (CPSS), because the human being is placed at the centre of manufacturing, the human being is the caretaker of processes, strongly assisted by technology to perform this function. Technology in Industry 5.0 should also be used in companies to build business resilience in the face of a labile environment. The keyword "Resilient" is as important, as human factors in the analyzed scientific publications on Industry 5.0.

When industrialization centred around the concept of development, a cloud was obtained (Fig. 9) depicting the importance of sustainability and the development of Society 5.0. It can be seen that there are links between the technologies of Industry 4.0 (AI, IIoT, SM, robots, Advanced Technologies, etc.), which marked the research

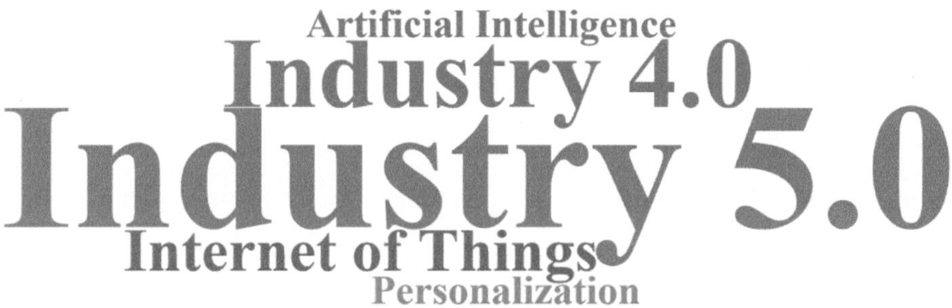

Fig. 7. Small cloud of keywords selected from the 10 highest cited publications (number of indications of 2 or above). Source: own analysis based on scientific publications with the highest citation rate in the WoS database (26, Dec. 2022).

Fig. 8. Big Cloud from key words centred around Industry 4.0 and Industry 5.0. Source: own analysis based on scientific publications from the WoS database (number of indications 2 and above, 26 Dec. 2022).

Fig. 9. Big cloud of keywords for technologies and trends in Industry 5.0. Source: own analysis based on scientific publications from the WoS database for the keyword: Industry 5.0 (number of indications 2 and above, 26 Dec. 2022).

areas of Industry 4. 0 in industries, with Sustainability and Society 5.0. In addition, the importance of blockchain, as a virtual data chain, which in industries can be used to transfer and store information about transactions and LCP (life cycle products), becomes apparent.

The concept of the business model in the Industry 5.0

Business models are changing according to changes in companies and economies. The changes over the last two decades have been very important for business. The term 'business model' often encompasses everything, including strategy, trends, value concept, economic model and revenue model. The strategic management community is constantly establishing the role of the business model in theory and practice (DaSilva et al., 2020). In the section, the next research question was connected with business model: RQ3: What is the architecture of the business models in Industry 5.0.

On the basis of literature and conceptual analysis, a business model concept was developed for Industry 5.0. The concept is based on the technologies of the Fourth Industrial Revolution, called the pillars of Industry 4.0 and the values of Industry 5.0. There are 9 pillars and 3 values. The pillars of Industry 4.0 are: Internet of Things, Big data, incremental manufacturing (3D printing), augmented reality, system integration, cloud computing, silutaion and cybersecurity (Erboz, 2017; Burrell, 2019; Senn, 2019; Piccarozzi et al., 2022; Dubey et al., 2022). The values of Industry 5.0 are: human-centricity, sustainability, resiliency.

The pillars of Industry 4.0 and values of Industry 5.0 create the matrix with interaction between them (Fig. 10).

Description of interactions:

1. Human-centricity and Industry 4.0 pillars: the interactions between the nine pillars of Industry 4.0 and the three pillars of Industry 5.0 create cyber-physical production systems that also involve humans. Prior to the European Commission document (Jan. 2021), which used the phrase 'human-centric', this statement had already appeared in studies by Romero et al. (2015), who used the term: human-automation symbiosis. In 2016, Romero et al. introduced "Operator 4.0" in "A Human-Centric Perspective on the Fourth Industrial Revolution Technologies"

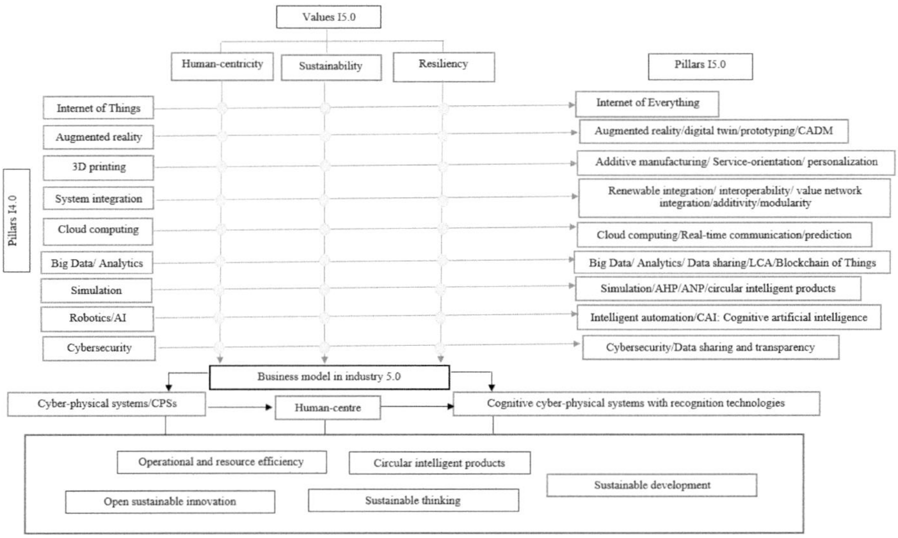

Fig. 10. Matrix of relations between I4.0 pillars and I5.0 values. Source: own analysis.

(Romero et al., 2016a,b). In a cyber-physical space, people operate and supervise technologies, teach machines to be intelligent, track processes through real-time data provided from machines and increasingly interact with machines (Gajdzik, 2023). In the industrial revolution is needed the humanization (Kalateh et al., 2022). The collaboration modern technologies with human, or human with modern technologies is needed to achieve zero defects in manufacturing (Wan and Leirmo, 2023). Modern factory is the combination of key technologies, information and computer systems, processes with their visualisation, intelligent products, and the competences of people into a single network that oversees itself increasing the efficiency of work execution. At the heart of smart factories are Cyber-Physical Production Systems (CPPS) (Lee et al., 2015; Lee, 2015; Liu et al., 2017). When a human is introduced into this system one gets an H-CPS (Human Cyber-Physical System) (Flores et al., 2020; Romero et al., 2015). Factories are business activities based on modern technologies with operators of them. Operator can be device teacher, solution mentor, process controller, robots assistant, machine learning programmer, robots manager, artificial intelligence operators, design engineers, wireless computer network operators, computer operators, etc. (Gajdzik, 2023). Ruppert et al. (2018), influenced by the study by Romero et al. (2016a,b), performed an analysis of the interaction of technologies and operators, identifying eight types of operators: super-strength operator, augmented operator, healthy operator, virtual operator, smarter operator, collaborative operator, social operator, analytical operator. In Industry 5.0 there is coexistence of humans and machines (Johri et al., 2021) and human-robot co-working (Demir et al., 2019). Human is in the centre of cyber-physical systems (Romero et al., 2016a,b) and an user is in the centre of blockchain (user-centric blockchain) (Yank et al., 2022). Industry 5.0 involves again humans in global industrial environments and intends to empower them through the incorporation of innovative technologies. The main idea of this strategy is the convergence of several aspects of human centrality, through industrial harmonization between machines and humans (Leng et al., 2022; Alves et al., 2023). Industry 5.0 operators should strategically use technology to improve the quality of the working environment. In this way, the idea addresses the central role of humans in production processes, where technology supports humans. In this way, synergies are achieved with regard to the interaction of humans and robots, where the human factor can cooperate, integrate and cope with new digital technologies (Wan and Leirmo, 2023). In parallel with the introduction of Industry 5.0, the concept of Operator 5.0 also emerged, representing the Operator 4.0 of the future, i.e., a more resilient Operator 5.0 to the adversities encountered in digital industrial environments (Romero et al., 2021).

2. Sustainability and Industry 4.0 pillars: a business cannot be realized without sustainability. Sustainability is a business paradigm and key direction in business strategy. High technologies can be used to solve environmental problems. In line with European policy, the new technologies of the Fourth Industrial Revolution must have a stronger impact on the reduction of negative aspects of the environment through the reduction of natural resources, materials, energy, decarbonisation (reduction of carbon emissions), etc. Sustainable Development Goals (2030 are realized by better and better technologies. Modern technological transformation is more strongly integrated (than even a decade ago) with Industry 5.0, Society 5.0, Smart Cities and villages (Kasinathan et al., 2022). Industry 5.0 is a socio-technological phenomenon that relies on technological advances and stakeholder collaboration to move beyond economic development and address prevailing environmental and social issues. Industry 5.0 is driven by two main classes of technologies, including (1) enabling technologies that have matured since the third revolution of the Industrial Revolution and were largely commercialised during the Industry 4.0 and (2) new technologies representing the most disruptive technological innovations, such as CAI (Cognitive artificial intelligence) or adaptive robots. The technological aspect of Industry 5.0 also includes the development of the necessary techno-functional design principles, such as real-time capability or decentralisation. These principles allow the technological components of Industry 5.0 to perform optimally and ensure their intended functionality. Industry 5.0 goes well beyond the manufacturing industry and smart factories. Industry 5.0 is shifting towards a stakeholder perspective when defining the components and scope of the business. Intelligent customers, stakeholders (e.g., governments or trade unions), suppliers, adaptive production facilities and technology providers, adaptive production plants and technology providers are examples of components that should be digitised and integrated to create the hyper-connected value ecosystem of Industry 5.0 (Ghobakhloo et al., 2022).
3. Resiliency and Industry 4.0 pillars: after the COVID-19 pandemic, the European Commission pointed out that the industry was vulnerable to various geopolitical upheavals and natural disasters and therefore introduced the principle of stability (resilient) (EC Document, Jan. 2021). The effect of the restrictions imposed,

during the COVID-19 pandemic, on the world was to disrupt supply chains. The COVID-19 pandemic made companies (manufacturers) realise how vulnerable (not resilient) global supply chains are to disruption. In response to the situation, the European Commission created an advisory 'Recovery and Resilience Instrument' (12 February, 2021). Resilience is defined based on the capability of an SC to reduce the impacts or likelihood of possible disruptions and decrease the resuming and restoring times (Hasan et al., 2020). Business resilience is the process of learning from historical events and predicting future events. Smart technologies using historical data for learning seem to be helpful in acquiring resilience, e.g., Big Data and analysis can decrease potential risks, predictive maintenance can stabilise manufacturing, blockchain and Internet of Things (Blockchain of Things, BCoT) (Karmakar et al., 2022) can help in building the agility (Sriman et al., 2022).

Three values of Industry 5.0 and nine pillars of Industry 4.0 the conceptions have many relations but the Industry 4.0 is concentrated mainly on technical aspect and is developed from operational management point of view. The Industry 5.0 is prepared from strategic management point of view. The Industry 4.0 view is the implementation of various new technical solutions into business entities especially in production to increase their level of innovativeness and effectiveness. In many companies not always the effectiveness on tactical level is connected with effectiveness on strategic level of company (Miyake, 2022; Sultan et al., 2021). Sometimes the company can implement new technological solution but it's effectiveness will not increase in long term due to lack of strategical view, strategical thinking and strategical approach. The tactical level is something between Industry 4.0 and Industry 5.0—on this level we can observe many activities connected with both of those conceptions.

The implementation of development strategies is based on the concept of cyber-physical production systems, so in Fig. 11, places it at the centre of the business model. Existing factories, in the future, will become smart factories with collaborative cyber-physical systems. Cyber-physical systems collect and process data in real time in order to optimise processes for the customer (product personalisation). In the cyber-physical systems, there is a human being who supervises and coordinates the processes.

Factories with cyber-physical production systems, benefit from innovations embedded in the pillars of Industry 4.0 and Industry 5.0. Because, everything was started from Internet, so IoT and IoE were separated from the pillars. According to a global report by Deloitte (2020), the impact of Industry 4.0 technologies on business will grow. The report is based on a face-to-face survey of organisation leaders (N=2,029). In their opinion, the key technologies include IoT (cited by 72% of business leaders), artificial intelligence technologies (cited by 68% of them), cloud computing (64%), Big Data and Big data Analytic (54%). Less than 50% of indications were given to the following technologies: nano-technology (44%), advanced robotics and intelligent robots (40%), sensors (40%), block chain (14%), 3D printing (10%), augmented reality (9%), quantum computing (7%), edge computing (6%).

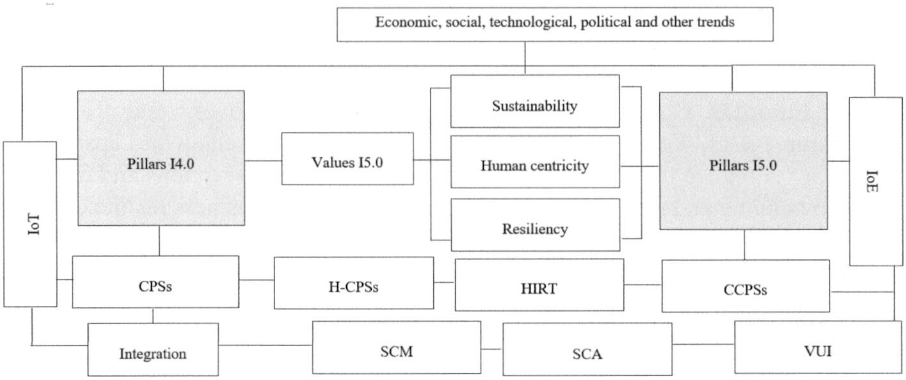

Fig. 11. The concept of business model in Industry 5.0. Source: own analysis.

Above cyber-physical systems are placed the values of Industry 5.0, which set the strategic direction for business and the ability to acquire business resilience to the labile environment. The modern world, including business, is becoming less and less comprehensible to humans. Nassim Taleb, in both of his works (2007, 2012), points out possible directions and courses of action, as well as tools to help meet difficult challenges, suggesting how to live in a world that humans do not understand (this is the slogan under which he popularises his works, above all 'Antiquity'). Taleb (2012) posits that histories are primarily created by Black Swan events, while humans focus on understanding the ordinary as accurately as possible, so models, theories and interpretations cannot capture the 'Black Swan' or measure the possibility of such shocks. Since humans are failing, maybe smart technologies and Big Data with Analytics can help predict business shocks.

The result of the collaboration of new technologies and the ubiquitous communication of intelligent and mechatronic resources (machines, robots, means of transport, etc.), with little human input, performing functions to coordinate the functioning of the systems, so that the solutions used do not escape human control (innovations must be applied wisely), are new value chains. M.E. Porter's (1990) traditional value chain will be replaced by flexible value networks. The networks are formed by: suppliers, producers, distributors, supported by data and technologies that enable closer cooperation between them, as well as between them and customers and business partners (stakeholders) (Hasan et al., 2020).

'Agility' is the key word for building new value chains on the basis of Fourth Industrial Revolution technologies (Santhi and Muthuswamy, 2023). Only such technologies will be able to meet the increasing demands of customers for the appearance, quality and use of products. The personalisation of products through flexible processes in cyber-physical production systems is the most essential bond between the customer and the manufacturer, but must be realised along the entire value chain (Pizon and Gola, 2023).

Business models cannot operate in isolation from the mega trends in the environment, which is why, in addition to the mega trend of industrial concepts, other trends have been included in the model, which are sustainable consumption, sustainable production, the sharing economy, the circular economy, deep decarbonisation and many others. Trends and mega-trends are business determinants. Every business operates in an environment that is increasingly dynamic and even, as the pandemic has shown, labile. "Black Swan" (Taleb, 2007) occurred and was quite a surprise for business. The experience acquired, after the COVID-19 pandemic, should be directed towards building business resilience to difficult-to-predict situations. New technologies combining the physical and digital worlds can help companies build resilience. "Marrying" the physical and digital worlds (a name used by Peters, 2016, 2017) enables business to create cyber-physical systems that aim to produce personalised, but sustainable and in collaboration with humans.

Nomenclature: CCPSs Cognitive cyber-physical systems, HIRT Human interaction and recognition technologies, IoE Internet of everything, IoT Internet of things, SCA Supply chain adaptability SCM Supply chain modularity VUI Value network integration, H-CPPs Human Cyber- Physical Systems, CPSs Cyber- Physical Systems.

There are, however, quite a few decision-making dilemmas in the proposed business model concept. One may wonder about the effects of product personalisation. This is because it is assumed that the personalisation of products, over time, will become mass, and mass personalisation can increase the environmental wastes (Saniuk et al., 2020). Another dilemma, still unresolved, is the role of the human factor in the relationship with smart technologies. While one may agree with the placement of the human factor at the centre of technological change, it raises doubts about the role of humans when human algorithm is handed over to machines (Krzysztofek, 2015). Will advanced robotics change humans? Are humans ready to cooperate with intelligent robots? Business dilemmas cannot be solved ad hoc. The concept of Industry 5.0 forces business to take a fresh look at business from the side of many predictable and unpredictable factors (black swan). It can be assumed that the accumulation of factors around business will force business to answer the question: is business a business? Perhaps, as advocated by social responsibility (CSR) researchers, this question should be changed to: business is not just business (Sen et al., 2006, 2009).

Conclusion

In the new development concept, Industry 5.0. factories of the Future will be more strongly oriented toward people, values and ethics. Although manufacturing companies are currently at a transition point between Industry 4.0 and Industry 5.0, a new age of industry is already emerging. Using the nomenclature of Longo et al. (2020) this is the "Age of Amplification" of the role of technology vis-à-vis humans and complex social, economic and environmental problems. Industry 5.0 will emerge when man and machine reconcile and work in perfect symbiosis with each other. Recent years have indeed helped to draw attention to humans in cyber-physical production systems (CPPS) and to the genesis of "Operator 4.0" (Romero et al., 2016a,b; Romero et al., 2015; Ruppert et al., 2018). Many scientists argue that value-oriented engineering of technology in Industry 5.0 is an urgent and sensitive topic. Industry 5.0 is considered the next industrial evolution, its goal is to leverage the creativity of human experts in collaboration with efficient, intelligent and accurate machines to achieve resource-efficient and user-preferred manufacturing solutions compared to Industry 4.0 (Maddikunta et al., 2022). For Longo et al. (2020) Industry 5.0 is the next wave revolution building a new paradigm for the business model of robot-human symbiosis. An apt summary of the considerations carried out is the statement of Xu, X. with his team (2021), namely that Industry 4.0 is driven by technology, while Industry 5.0 is driven by values. Both, the Industry 4.0 concept and Industry 5.0 concept have to develop the sustainable production (Gajdzik et al., 2021).

References

Akundi, A., Euresti, D., Luna, S., Ankobiah, W., Lopes, A. and Edinbarough, I. 2022. *State of Industry 5.0-analysis and identification of current research trends.* Applied System Innovation 5(1): DOI: 10.3390/asi5010027.

Albur, W., Arvind, C. J. and Bigghe, R. 2016. *Skill development for Industry 4.0.* Whitepaper, FOCCI, Roland Berger.

Alves, J., Lima, T.M. and Gaspar, P.D. 2023. *Is Industry 5.0 a human-centred approach? A systematic review*. Processes 11(1): 193. https://doi.org/10.3390/pr11010193.

Aslam, F., Wang, A. M., Li, M. Z. and Rehman, K. U. 2020. *Innovation in the Era of IoT and Industry 5.0: Absolute Innovation Management (AIM) framework.* Information 11(2), DOI:10.3390/info11020124.

Broo, D. G., Kaynak, O. and Sait, S. M. 2022. *Rethinking engineering education at the age of Industry 5.0*. Journal of Industrial Information Integration 25, DOI: 10.1016/j.jii.2021.100311.

Burrell, D. 2019. *Principles of Industry 4.0 and the 9 Pillars*, https://www.plextek.com/insights/insights-insights/industry-4-0-and-the-9-pillars/ (accessed on 07.02.2019).

Business dictionary: Digitalization, [online:] http://www.businessdictionary.com/definition/ digitization.html (2020-01-15).

COM. 2023. Communication from the commission to the European parliament, the European council, the council, the European economic and social committee and the committee of the regions. A Green Deal Industrial Plan for the Net-Zero Age. European Commission, Brussels, 1.2.2023 COM(2023) 62 final. Available online: https://commission.europa.eu/system/files/2023-02/COM_2023_62_2_EN_ACT_A%20Green%20Deal%20Industrial%20Plan%20for%20the%20Net-Zero%20Age.pdf.

Czakon, W. 2011. *Metodyka systematycznego przeglądu literatury*. Przegląd Organizacji, No. 3: 57–62.

DaSilva, C. M. and Trkman, P. 2020. *Business Model: What It Is and What It Is Not*. Available online: http://boilingice.com/wordpress/wp-content/uploads/2020/01/BP-DaSilva-Trkman-Business-Model.pdf.

De Bellis, N. 2009. *Bibliometrics and Citation Analysis: From the Science Citation Index to Cybermetrics.* Scarecrow Press.

Barata, J. and Kayser, I. 2023. *Industry 5.0 – Past, Present, and Near Future*. Procedia Computer Science 219: 778–788, doi 10.1016/j.procs.2023.01.351.

Demir, K. A., Döven, G. and Sezen, B. 2019. *Industry 5.0 and human-robot co-working*. Procedia Computer Science 158: 688–695.

Digital Skills in the EU Labour Market. European Parliamentary Research Service 2017.

Dubey, G., Gupta, R. K., Kumar, S. and Kumar, M. 2022. *Study of Industry 4.0 pillars and their uses in increasing productivity and reducing logistics defects*. Materials Today: Proceedings 63: 85–91.

Encyclopedia MDPI [encyclopedia.pub] based on: Hisashi, S., Yoichi, T., Hirco, K. and Hisanori, H. 2017. *International standardization for smarter society in the field of measurement, control and automation.* 56 Annual Conference of the Society of Instrument and Control Engineers of Japan (SICE), 10: 263–266. DOI: 10.23919/sice.2017.8105723.

Erboz, G. 2017. *How to define Industry 4.0: Main pillars of Industry 4.0. In*: Conference: 7th International Conference on Management (ICoM 2017). At Nitra, Slovakia. https://www.researchgate.net/publication/326557388_How_To_Define_Industry_40_Main_Pillars_Of_Industry_40 (2019-06-09).

Flores, E., Xu, X. and Lu, Y. 2020. *Human cyber-physical Systems: A skill-based correlation between humans and machines*. *In*: 16th IEEE International Conference on Automation Science and Engineering (CASE) August 20-21: 1313–1318.
Gajdzik, B. 2022. *A decade of research on Industry 4.0: A bibliometric study of key research areas with life cycle analysis of publication dynamics*. European Research Studies Journal 25(2): 118–134.
Gajdzik, B. 2023. *Industry 5.0 as a new concept of development within high volatility environment: about the Industry 5.0 based on political and scientific studies*. Scientific Papers of Silesian University of Technology – Organization and Management Series, No. 169. DOI: http://dx.doi.org/10.29119/1641-3466.2023.169.15.
Gajdzik, B., Grabowska, S. and Saniuk, S. 2021. *Key socio-economic megatrends and trends in the context of the industry 4.0 framework*. Forum Sci. Oecon 9: 5–21.
Gajdzik, B., Grabowska, S., Saniuk, S. and Wieczorek, T. 2020. *Sustainable development and Industry 4.0: A bibliometric analysis identifying key scientific problems of the sustainable Industry 4.0*. Energies 13(16) (art. no. 4254): 1–27. DOI:10.3390/en13164254.
Gajdzik, B. and Wolniak, R. 2022. *Smart production workers in terms of creativity and innovation: The implication for open innovation*. J. Open Innov. Technol. Mark. Complex 8(68). https://doi.org/10.3390/joitmc8020068.
Glenszczyk, M. (2022). (title in Polish) *Wartość jako czynnik uodparniający model biznesu przedsiębiorstwa w sytuacji dużej labilności otoczenia*. pp. 11–28. *In*: Barszczowska, B., Kot-Radojewska, M. and Sobczyk-Kolbuch, E. (eds.). (Title in Polish) Gospodarka w pandemii. Wyzwania i działania. Dąbrowa Górnicza. Publisher: Wydawnictwo Naukowe Akademii WSB.
Grabowska, S., Saniuk, S. and Gajdzik, B. 2022. *Industry 5.0: Improving humanization and sustainability of Industry 4.0*. Scientometrics 127(6): Art. 3117–3144, https://doi.org/10.1007/s11192-022-04370-1.
Ghobakhloo, M., Iranmanesh, M., Mubarak, M. F., Mubarik, M., Rejeb, A. and Nilashi, M. 2022. *Identifying Industry 5.0 contributions to sustainable development: A strategy roadmap for delivering sustainability values*. Sustain. Prod. Consum 33: 716–737.
Hain, D., Jurowetzki, R., Lee, S. and Zhou, Y. 2023. *Machine learning and artificial intelligence for science, technology, innovation mapping and forecasting: Review, synthesis, and applications*. Scientometrics, https://doi.org/10.1007/s11192-022-04628-8.
Hamdani, N. A., Herlianti, A. O. and Amin, A. S. 2019. *Society 5.0: Feasibilities and challenges of the implementation of fintech in small and medium industries*. Journal of Physics Conference Series 1402(77053). DOI: 10.1088/1742-6596/1402/7/077053.
Hasan, M. M., Jiang, D., Ullah, S. and Noor-E-Alam, Md. 2020. *Resilient supplier selection in logistics 4.0 with heterogeneous information*. Expert Systems with Applications.
Industry 5.0. Towards a sustainable, human centric and resilient European industry. Document of The European Commission, Brussels, Manuscript completed in January, 14, 2021.
Industry 5.0, a transformative vision for Europe. Governing Systemic Transformations towards a Sustainable Industry. Document of The European Commission, Brussels, Manuscript completed in 2022.
Jabłoński, A. and Jabłoński, M. 2018. *Modele biznesu przedsiębiorstw perspektywa rozwoju – ujęcie koncepcyjne*. CeDeWu, Warsaw.
Javaid, M. and Haleem, A. 2020. *Critical components of Industry 5.0 towards a successful adoption in the field of manufacturing*. Journal of Industrial Integration and Management-Innovation and Entrepreneurship 5(2): 327–348, DOI: 10.1142/S2424862220500141.
Javaid, M., Haleem, A., Singh, R. P., Haq, M. I. U., Raina, A. and Suman, R. 2020. *Industry 5.0: potential applications in COVID-19*. Journal of Industrial Integration and Management-Innovation and Entrepreneurship 5(4): 507–530. DOI:10.1142/S2424862220500220.
Johr, P., Singh, J. N., Sharma, A. and Rastogi, D. 2021. *Sustainability of coexistence of humans and machines: An evolution of Industry 5.0 from Industry 4.0*. Proceedings of the 10th International Conference on System Modeling and Advancement in Research Trends, SMART, pp. 410–414.
Kagermann, H. 2015. *Change through digitalization – value creation in the age of Industry 4.0*. pp. 23–45. *In*: Albach, H., Meffert, H., Pinkwart, A. and Reichwald, R. (eds.). Management of Permanent Change. Springer Fachmedien Wiesbaden.
Kagermann, H., Wahlster, W., Helbig, J. (eds.). April 2011. *Recommendations for implementing the strategic initiative Industrie 4.0: Final report of the Industrie 4.0*. Working Group: Industrie 4.0: Mit

dem Internet der Dinge auf dem Weg zur 4. industriellen Revolution, VDI-Nachrichten, Acatech-National Academy of Science and Engineering: München, Germany. Available online: http://forschungsunion.de/pdf/industrie_4_0_final_report.pdf.

Kalateh, S., Estrada-Jimenez, L. A., Pulikottil, T., Hojjati, S. N. and Barata, J. 2022. *The human role in Human-centric Industry*, IECON Proceedings: Industrial Electronics Conference, October.

Kang, J. (2018). *Change: From Industry 4.0 to Society 5.0-Taking the comparison of related development strategies between Germany and Japan as an example*. Book series: Advances in Social Science Education and Humanities Research: ADV SOC SCI EDUC HUM 213: 569–573, Proceedings Paper. In 4th International Conference on Humanities and Social Science Research (ICHSSR), APR 25–27, 2018, Jiangnan Univ, Int Acad Exchange Ctr, Wuxi, PEOPLES R China (Book editor: Du, X, Huang, C, Zhong, Y.)

Kasinathan, P., Pugazhendhi, R., Elavarasan, R. M., (...), Devendiran, R. and Alsharif, M. H. 2022. *Realization of sustainable development goals with disruptive technologies by integrating Industry 5.0, Society 5.0, smart cities and villages*. Sustainability (Switzerland) 14(22) Art. 15258.

Kong, D., Yang, J. and Li, L. 2020. *Early identification of technological convergence in numerical control machine tool: a deep learning approach*. Scientometrics 125(3): 1983–2009. DOI: 10.1007/s11192-020-03696-y.

Krzysztofek, K. 2015. *Człowiek – Społeczeństwo – Technologie*. Ethos 28(3/111): 191–213. DOI 10.12887/28-2015-3-111-12.

Kwiotkowska, A., Wolniak, R., Gajdzik, B. and Gębczyńska, M. 2022. *Configurational paths of leadership competency shortages and 4.0 leadership effectiveness: An fs/QCA study*. Sustainability Vol. 14, Art. 2795. https://doi.org/10.3390/su14052795.

Lee, J. 2015. *Smart factory systems*. Informatik Spektrum 38: 230–235.

Lee, J., Bagheri, B. and Kao, H. 2015. *Research Letters: A Cyber-Physical Systems architecture for Industry 4.0-based manufacturing systems.* Manuf. Lett. 3: 18–23.

Leng, J., Sha, W., Wang, B., Zheng, P., Zhuang, C., Liu, Q. et al. 2022. *Industry 5.0: Prospect and retrospect*. J. Manuf. Syst. 65: 279–295.

Liu, Y., Peng, Y., Wang, B., Yao, S. and Liu, Z. 2017. *Review on cyber-physical systems. IEEE/CAA J.* Autom. Sin. 4: 27–40, DOI:10.1109/jas.2017.7510349.

Longo, F., Padovano, A. and Umbrello, S. 2020. *Value-oriented and ethical technology engineering in Industry 5.0: A human-centric perspective for the design of the factory of the future.* Applied Sciences-BASEL 10(12). DOI: 10.3390/app10124182.

Lorenz, M., Rüfimann, M., Strack, R., Luetk, K. L. and Bolle, M. 2015. *Man and machine in Industry 4.0. how will technology transform the industrial workforce through 2025?* BCG Perspectives, 51.

Maddikunta, P. K. R., Pham, Q. V., Prabadevi Deepa, N., Dev, K., Gadekallu, T. R., Ruby, R. et al. 2022. *Industry 5.0: A survey on enabling technologies and potential application. Industry 5.0: A survey on enabling technologies and potential applications*. Journal of Industrial Information Integration, Vol. 26. DOI: 10.1016/j.jii.2021.100257.

Miyake, D. 2022. *Strategic planning Vs. operational planning: 7 main differences*, https://www.clearpointstrategy.com/strategic-planning-vs-operational-planning/, (accessed on 23 January 2023).

Moher, D., Liberati, A., Tetzlaff, J. and Altman, D. G. 2009. *Preferred reporting items for systematic reviews and meta-analyses: The PRISMA statement*. Annals of Internal Medicine 151(4): 264–269.

Nahavandi, S. 2019. *Industry 5.0-A Human-Centric Solution*. Sustainability 11(16), Art. 4372, DOI: 10.3390/su11164371.

Nayeri, S., Sazvar, Z. and Heydari, J. 2023. *Towards a responsive supply chain based on the Industry 5.0 dimensions: A novel decision-making method*. Expert Systems with Applications, 213, Part C, 119267.

Ozdemir, V. and Hekim, N. 2018. *Birth of Industry 5.0: Making sense of big data with artificial intelligence, the internet of things and next-generation technology policy.* OMICS-A Journal of Integrative Biology 22(1): 65–76. DOI: 10.1089/omi.2017.0194.

Peters, H. 2016. *Application of Industry 4.0 concepts at steel production from an applied research perspective. Presentation at 17th IFAC Symposium on Control, Optimization, and Automation in Mining*. Mineral and Metal Processing, [online:] https://tc.ifac-control.org/6/2/files/symposia/vienna-2016/mmm2016_keynotes_peters.PowerPoint-Präsentation (ifac-control.org).

Peters, H. 2017. *How could Industry 4.0 transform the Steel Industry*? Presentation at Future Steel Forum, Warsaw, 14.-15.6.2017. Available online: https://futuresteelforum.com/content-images/speakers/Prof.-Dr-Harald-Peters-Industry-4.0-transform-the-steel-industry.pdf.

Piccarozzi, M., Silvestri, C., Aquilani, B. and Silvestri, L. 2022. *Is this a new story of the 'Two Giants'? A systematic literature review of the relationship between Industry 4.0, sustainability and its pillars*. Technological Forecasting and Social Change, Vol. 177, Art. 121511.

Pizoń, J. and Gola, A. 2023. *Human–machine relationship—perspective and future roadmap for Industry 5.0 Solutions*. Machines 11: 203. https://doi.org/10.3390/machines11020203.

Potocan, V., Mulej, M. and Nedelko, Z. 2021. *Society 5.0: Balancing of Industry 4.0, economic advancement and social problems*. KYBERNETES 50(3): 794–811, DOI: 10.1108/K-12-2019-0858.

Porter, M. 1990. *Competitive Advantage of Nations: Creating and Sustaining Superior Performance*. New York: The Free Press.

Porter, M. and Heppelmann, J. E. 2014. *How smart, connected products are transforming competition. In*: Harvard Business Review 92(11): 64–88. Available online: https://hbr.org/2014/11/how-smart-connected-products-are-transforming-competition (accessed on 12 November 2022).

Regulation establishing the Recovery and Resilience Facility. 12 Feb. 2021. European Commission, Brussels. Available online: https://commission.europa.eu/business-economy-euro/economic-recovery/recovery-and-resilience-facility_en.

Romero, D., Bernus, P., Noran, O., Stahre, J. and Fast-Berglund, Å. 2016a. *The Operator 4.0: human cyber-physical systems & adaptive automation towards human-automation symbiosis work systems*. In APMS 2016, Advances in Production Management Systems: Initiatives for a Sustainable World, IFIP International Conference on Advances in Production Management Systems; Springer: Cham Switzerland: 677–686. Retrieved from: https://link.springer.com/chapter/10.1007/978-3-319-51133-7_80.

Romero, D., Noran, O., Stahre, J., Bernus, P. and Fast-Berglund, Å. 2015. *Towards a human-centred reference architecture for next generation balanced automation systems: human-automation symbiosis*. In IFIP International Conference on Advances in Production Management Systems–APMS. Advances in Production Management Systems: Initiatives for a Sustainable World: 556–566. Retrieved from https://link.springer.com/chapter/10.1007/978-3-319-22759-7_64 .

Romero, D., Stahre, J., Wuest, T., Noran, O., Bernus, P., Fast-Berglund, Å. et al. 2016b. *Towards an Operator 4.0 Typology: A human-centric perspective on the fourth industrial revolution technologies*. In Proceedings of the International Conference on Computers and Industrial Engineering (CIE46), Tianjin, China, October 11 (29–31): 1–11.

Romero, D. and Stahre, J. 2021. *Towards the resilient Operator 5.0: The future of work in smart resilient manufacturing systems*. Procedia CIRP, 104: 1089–1094.

Ruppert, T., Jaskó, Sz., Holczinger, T. and Abonyi, J. 2018. *Enabling technologies for Operator 4.0: A Survey*. Apply Science 8, No. 1650, DOI:10.3390/app8091650.

Sachsenmeier, P. 2016. *Industry 5.0-The relevance and implications of bionics and synthetic biology*. Engineering 2(2): 225–229, DOI: 10.1016/J.ENG.2016.02.015.

Salimova, T., Guskova, N., Krakovskaya, I. and Sirota, E. 2019. *From Industry 4.0 to Society 5.0: Challenges for sustainable competitiveness of Russian industry*. IOP Conference Series: Materials Science and Engineering, Vol. 497, No. 1, Art. 012090.

Saniuk, S., Grabowska, S. and Gajdzik, B. 2020. *Personalization of products in the Industry 4.0 concept and its impact on achieving a higher level of sustainable consumption*. Energies, Vol. 13, Art. 5895.

Santhi, A. R. and Muthuswamy, P. 2023. *Industry 5.0 or industry 4.0S? Introduction to industry 4.0 and a peek into the prospective industry 5.0 technologies*. Int. J. Interact. Des. Manuf. 17(2): 947–979. DOI: 10.1007/s12008-023-01217-8.

Sen, S., Bhattacharya, C. B. and Korschun, D. 2006. *The role of corporate social responsibility in strengthening multiple stakeholder relationships: A field experiment*. Journal of the Academy of Marketing Science 34: 158–166.

Sen, S., Du, S. and Bhattacharya, C. B. 2009. *Building relationships through corporate social responsibility*. pp. 195–211. *In*: MacInnis, D. J., Park, C. W. and Priester, J. R. (eds.). Hand-book of Brand Relationships. Armonk, NY: M.E. Sharpe.

Senn, C. 2019. *The nine pillars of Industry 4.0*. Available online: https://www.idashboards.com/ blog/2019/07/31/the-pillars-of-industry-4-0/ (2019-02-07).

Sriman, B., Annie Silviya, S. H., Santhosh Kumar, E., Suryaa Narayanan, K. and Nishaalu, S. 2022. *Blockchain Industry 5.0: Next generation smart contract and decentralized application platform. Proceedings of the 2022 International Conference on Innovative Computing*. Intelligent Communication and Smart Electrical Systems, ICSES.

Sultan, S., Acharya, Y. and Hynes, N. 2021. *Commentary: When promising innovators lack strategic vision: The concept of flow modulation in aortic dissection*. Journal of Endovascular Therapy 28(1): 32–35.

Taleb, N. 2007. *The Black Swan: The Impact of Highly Improbable*. Kurhaus.

Taleb, N. 2012. *Antifragile: Things That Gain from Disorder*. Kurhaus.

The Fourth Industrial Revolution. At the intersection of readiness and responsibility. Deloitte, 2020.

Transforming our world. The 2030 Agenda for Sustainable Development. 2015. UN, A/RES/70/1. Available online: https://sustainabledevelopment.un.org/content/documents/21252030%20Agenda%20for%20Sustainable%20Development%20web.pdf.

Wan, P. K. and Leirmo, T. L. 2023. *Human-centric zero-defect manufacturing: State-of-the-art review, perspectives, and challenges*. Computers in Industry Vol. 144, Art. 103792.

Yang, H., Asheralieva, A., Zhang, J., (...), Niyato, D. T. and Raza, K. A. 2022. *User-centric blockchain for Industry 5.0 applications*. IEEE International Conference on Communications Workshops, ICC Workshops: 25–30.

Xu, X., Lu, Y. Q., (...) and Wang, L. H. 2021. *Industry 4.0 and Industry 5.0-Inception, conception and perception*. Journal of Manufacturing Systems 61: 530–535.

Chapter 4

The Impact of Digital Technology and Climate Transformation on Business Models of Enterprises in the Energy Sector in Poland (On the Example of Jastrzębska Spółka Węglowa SA)

Anna Bałamut

Introduction

Climate change brings many opportunities and threats to the environment, society and business world. An example may be ensuring fluidity for the functioning infrastructure, uninterrupted supply chain or efficiently operating energy sector. This affects the competitiveness of the industry, the quality and availability of services and the standard of living of the population. Challenges are not only risks, but also new opportunities and possibilities. Ability to adapt to changes. What matters is not only the speed, but also the ease of adapting to the conditions of a changing (turbulent) environment and extent to which companies use their material or human resources. The whole situation is interesting from the point of view of the imperative strategic management and the creation of business models.

The aim of this the study is to indicate the impact of digital and climate transformation on business models. Following research question was asked: is the European Union—EU a leader in terms of carbon neutrality and digitalization? The following hypothesis was assumed: Jastrzębska Spółka Węglowa SA takes into account the guidelines imposed by the EU on low-emission and digitalization and adapts selected business models.

Andrzej Frycz Modrzewski Krakow University, Faculty Of Management and Social Communication, Gustawa Herlinga-Grudzińskiego 1, 30-705 Kraków, Poland.
Email: anka.piziak@gmail.com, ORCID: 0000-0001-7300-7367

The text is divided into two parts, introduction and conclusion. The first part: EU low-emission policy and the issue of digitalization. Consequences for the Polish energy sector. The second part: Enterprise management models in the energy sector and digitalization on the example of JSW SA.

The article uses the method of content analysis of documents, press releases and websites. The following were used, among others: empirical methods, i.e., observation, description, and general logical methods, i.e., analysis, synthesis, induction and deduction. The article uses: primary sources, monographs, articles and publications posted on the websites of individual ministries, organizations, entities, etc.

EU low-emission policy and the issue of digitalization. Consequences for the polish energy sector

Energy Union document from 2015 talks about: diversification of European energy sources, a fully integrated energy market, appropriate infrastructure and stable energy transmission, improving energy efficiency, reducing the issue of importing raw materials in favor of own solutions, reducing carbon dioxide emissions (low-emission), while at the same time economic growth , promoting research in the field of clean technologies and solutions supporting environmental protection. Membership in the European Union (EU) obliges countries to accept and implement the indicated solutions. However, Article 194 of the TFEU states that individual member states remain free to choose the shape of their energy mix. Additionally, geographical conditions, political and legal aspects significantly influence the nature of a given market (COM, 2015).

Currently, the EU strategy is to adapt energy goals to climate goals, which is visible in the so-called document from 2021—Fit for 55 (COM, 2021 550 final). It includes reducing greenhouse gas emissions by 55% before 2030 compared to 1990 levels and reducing net greenhouse gas emissions to zero by 2050. In March 2023, the EU energy targets for 2030 were agreed: increasing the share of energy from renewable sources in all sources of energy consumed to 42.5%, aiming to achieve a share of 45% and reducing primary and final energy consumption in the EU by 11.7% compared to 2020 projections for 2030 (EP, 2023). Under the current energy framework, EU Member States must: establish 10-year integrated national energy and climate integrated plans for 2021–2030, report on progress every two years and develop coherent long-term national strategies to achieve the agreed energy targets and the goals of the Paris Agreement. Returning to the 2021 document, it included a number of previous arrangements: the Renewable Energy Directive (COM/2021/557), the Energy Efficiency Directive (COM/2021/558), the Energy Taxation Directive (COM/2021/563), the Energy Performance of Buildings Directive (COM/2021/802), and the Gas Directive (COM/2021/803) and Regulation (COM/2021/804). The revision introduced new decarbonized gas markets, such as hydrogen, and included new transport regulation proposals,such as the Regulation on the deployment of alternative fuels infrastructure (COM/2021/559), the ReFuelEU Aviation Initiative (COM/2021/561) and the FuelEU Maritime Initiative (COM/2021/562).

To sum up, the EU talks about so-called the energy trilemma, i.e., security, availability of energy raw materials at low prices and renewable energy sources and their share in the energy mix of countries. Russia's invasion of Ukraine in 2022 showed that the EU has a serious problem with maintaining energy and ecological security. Member countries are struggling with, among others: with inflation, record gas prices and the energy poverty (households increasingly report that they are unable to provide adequate heating of buildings—at a price acceptable to the user). Therefore, the energy transformation should be implemented based on energy resources available in a given country. The question therefore arises whether, in the face of the destabilization of the European energy market, governments, coalitions and enterprises will choose environmental protection or job protection. Additionally, remain the issue of competitiveness and, consequently, the choice of technological solutions. Whether because of the quality and speed of production and its price.

12 September 2023, the European Parliament decided to increase the use of energy from renewable sources to implement the assumptions of the Green Deal and REPowerEU. According to the amendment, Member States must obtain 45% of energy from renewable energy sources by 2030. Changes regarding the EU's low emission are key for energy and ecological security, but they are happening too quickly due to the diversity of energy mixes of the member states, including Poland. Low-emission brings sacrifices and high costs for the economy, such information appears even in the German press, where it is said that the energy transformation will cost not only state governments, but also entrepreneurs and public. On the one hand, Member States are free to choose their energy mix, but on the other they must implement EU guidelines. So are we talking about competitiveness or its disruption? RED I from 2009 talked about obligations regarding the use of renewable energy in the energy mix (EC, 2009), RED II about goals and support instruments (EU, 2018, 2001). Meanwhile, RED III (EU, 2023) streamlines the procedures for issuing permits for the construction of new renewable energy power plants. A period of 12 months has been indicated for the approval of new installations using green energy in areas with accelerated renewable energy investments—renewables go to areas. Outside of those areas, this period should not exceed 24 months.

Additionally, discussions are taking place at the EU forum on the following topics: a proposal to make e-fuels for combustion cars climate neutral from 2035; by decision of the European Parliament (EP), road transport was included in the EU carbon dioxide emission allowance trading system - EU ETS, which was welcomed by the European Automobile Manufacturers' Association ACEA. However, distribution companies are afraid of this solution. The problem is the costs that may be incurred by the consumer in the future. New construction is to be zero-emission, and urban transport, such as buses, is to be emissions-free. There is only one question: whether the EU's desire to be a leader in climate issues encourages member states to be competitive or whether it influences the shape of the energy mix. Therefore, they are perceived only as a financial burden.

Poland, as an EU member, is forced to comply with EU guidelines on low emission, and enterprises, as market participants, must pursue an active climate policy. This affects on the management at all levels of the organization. Companies that effectively adapt their management models to the imposed requirements are more competitive. Low-emission policy, however, affects management models. Companies and enterprises are integrating greenhouse gas reduction targets into their business strategies. It is important to take climate goals into an account in strategic planning and operational management processes. Such action is not possible without the use of modern technologies, e.g., renewable energy, energy efficiency and electromobility. Companies must adapt their management models to effectively keep up with current trends. Both climate change and emissions regulations may create new types of risks, such as climate and regulatory risks. Management models must take into account the variability of the environment, take into account possible risks and develop strategies to minimize them.

The low-emission strategy requires not only active monitoring of greenhouse gas emissions, but also the issue of their reduction. Management models must include measurement and reporting systems that enable tracking of low-carbon progress. Low-emission policy is often perceived as an element of CSR—Corporate Social Responsibility. Companies must engage in social activities related to climate protection, which affects management models in the area of sustainable development. It is worth emphasizing that the development of low-emission technologies and climate regulations create new markets and business opportunities. If companies want to be competitive, they must adapt their management models to take advantage of these new markets and develop sustainable sources of revenue. This also has implications for supply chain management, such as monitoring and assessing suppliers for their impact on greenhouse gas emissions. An additional aspect is education and involvement of employees themselves in low-emission goals. Therefore, human resources management models must take into account: cyclical processes of education of employees for different generations. Poland, as an EU member, is obliged to comply with the low-emission policy. Despite the belief that the Community's path to leadership is too fast, Poland has a number of documents confirming commitment and acceptance of the indicated solutions.

The first of them is the *Strategy for Responsible Development 2020 with a perspective until 2030*: This document is a key development plan for Poland, covering a number of activities related to creating conditions for the growth of residents' incomes, while increasing cohesion in the social, economic and environmental dimensions, as well as goals related to renewable energy, energy efficiency and low-emission transport (MFiPR, 2017).

Another key document is Poland's Energy Policy until 2040 (MKiŚ, 2021), which indicates areas such as: optimal use of energy resources, expansion of electricity generation and network infrastructure; diversification of supplies, expansion of the network infrastructure of natural gas, crude oil and liquid fuels; development of energy markets; construction of a nuclear power plant, development of renewable energy sources; development of heating and cogeneration and improvement of the energy efficiency of the economy. This document also highlights the role of intelligent power grids, i.e., intelligent electric power systems, automatic monitoring, control, regulation and network security systems. An important issue is the exchange of data between devices, the so-called Internet of Things technology.

The next document is the National Energy and Climate Plan 2021–2030 - NECP (MAP, 2019). This is a document that defines Poland's goals in terms of reducing greenhouse gas emissions and developing renewable energy sources. Poland is preparing this plan as part of EU regulations and climate commitments.

Specifies, among others: 5 dimensions of the Energy Union: energy security, internal energy market, energy efficiency, decarbonisation and research, innovation and competitiveness. It indicates, for example, a 7% reduction of greenhouse gas emissions in sectors that are not covered by the ETS system compared to 2005. Also 21–23% share of renewable energy in final gross energy consumption and 14% share of renewable energy in transport.

A low-emission economy plan is a mandatory element in a situation where a city or commune plans to apply for financial support in projects related to Energy Efficiency and Renewable Energy Sources. The plan includes specific steps and goals related to: emission reduction, energy efficiency, renewable energy sources and transformation of the industrial sector. These plans are still needed by local governments due to the data collection and the ability to properly evaluate investments. Low-emission activities must be complementary to the company's strategic documents and the National Urban Policy 2030, the aim of which is to coordinate sectoral policies, including energy policy.

Poland uses EU structural funds and operational programs that support low-emission projects, including the modernization of energy infrastructure, improving energy efficiency and developing low-emission transport, in 2021–2027, e.g., European Funds for Infrastructure, Climate and Environment, budget 113, PLN 4 billion, European Funds for the Modern Economy - PLN 37.1 billion, European Funds for Social Development - PLN 18.9 billion, European Funds for Digital Development - PLN 9.2 billion, European Funds for Eastern Poland - PLN 12.3 billion, European Funds for Food Aid - PLN 2.4 billion, European Funds for Fisheries - PLN 2.3 billion, Technical Assistance for European Funds - PLN 2.5 billion, 16 regional programs, e.g., social infrastructure and environment PLN 0-155.4 billion and the Interreg Program European Territorial Cooperation - PLN 2.2 billion (MFIPR, 2022).

Another important document is the Strategy for the Responsible Development of Low-Emission Transport adopted in 2017 (RM, 2017). This is a document specifying goals and measures for the development of low-emission transport in Poland, including the promotion of low-emission transport means, e.g., electric or hydrogen vehicles.

Veolia Energia Polska SA, in cooperation with the foresight company 4CF, developed the Energy 2050 project, in which they not only presented, but also confronted with market participants (energy, telecommunications companies and electronics industry organizations) and market scenarios, their solutions regarding the impact of digitalization on the energy sector in Poland. The key is to be the supply of innovations and new solutions based on : Industrial Internet of Things—sensors in the network allowing monitoring of individual elements, e.g., system, storage, AI as a tool for managing supplies and optimizing energy storage, digital technologies, e.g., blockchain, which can improve the property and fixed assets management process, document circulation and logistics. They can also improve the flow of information and the security of supply chains. Intelligent networks supported by demand response models (Demand Response models) enable monitoring of changes, Virtual Power Plants (VPP) as systems integrating various energy sources used to manage energy distribution by monitoring and controlling its production and demand. Production optimization systems use data from smart meters and IoT devices on the consumer side. Reporting to the consumer, e.g., via a mobile application. As part of an intelligent local energy network, nearby energy-producing buildings. Virtual models built on data obtained from existing, real energy networks will reduce the time and cost of designing new installations, Securing and automating transactions within the energy network and virtual energy exchanges as digital platforms that would enable individual consumers to purchase energy (Transformation, 2050, 2020).

The European Union's digital transformation is a strategic initiative. Its goal is to make the best use of digital technologies in all economic processes, improve competitiveness and increase innovation. Digital Europe Strategy: launched in 2020, aims to strive for the EU to be a leader in digital technologies, an example is 5G and 6G (EC, 2023). Another program is NextGenerationEU, an economic recovery plan for the Member States, which, among others, investments in the area of digitalization are a priority. It can be said that it is the driving force of the ecological and digital transformation in the EU. The funds from this plan allow for an effective response in the event of such a need (EU, 2023). The EU promotes Industry 4.0 solutions: automation, robotization, augmented reality to improve the competitiveness of sectors. Such solutions appear, among others, in the European Union Green Deal document. The EU is leading the data protection and privacy initiative by introducing detailed data protection rules (GDPR) to strengthen privacy protection for consumers and citizens. On 30 September 2020, the EU adopted the *Digital Education Action Plan 2021–2027* (EU, 2020). The main assumption is digital education in Europe. The plan is intended to support and adapt education and training systems in EU countries to the requirements of the so-called digital era. These assumptions result from the EU's priority goal, which is *A Europe fit for the digital age*. It is also consistent with the assumptions of *Next Generation EU* (EU, 2020). It also supports the implementation of the goals of *The Recovery and Resilience Facility* RRF (EU, 2021), which serves to build a greener, digital and more resilient European Union. This confirms the EU's position on artificial intelligence, which believes that both enterprises and citizens should be able to access such a solution.

Enterprise management models in the energy sector and digitalization—on the example of JSW S A

The key task of modern managers is to increase shareholder value while taking into account the needs of other stakeholders. They use a number of management tools and methods. The essence is the return of invested capital. This creates a situation in which the most important element is the creation of value through appropriate strategic and operational decisions. Models are created that support the above-mentioned creation and constitute a specific combination of material assets and intellectual capital and are used to respond to the appropriate market situation. The variability of business models is emphasized due to financial and intellectual capital, networking of enterprises (clustering), innovation and management of enterprise results (Jabłoński, 2013). The business model design procedure includes the following elements: designing a value proposition, designing the value chain of production or service provision, defining key actors in the value chain, analyzing competition, designing an economic model, designing the relationships between individual actors of the business model. Gaining a competitive advantage means: treating the organization as a system (organizational and management structure), dynamic marketing focused on business partnership, but taking into account the impact of stakeholders, focusing on internal and external communication and the so-called resource orientation taking into account all members of the organization (Jabłoński, 2008). It is important to treat both qualitative and ecological criteria jointly. Ecological quality significantly influences strategic decisions and, consequently, influences the choice of the company's development direction (Chodyński, 2007). The solution may be, for example, benchmarking, which involves improving the efficiency of one's own organization through processes such as identifying, analyzing, adopting and implementing solutions used by the most effective organizations. There are qualitative and ecological benchmarking. Both can be an excellent tool for reducing the company's competence gap (Brillman, 2002). It can be an excellent tactical and operational tool, e.g., searching for appropriate solutions to protect (limit) the impact on the natural environment. Process management therefore includes: management of goals, efficiency, resources and the so-called contact between departments—white spots in the case of activities that cross the boundaries of certain departments (Rummler and Brache, 2000). The business model is therefore a key element of a modern management system. Information systems are used to exchange information on business events regarding business processes, models and strategies. There are strong feedback loops between the information system, strategy, processes and business models (Jabłoński, 2014).

The quality of products depends on the organization's management, and market success depends on the quality of management, which translates into a direct relationship with a possible crisis situation. Organizational responses are described within the concepts of organizational resilience and resilience strategy. The importance of non-economic impacts, including ecological ones, is emphasized. They should be accompanied by resilient behavior at various stages of the so-called resilience curve—a bathtub curve describing the course of the phenomenon. The concept of resilience is associated with the so-called rebirth of an organization after a crisis or failure and is most often associated with concepts such as resilience and resilience. Therefore, a resilient organization has the elements of a creative, intelligent and flexible organization.

Management of a mining company in Poland may be based on various management models that take into account the specificity of this industry and its challenges. In the context of increasing ecological awareness and environmental protection requirements, many mining companies in Poland are focusing on sustainable development. The sustainable development model assumes simultaneous consideration of economic, social and environmental aspects. Companies try to minimize the impact of mining on the natural environment and actively engage in local communities. The next one is the Lean Management Model, under which mining companies strive to optimize processes and eliminate waste (including human and material resources). They focus on operational efficiency, eliminating waste and delivering value to customers while reducing costs. Another may be a risk management model. Mining is an industry with many risks, both operational and market. It focuses on identifying, assessing and minimizing risks in mining activities. Creating emergency plans and managing crisis risk is also valuable. It is also worth mentioning the technological model. Mining companies in Poland can focus on investing in modern technologies such as automation, monitoring systems, data analysis and artificial intelligence. The use of advanced technologies can improve efficiency and safety in mining. Another is the partnership model. In some cases, mining companies enter into partnerships with other companies to increase operational efficiency or diversify their operations. This may include cooperation in the development of new mining projects or product diversification. The corporate social responsibility (CSR) model is also important, especially in the context of mining activities in Poland, which is often associated with difficult working conditions and the impact on the local community. It involves taking social actions that contribute to the development of local communities, ensuring employee safety and promoting a positive image of the company. However, due to changing market and raw material conditions, many mining companies in Poland use an adaptive model. This means being able to adapt to changes in raw material prices, market demand and government regulations. Each mining company can choose or adapt the appropriate management model depending on its specificity, business goals and operating environment. It is also important to monitor and evaluate the effectiveness of the selected model and adapt it to changing conditions.

The Capital Group Jastrzębska Spólka Węglowa SA is the largest producer of high-quality hard coking coal in the European Union and one of the leading producers of coke used to melt steel. JSW SA was established on April 1, 1993, and included seven mining companies, which were transformed into a sole-shareholder company of the State Treasury. On July 6, 2011, it debuted on the Warsaw Stock Exchange. JSW SA uses the following management models (JSW, 2023):

- Sustainable development: JSW SA is committed to sustainable development, which means simultaneous consideration of economic, social and environmental aspects in its activities. The company takes actions to minimize the impact of coal mining on the natural environment and support local communities, and from 2021 it reports its activities in the field of sustainable development as part of the Integrated Report available on the website.
- Safety: In the mining industry, employee safety is of paramount importance. JSW SA places emphasis on ensuring the highest level of safety in workplaces. It implements rigorous procedures and training programs (realistic representation of underground work in digital space - VR technology) to minimize the risk of accidents. Audits are an additional form of control. There is an Occupational Health and Safety Management System in place at JSW SA plants.
- Technologies and innovations: JSW SA invests in modern technologies that improve the efficiency of mining processes and ensure safety. This includes automation, monitoring systems, data analysis and the development of innovative solutions in the mining industry.
- Diversification of activities: JSW SA is involved not only in hard coal mining, but also in other areas, such as coke production, electricity production and

construction. Diversification of activities allows us to reduce the risk related to coal prices and adapt to changing market conditions.

- Risk management: JSW SA takes steps to identify, assess and manage various types of risks related to mining activities, including market, financial and operational risks. This includes creating contingency plans and crisis management.
- Stakeholder relationship management: JSW SA maintains good relationships with stakeholders, including local communities, local authorities, suppliers, customers and investors. Maintains dialogue and cooperation with various stakeholder groups.
- Corporate social responsibility (CSR): JSW SA is actively involved in social activities for the local communities in which it operates. This may include support for education, culture, health care and other areas important to society.
- Human resources management: Human resources management plays a key role in JSW SA. The company takes care of developing and training its employees, providing them with appropriate competences to work in a difficult and demanding mining environment.
- Regulatory supervision: JSW SA must strictly comply with mining laws and regulations, including environmental protection requirements, employee health and safety, and labor rights.
- Reporting and transparency: The company regularly reports its activities and financial results, which contributes to increasing the transparency of its activities and building stakeholder trust.

Digital transformation includes, among others: automation of mining processes (robotics and remote control systems), data monitoring and management (data analysis tools), employee safety and health (tracking devices, alarm systems, communication), supply chain optimization, employee training. JSW is implementing, for example, a reactive power compensation program. It is expected to bring the company PLN 15 million in annual savings. The program was developed and implemented by the Energy Management Office of JSW SA. It should be emphasized that it has been implemented since 2021. The first reactive power compensation systems have been installed and operate in the Pniówek Coal Mine and the Borynia-Zofiówka-Bzie Coal Mine in the Zofiówka and Borynia sections. Full digitization allows for an unmanned process. It is aimed at economic and ecological effects, e.g., Jastrzębska Spółka Węglowa will no longer pay fees for passive energy.

Another example is the project of an intelligent methane drainage system in the "Pniówek" mine. It received funding under the European MASTERMINE program for producers of critical raw materials, financed by the EU Horizon Europe research fund (EC, 2021). Its goal is to: optimize and improve the efficiency of the mine methane drainage system through its automation and digitization. The essence is the effective capture of methane released during operation. The implementation of this project takes into account the international aspect. The project consortium includes 22 units (including 2 from Poland): JSW SA and the Central Mining Institute. The project budget is: €13,840,490, co-financing €11,963,526, budget of

GIG and JSW S.A. - €1,130,988 and co-financing for GIG and JSW S.A. - €962,309. The investment is aimed at implementing the entire process, from the inventory of the methane drainage network to the determination of parameters. A project of a new network of sensors and control devices will be created. Additionally, algorithms will be developed for the system, which will enable the process to be autonomous without constant operator supervision. It should be emphasized that the methane drainage process is very complicated. Atmospheric pressure is problematic because the lower the barometer readings, the more methane can be released from the rock mass. The essence is therefore to create an intelligent system that responds flexibly to the situation occurring at a given time (CMM Energy, 2023).

SW Szkolenie i Górnictwo was established on February 4, 2014 as an entity dependent on JSW. Initially, the business profile concerned courses and training. Currently, he cooperates with entities such as the AGH University of Science and Technology in Kraków, the Institute of Industrial Technology in Radom, the Educational Research Institute in Warsaw and the Gomułka Group. It implements the following projects: The aim of the project is to increase the professional activity of residents of the Silesian Voivodeship, especially employees of coal companies. Additional qualifications and competences in the form of training, vocational courses, postgraduate studies, career counseling, and internships are intended to help employees find their way in the labor market during the energy transformation. The value of the project is 2 695 134,89 PLN (JSW SA, 2023). The second project is titled Improving work safety and communication of small work teams using a network VR environment (SENSE VR). The aim of the project is to develop a training method for miners based on the use of an adaptive VR network environment. A novelty in the project is the ability to adapt the training to the employee's knowledge—this process is to be carried out individually. The Central Mining Institute aims to analyze reports on mining accidents and then isolate key situations for which special training programs will be prepared. The project was implemented in the years 2000–2022 and had a value of PLN 3 239 990,72, of which PLN 2 321 979,71 were EU funds (European Regional Development Fund) (JSW SA, 2023). The last project is Preparation of solutions for engaging employers in the organization of practical training in professions in the protection and safety of persons and property (BPO). They cooperate here: Przemysłowa Akademia Rozwoju Sp. z o. o. in cooperation with JSW Szkolenie i Górnictwo Sp. z o. o. is implementing a project co-financed by the European Social Fund under the Knowledge Education Development Operational Program 2014–2020, Measure: 2.15 Vocational education and training adapted to the needs of the changing economy no. POWR.02.15.00-IP.02-00-002/20. The project was implemented in 2021–2022 and was aimed at the so-called practical vocational training: occupational health and safety technician, physical protection technician of people and property, and firefighting technician. The EU funds amounted to PLN 678 725,00 (JSW SA, 2023).

4 October 2023, at the headquarters of JSW SA. A project with a total cost of PLN 88,165,130.00 was signed between the National Fund for Environmental Protection and Water Management. The investment in the 'Budryk' coal mine consisted in the construction of specialized infrastructure enabling the management

of methane, which is obtained in the mine in the methane drainage process. The essence will be its use to generate energy for coal use (NFOŚiGW, 2023).

Conclusions

Jastrzębska Spółka Węglowa SA, due to the changing environment in which it finds itself, faces the challenge of maintaining current or choosing new future management models. Sustainable and more competitive solutions will certainly be the essence. However, it is important that the company is flexible and ready to invest in new solutions and technologies. This can be a key element to success. Therefore, solutions such as:

- diversification - reducing CO_2 emissions and investing in renewable energy sources,
- operational efficiency - based on modern technologies, process automation, etc.,
- environmental protection - pro-ecological solutions that protect not only the natural environment,
- modern technological solutions - JSW SA should improve processes by using modern, effective solutions, e.g., blockchain, data analysis, artificial intelligence,
- sustainable development of local communities - lasting relationships with stakeholders,
- research and development - not only imposed EU guidelines, but our own analysis of customer needs,
- human resources management - recruitment and training of employees, adapted to market needs, including the energy transformation. All activities should be included in a modern top-down and bottom-up strategy. The top strategy takes into account the management and the definition of: mission, goals, vision of the company. Functional areas are indicated, goals are set, and then projects are implemented. In the case of a down strategy, the knowledge that has already been used in previous situations is important, i.e., the so-called indicators, statistics. This could be a resource for future projects.

References

Brillant, J. 2002. *Nowoczesne koncepcje i metody zarządzania,* PWE, Warszawa.

Communication from the Commission to the European Parliament, the Council, the European Economic and Social Committee, the Committee of the Regions and the European Investment Bank A Framework Strategy for a Resilient Energy Union with a Forward-Looking Climate Change Policy, 2015. COM/2015/080 final, https://eur-lex.europa.eu/legal-content/EN/ALL/?uri=celex%3A52015DC0080 (accessed on 15 October 2023).

Communication from the Commission to the European Parliament, the European Council, the Council, the European Economic and Social Committee and the Committee of the Regions Artificial Intelligence for Europe COM/2018/237 final. 2018. Available online: https://eur-lex.europa.eu/legal-content/EN/TXT/?uri=COM:2018:237:FIN (accessed on 15 October 2023).

Chodyński, A. 2007. *Wiedza i kompetencje ekologiczne w strategiach rozwoju przedsiębiorstw*. Difin. Warszawa. 128–129.

Directive 2009/28/EC of the European Parliament and of the Council of 23 April 2009 on the promotion of the use of energy from renewable sources and amending and subsequently repealing Directives

2001/77/EC and 2003/30/EC, 2009. Available online: https://eur-lex.europa.eu/eli/dir/2009/28/oj (accessed on 15 October 2023).

Directive (EU) 2018/2001 of the European Parliament and of the Council of 11 December 2018 on the promotion of the use of energy from renewable sources (recast), 2018. Available online: https://eur-lex.europa.eu/legal-content/EN/TXT/?uri=uriserv:OJ.L_.2018.328.01.0082.01.ENG&toc=OJ:L:2018:328:TOC (accessed on 15 October 2023).

Energy efficiency, EP. 2023. Available online: https://www.europarl.europa.eu/factsheets/en/sheet/69/efektywnosc-energetyczna(accessed on 15 October 2023).

EC, 2023. *Energy*. Available online: https://energy.ec.europa.eu/topics/energy-strategy/national-energy-and-climate-plans-necps_en (accessed on 16 October 2023).

EC, 2023. *Shaping Europe's digital future*. Available online: https://energy.ec.europa.eu/topics/energy-strategy/national-energy-and-climate-plans-necps_en (accessed on 16 October 2023).

EC, 2023. *Horizon Europe is the EU's leading initiative for research and development*. Available online: https://www.consilium.europa.eu/en/policies/horizon-europe/ (accessed on 16 October 2023).

EC, 2023. *A Europe fit for the digital age. Empowering people with a new generation of technologies*. Available online: https://commission.europa.eu/strategy-and-policy/priorities-2019-2024/europe-fit-digital-age_en (accessed on 16 October 2023).

EC, 2023. *The Recovery and Resilience Facility*. Available online: https://commission.europa.eu/business-economy-euro/economic-recovery/recovery-and-resilience-facility_en (accessed on 16 October 2023).

EU, 2023. *NextGenerationEU*. Available online: https://next-generation-eu.europa.eu/index_pl (accessed on 16 October 2023).

EU, 2023. *Recovery plan for Europe*. Available online: https://commission.europa.eu/strategy-and-policy/recovery-plan-europe_en (accessed on 16 October 2023).

Jabłoński, A. 2008. *Modele biznesu w sektorach pojawiających się i schyłkowych, tworzenie przewagi konkurencyjnej przedsiębiorstwa opartej na jakości i kryteriach ekologicznych*. WSB. Dąbrowa Górnicza. p.25.

Jabłoński, M. 2013. *Kształtowanie modeli biznesu w procesie kreacji wartości przedsiębiorstw*. Difin. Warszawa. p. 29.

Jabłoński, M. 2014. *Współczesne trendy i wyzwania w zarządzaniu wartością przedsiębiorstw*. WSB. Dąbrowa Górnicza. p. 19.

JSW, 2023. Available online: https://www.jsw.pl/ (accessed on 16 October 2023).

MFiPR, 2022. Fundusze Europejskie 2021–2027. Available online: https://www.gov.pl/web/fundusze-regiony/fundusze-ue-2021-27(accessed on 15 October 2023).

MKiŚ, 2019. Krajowy plan na rzecz energii i klimatu na lata 2021-2030.Warszawa.

MFiPR, 2017. Strategia na rzecz Odpowiedzialnego Rozwoju 2020 z perspektywą do 2030. Warszawa.

MFiPR, 2021. Instrument na rzecz Odbudowy I zwiększenia Odporności (Recovery and Resilience Facility – RFF. Warszawa.

MKiŚ, 2021. Polityka Energetyczna Polski do roku 2040. Warszawa.

National long-term strategies. EU countries' long-term strategies to meet their Paris Agreement commitments and the energy union objectives, EC, 2023. Available online: https://commission.europa.eu/energy-climate-change-environment/implementation-eu-countries/energy-and-climate-governance-and-reporting/national-long-term-strategies_pl#:~:text=EU%20long%2Dterm%20strategy,-The%20Commission%20put&text=The%20European%20Council%20endorsed%20in,(UNFCCC)%20in%20March%202020 (accessed on 15 October 2023).

NFOŚiGW, 2023. Available online: https://www.gov.pl/web/nfosigw/narodowy-fundusz-ochrony-srodowiska-i-gospodarki-wodnej?utm_source=GA&utm_medium=cpc&utm_campaign=Inwestycje_reportaze_II_Tura&utm_content=bokstekstowy&gclid=CjwKCAjwysipBhBXEiwApJOcu1V1bMo8as787olBsaOcNW7L7JFcqKaHFNpjJuqnuD4BqEn2g5t5EhoCPnQQAvD_BwE (accessed on 15 October 2023).

Proposal for a Directive of the European Parliament and of the Council amending Directive (EU) 2018/2001 of the European Parliament and of the Council, Regulation (EU) 2018/1999 of the European Parliament and of the Council and Directive 98/70/EC of the European Parliament and of the Council as regards the promotion of energy from renewable sources, and repealing Council Directive (EU) 2015/652,COM/2021/557 final. 2021. Available online: https://eur-lex.europa.eu/

resource.html?uri=cellar:dbb7eb9c-e575-11eb-a1a5-01aa75ed71a1.0001.02/DOC_1&format=PDF (accessed on 15 October 2023).

Proposal for a Directive of the European Parliament and of the Council on energy efficiency (recast) COM/2021/558 final, 2021. Available online: https://eur-lex.europa.eu/legal-content/EN/TXT/?uri=CELEX%3A52021PC0558 (accessed on 15 October 2023).

Proposal for a Council directive restructuring the Union framework for the taxation of energy products and electricity (recast) COM/2021/563 final. 2021. Available online: https://eur-lex.europa.eu/legal-content/en/TXT/?uri=CELEX%3A52021PC0563 (accessed on 15 October 2023).

Proposal for a Directive of the European Parliament and of the Council on the energy performance of buildings (recast) COM/2021/802 final, 2021. Available online: https://eur-lex.europa.eu/legal-content/EN/TXT/?uri=CELEX:52021PC0802(accessed on 15 October 2023).

Proposal for a Directive of the European Parliament and of the Council on common rules for the internal markets in renewable and natural gases and in hydrogen, COM/2021/803 final.2021. Available online: https://eur-lex.europa.eu/legal-content/EN/TXT/?uri=CELEX:52021PC0803(accessed on 16 October 2023).

Proposal for a Regulation of the European Parliament and of the Council on the internal markets for renewable and natural gases and for hydrogen (recast) COM/2021/804 final. 2021. Available online: https://eur-lex.europa.eu/legal-content/EN/TXT/?uri=COM:2021:804:FIN (accessed on 16 October 2023).

Proposal for a Regulation of the European Parliament and of the Council on the deployment of alternative fuels infrastructure, and repealing Directive 2014/94/EU of the European Parliament and of the Council COM/2021/559 final.2021. Available online: https://eur-lex.europa.eu/legal-content/EN/TXT/?uri=COM:2021:804:FIN (accessed on 16 October 2023).

Proposal for a Regulation of the European Parliament and of the Council on ensuring a level playing field for sustainable air transport COM/2021/561 final. 2021. Available online: https://eur-lex.europa.eu/legal-content/EN/TXT/?uri=COM:2021:804:FIN (accessed on 16 October 2023).

Proposal for a Regulation of the European Parliament and of the Council on the use of renewable and low-carbon fuels in maritime transport and amending Directive 2009/16/EC. 2009. https://eur-lex.europa.eu/legal-content/EN/TXT/?uri=COM:2021:804:FIN (accessed on 16 October 2023).

Rummler, G. A. and Brache, A. P. 2000. Podnoszenie efektywności organizacji, PWE. Warszawa. pp. 51–52.

RM, 2017. Strategia na rzecz Odpowiedzialnego Rozwoju. Warszawa.

Veolia, 4FC. 2020. Transformation 2050. Available online: https://transformacja2050.pl/project/cyfryzacja-w-energetyce-analiza/(accessed on 16 October 2023).

Chapter 5

Value Creation for the Digital Consumer

A Management Guide

Bożena Gajdzik,[1,*] *Magdalena Jaciow*[2] and *Robert Wolny*[2]

Introduction

The advent of the 21st century heralds the onset of the fourth industrial revolution, with digital transformation serving as a cornerstone. This transformation affects all sectors, including societal, economic, and international relationships. The digital economy is underpinned by datafication and networking procedures that generate new digital representations of real-world phenomena. Both businesses and consumers must navigate and establish their roles within this novel paradigm.

In the digital economy, consumers are characterized by their active use of digital technologies. Generation Y and Generation Z represent the driving forces of this economy. Varieties of such active consumers encompass e-consumers, m-consumers, and c-consumers. E-consumers fulfill their needs by purchasing products online, m-consumers achieve the same via mobile devices, while c-consumers embody fully digital entities that express and meet their needs through personalized digital goods acquired online.

The traits of consumers in the digital economy range widely, from a comprehensive acceptance of digital technologies to convenience, innovation,

[1] Faculty of Materials Engineering, Department of Industrial Informatics, The Silesian University of Technology, Gliwice, 44-100, Poland.

[2] Faculty of Economy, Department of Digital Economy Research, The University of Economics in Katowice, 1 Maja 50, 40-287 Katowice, Poland.
Email: magdalena.jaciow@ue.katowice.pl, ORCID: 0000-0003-3518-923X
Email: robert.wolny@ue.katowice.pl, ORCID: 0000-0003-4088-718X

* Corresponding author: bozena.gajdzik@polsl.pl, ORCID: 0000-0002-0408-1691

mobility, personalization, omnichannel behavior, community involvement, trend-following, desire for control, and a conscious choice of overpayment during the purchasing process. These characteristics underscore how digitalization is reshaping consumer behaviors and preferences.

Given the escalating competition and the volatile nature of market landscapes, gaining a profound understanding of consumer behaviors and value perceptions is imperative. Factors influencing consumer buying decisions stem both from internal (consumer-related) and external (environmental) sources. Technological advancements, particularly in the realms of internet and mobile telephony, have upended conventional consumption patterns. The surge of e-commerce and the digital economy has further morphed how consumers shop and engage with businesses. This chapter underscores the significance of personalization and value co-creation within the digital economy, as well as the impact of digital technologies and social media on consumer behaviors.

The objective of this chapter is to articulate strategies and managerial practices that will capacitate companies to effectively create value for digital consumers. The aim is to offer insights and practical knowledge on measures that can be employed to fulfill the needs and expectations of online consumers, guarantee customer satisfaction, and cultivate enduring relationships with them.

This chapter explores the core values that digital consumers seek in online shopping, the significance of customer segmentation, strategies for digital customer acquisition and retention, challenges in handling digital consumer relationships, and methods of creating value for customers in e-commerce. The necessity of effective communication, fostering customer relationships, and leveraging technology to thrive in the online market is emphasized.

The consumer in the digital economy

Digital transformation represents a unique type of organizational change impacting various entities, including businesses, sectors, supply chains, public administration, and entire economies. In broad terms, it signifies a "structural alteration in the operational model of the market, consumers, businesses, and other organizations (including governmental bodies), employees, and the global economy, driven by datafication" (Śledziewska and Włoch, 2020). It encompasses "modifications associated with the deployment of digital technology across all facets of human society" (Leodolter, 2017). Core drivers of the digital transformation process are commonly acknowledged as digital data, automation, connectivity, and digital consumer access. The concept of a "digital economy" was first introduced in 1996 by D. Tapscott, who termed it the "era of network intelligence" (Tapscott, 1996). An encompassing definition of the digital economy proposes that it "refers to a broad range of economic activities that include using digitized information and knowledge as the key factor of production, modern information networks as an important activity space, and the effective use of information and communication technology (ICT) as an important driver of productivity growth and economic structural optimalization" (G20 DETF, 2016).

The evolution of the information society has stimulated modifications in the consumer category. The initial references to the information society can be traced back to the 1960s. The evolution of the concept of the information society underscores the fundamental factors of its development:

- Proliferation and popularization of modern information and communication technologies,
- Advancement of a knowledge-based economy,
- Sustainable, balanced development wherein economic growth, environmental conservation, and efforts to maintain social bonds should harmoniously align.

The consumer within the digital economy is an individual actively employing digital technologies. Generation Y (commonly referred to as the network generation, born between 1980 and 1994, brought up in the age of globalization and universal internet access) and Generation Z (iGeneration, born between 1995 and 2009, who engage with new technologies that have pervaded all facets of their existence) are typically considered the active entities of the digital economy (Kryvachuk, 2021). Active consumers in the digital economy include:

- e-consumers,
- m-consumers,
- c-consumers.

An e-consumer is a person who expresses and satisfies their consumer needs through products (goods and services) purchased online (Wolny, 2023). The e-consumer is a party to transactions in e-commerce. Due to the dynamic development of the mobile device market, a category of mobile commerce appeared in the literature (Chmielarz and Łuczak, 2016), in which the m-consumer is the party.

An m-consumer is a person who expresses and satisfies their consumer needs with goods and services purchased using mobile devices (Wolny, 2023). The fundamental difference between an e-consumer and an m-consumer is the abolition of restrictions associated with using stationary devices connected to the internet, and the availability of access to sales channels through mobile devices (tablets and smartphones).

The fully integrated subject of the digital economy is the digital consumer (c-consumer). The c-consumer is a person who expresses and satisfies their consumer needs through personalized digital products purchased online (Jaciow and Wolny, 2022). In the case of e-consumers and m-consumers, their purchasing behaviors may take place both online and offline, but for traditional purchases, at least one stage of the purchase process had to be associated with online behaviors (e.g., product search, information search, etc.). The digital consumer manifests buying behaviors exclusively through the internet, and digital products, often personalized, are the object of purchase, usually through mobile applications.

Several characteristics can be listed for consumers in the digital economy (Jaciow and Wolny, 2022):

- Full acceptance of digital technologies (including chatbots, virtual reality, voice control, artificial intelligence, the Internet of Things, and blockchain),

- Convenience (wants to shop or pay bills at any time/round the clock and receive deliveries at times convenient for them),
- Innovation (seeks what's new, different, unique; values the latest technological solutions, likes to experiment, is capable of co-creating new solutions),
- Mobility (not limited by either place or time; uses mobile devices),
- Personalization (wants to feel important, wants to be treated individually, wants goods/e-services tailored to their preferences),
- Omnichannel (moves from one channel to another – from the online channel to the offline channel and vice versa – and expects a uniform, consistent experience and smooth integration of both channels),
- Engagement (speaks up, expresses their opinions, comments, recommends),
- Participation in communities (is a member of groups/internet communities focused around the purchased and used products and brands),
- Trend-following (thanks to unlimited access to information, and often being a co-creator of information, they become a propagator of trends, and even a promoter – trendsetter, e.g., creating network communities, avatarization, trisumerism),
- Need for control (in online shopping they have full control over such activities as: information search, order placement, tracking (tracking) the parcel, etc.),
- Conscious overpayment in the purchase process (pays extra for transaction security on the internet, for the certainty of delivery of the parcel, or for shortening its delivery time).

In the digital economy, consumer behavior is undergoing considerable transformation, with factors influencing online purchasing behavior concurrently evolving. Much of this evolution stems from shifts in consumer trends, which can be short-term or long-term, global or regional. Current trends that are molding the purchasing behaviors of e-consumers comprise (Jaciow et al., 2013; Jaciow and Wolny, 2022; Błoński and Witek, 2019):

- Individualization of lifestyles, manifested in unconventional dress style, behavior, and professed values,
- Presumption, manifested in the activity of consumers who willingly share their market knowledge, positive and negative experiences resulting from the use of the product, recommend or discourage others from buying the product,
- Technification of consumption, i.e., the development of e-commerce and m-commerce,
- Platformization of consumption, i.e., the development of platforms enabling e-consumers purchasing processes,
- Shared consumption, a consumption model in which needs are satisfied by sharing owned products,
- Minimalism, based on the quantitative limitation of the status of owned products, as well as choosing better quality products,
- Ecologization of consumption, i.e., the process of popularizing the ecological awareness of consumption.

Creating value for customers in digital economies

Providing value to customers is important for business growth. For a customer to want to buy a product, they must derive value from it. The term value comes from the word to be valuable (valor or valere) (Ratajczyk, 2009). The value of a product to the consumer is the ability of that product to satisfy individually perceived needs. From a company's point of view, it is important to understand the customer's needs and identify what will constitute value for the customer. The concept of consumer value is strongly linked to value marketing and relationship marketing (Kotler, 1991; Doyle, 2000). The concept of consumer value appears in the definition of marketing management, by authors Kotler and Keller (2006). Although the primary carrier (source) of value for the consumer is the product (the product should be considered here as a carrier and provider of value), value must also be referred to the relationship with the producer or supplier, to the brand, to the consumer's trust in the producer, to the producer's image, etc. In recent years, the business world has seen the dominance of the value paradigm, and the concept of value is constantly being extended. The development of a company requires, above all, knowledge, the involvement of personnel, rapid decision-making and the exploration of new areas of solutions based, among other things, on the creation and introduction of innovations. Customers are a prerequisite for the existence of any enterprise.

In market economies, which are accompanied by increasing dynamics of change, value orientation is evident in the network of connections and interdependencies between business and consumer. The main objective of business activity is to build and enhance market value. Each business wants to build its own consumer value map, which is to be unique, original and different from the existing values offered to consumers. Consumers' needs, as well as their expectations and even their dreams, are the inspirations for business activity. The consumer, who is the primary user of the product, provides knowledge to the producer about his or her needs, experiences with the product, ways of using it, terms of purchase, forms of payment, time of purchase, and so on. Consumers are the main inspirers for business in the process of value creation. Therefore, it is correct to say that businesses are 'driven by customers' (Kotler 2005). Different consumers create different values. But while consumers judge offerings based on their use and experience (Holbrook, 1999), companies see value as profit (Ng 2013). Value is the result of two areas of value colliding, i.e., consumer value and business value, but business cannot exist without consumers (Hill et al., 1999).

In economies of intensified competition, the issue of consumer behaviour is of increasing importance. Flowing from needs and expectations, purchasing behaviour consists of making choices between available options with limited resources. Investigating consumers' perception of value is quite difficult. Many factors contribute to the prediction of consumer purchasing decisions. The consumer's behaviour in the market is influenced by both internal factors—related to the consumer himself, and external factors - inherent in his environment (Solomon et al., 1999). Among these, the technological factor deserves special attention. Advances in internetisation with mobile telephony and globalisation and internationalisation have revolutionised the sphere of consumption (Zhang et al., 2013). It is the information age that has contributed to the birth of the e-consumer. Consumers are different and their individual behaviours are difficult to compare. In addition, consumers think and behave dynamically. Consumer needs are complex and evolving. Value is the subjective assessment of each consumer (Armstrong and Kotler, 2000, p. 112-113). The determinants of consumers' purchasing decisions must (and are) analysed in detail, for only then can they form the basis of strategic decisions, becoming the foundation for tailoring the offer to their needs, and thus increasing the level of their satisfaction. In turn, a higher level of customer satisfaction determines a higher rate of loyalty, understood as both repeat purchases and recommendations.

Enterprises operate in a dynamic market environment, which means that they constantly have to keep track of consumer needs and get to know consumers. Companies need to combine business activities in the right proportions in order to operate effectively. There are two aspects of customer value: desired value and perceived value. Desired value refers to what customers expect in a product or service. Perceived value is the benefit that the customer believes he or she has received as a result of purchasing the product (Zupok, 2018). The entrepreneur should consider the product as a set/amalgam of features, benefits and values offered to satisfy needs and desires in the process of bringing about an exchange (Lrhmann and Winer, 2002). In the digital economy, another aspect of value is added, which is personalisation (Ardissono et al., 2002, Goy et al). The co-creation of value requires long-term partnerships between the consumer and the company (Humphreys and Grayson, 2008).

The digital economy is providing firms with new opportunities. One of these is that firms could potentially change the value but must allow customers to participate in the creation of the product. E-commerce is a highly dynamic business activity. This is due, on the one hand, to the development of new information technologies, the increase in the intensity of competition, the emergence of new business models and, on the other, to the development of the information society and the increasing accessibility of the web. Customers of online shops, as technological tools and means develop, are e-consumers of different ages. When doing e-shopping, customers are guided by price, product quality, convenience of purchase, speed of delivery, time saving, etc. (Jaciow and Wolny, 2022).

Modern consumers have adapted quite quickly to changing market realities and new mobile solutions. E-consumers are using digital technologies to make their lives easier and are thus redefining the way they shop. The digital consumer is a person who regularly shops in e-shops and uses the many applications available on IT platforms. The e-consumer purchases products and services through their platforms (Krzepicka, 2016). The digitisation of many areas of life, the development of communication tools and the possibility to analyse the huge amount of data obtained both from Internet users and the increasing number of devices connected to the Internet have provided the opportunity to both create value and share knowledge of preferred value (desired, target, future). Social media allow their participants to share, co-share and co-create information resources, including shopping preferences, fashion, shopping trends, etc.

New opportunities created by information and communication infrastructures have created the possibility of shopping, exclusively in cyberspace. Technical and economic barriers to the use of ICT are disappearing. A fundamental driver of ICT use is the cognitive skills of consumers. Through e-commerce, the consumer can find a better offer faster (Grzywińska-Rąpca and Grzybowska-Brzezińska, 2015). In the digital economy, the value provided by companies is understood very broadly. Values include product, service, price, place, forms of purchase, advertising, communication, partnerships, etc. (Dobiegała-Korona and Doligalski, 2010). The consumer in the digital economy is particularly interested in co-creating the product at the design and manufacturing stage (Berger and Piller, 2003). The consumer does not want to be a passive market participant. The consumer in the digital economy wants to be an active consumer. T. Levitt believes that the real competition is not between what companies produce in their factories, but between what they add to their products in the form of packaging, services, advertising, advice to buyers, pricing, storage, delivery methods and other treatments that have value for buyers. When software teams modify their engineering process they take into account the needs of consumers and their assessment of product quality. Implications in engineering processes are the results of consumer requirements (Gorschek and Davis, 2008). The result of customer, or consumer, activity is a highly personalised product (Kuksa et al., 2022). In digital personalisation, issues of privacy, design ethics and the designer's and creator's control over consumer freedom are challenges for organisations (Saniuk et al., 2020; Gajdzik et al., 2021). Access to new media technologies and software, as well as forms of communication and data storage and use (cloud) sites is open. Value co-creation occurs in context; empowering the consumer with the ability to dynamically reconfigure the offering the benefit is potentially increased (Humphreys and Grayson, 2008).

In the digital economy, value is becoming increasingly (more) personalised. Ubiquitous digital technologies are growing exponentially, changing the nature of products and services. Davies and Ng (2015) discuss in their publication, the concept of the incomplete product in transactions carried out in the digital economy. Companies can now provide digital offerings to consumers. The product can be designed to be incomplete, allowing consumers to complete the offering by applying their own resources. Product functionality can be added (reprogrammed) even after the product has been handed over to the customer. In this respect, the product will remain 'incomplete' for life (Yoo et al., 2010). An incomplete product will be constantly adapted to the changing needs of the consumer. In order to obtain a better 'fit' of value to his needs, incremental manufacturing technology supported by AI and machine learning algorithms, technology that communicates with the environment through the Internet of Everything (IoE) must be perfected. The direction set by Industry 4.0 (Kagermann et al., 2011; Schwab, 2016) of smart factories seems to be the right direction for consumer needs. The advance of ubiquitous digital technology has opened up a whole new picture of value in cyber-physical systems. The old image of the consumer and his or her decision-making behaviour in the shopping area in the 21st century, dominated by new internet-based technologies, is being obliterated. Today, the market is the e-consumer (Tkaczyk, 2016).

Development of digital technologies, firms are now able to serve context (value-in-use). The value corpus is a modular architecture, encompassing both product and service architecture, which is capable of dynamic reconfiguration. Personalisation is built on top of this modular architecture. This process is no longer linear, but is a system in which each party integrates resources to find the optimal fit between the subject, the offer and their value of use (Ardissono et al., 2002; Goy et al., 2007). Shaping the value of a product should take place at each stage of product management and should include: researching consumer needs, design, execution, delivery, market relations, communication, sharing, etc. At the product design stage, in order to ensure the success of the product in the market, sets of features and characteristics should be identified, in the context of being transformed and interpreted by the consumer, as value attributes (Ratajaczyk, 2009). The value attributes embodied in products are enriched by purchase accessibility, modes of use, product branding, corporate image, post-use product development, symbolic meaning, substitutability, complementarity, product function optimisation, LCA, etc. The multiplicity of commercial offerings and the availability of a variety of communicative and transactional solutions means that consumers are determining the fate of companies like never before, with full freedom of choice (Dennis et al., 2009).

Modern societies, the so-called network society, cannot imagine life without a computer and constant access to the World Wide Web. The integration and penetration of virtualisation is experienced by almost everyone in the modern world. In January 2022, the number of people using the Internet worldwide was almost 5 billion. At the beginning of 2000, it was only 350,000 people. Internet penetration is now 62.5 per cent of the world's total population (Digital 2022 Report). Internet use has become almost standard, regardless of age, education level, income or gender. More and more consumers are operating in a dual reality. In the information age, where access to IT is universal, the real and virtual worlds intermingle. For many consumers today, especially young consumers (generation Z), online shopping is part of their lives. Factories (manufacturers) are constantly looking for communication solutions that favour consumer acquisition. Companies produce products that build relationships with consumers. In order to win the consumer's trust, forms are outdoing themselves with market offers. In the digital economy, market offers encourage the consumer to be a business partner.

E-commerce is now international, so even national culture can influence customer behaviour. A model of consumer acceptance of e-commerce globally should consider the influence of culture on perceived usefulness, perceived ease of use, trust and intention to use (Featherstone, 1991; Yoon, 2009). Furthermore, there is a lack of understanding of the impact of culture on the value creation process of smart robots (Chi et al., 2023). Smart technologies have an important place in the concept of Industry 4.0. The transformation of services towards 'high-touch and high-tech' can only be successful if consumers accept the use of such technologies in service delivery (Belanche et al., 2020). Today's consumers (people from different cultural backgrounds) may exhibit different behaviours related to technology acceptance (Ameen and Willis, 2015; Lee et al., 2013) and perceptions of the place of robots in value creation and assisted shopping (Bartneck et al., 2007; Rau et al., 2009). In the context of the use of artificial intelligence technologies, culture may also be a key determinant of people's behavioural intentions (Belanche et al., 2020). E-consumers are supported in their purchases by intelligent shopping assistants (robots). Trust should be a belief that is the result of users' evaluation of robot-related factors such as robot performance, task environments or robot features (Chi et al., 2021; Tussyadiah et al., 2020).

In a digital economy strongly supported by Industry 4.0, value has many faces. Decision-making dilemmas arise, such as: what new value components can be developed for future smart factory offerings? What implications does a smart product have on the business model? What implications does personalisation have on offer design and delivery? Where can the boundary for personalisation be drawn? What Fourth Industrial Revolution technologies can be used to help companies serve the value proposition? What are the limits of material, digital and human resources in value creation? Can consumers trust robots and intelligent shopping assistants?

The technological dilemmas cited generate social and sustainability dilemmas. Therefore, Industry 4.0 will be followed by Industry 5.0, in which a balance between technology development and sustainability and humanisation is sought (Grabowska et al., 2021). The transformation of services towards 'high-tech' can only succeed if consumers accept the use of such technologies in service provision (Belanche et al., 2020).

Elements of relationship management in the process of creating value for digital customers

The development of online businesses depends, among other things, on the value of intangible assets they generate. Intangible assets are most commonly classified into three categories (Kaplan, Norton, 2011, p. 32-33):

1. Human capital: the knowledge, skills, and talents of employees.
2. Information capital: databases, information systems, networks, and technological infrastructure.
3. Organizational capital: culture, leadership, workforce alignment, teamwork, and knowledge management.

In the modern business model, value creation occurs through communication and customer relationship management processes. Referring to the strategy map, which is an extension of the Balanced Scorecard by Kaplan (Kaplan, Norton, 2011, p. 49-50), it should be noted that creating value from intangible assets is characterized by the following:

- Value creation is indirect because intangible assets rarely have a direct impact on business results but contribute to the improvement of various processes. These, in turn, can increase customer satisfaction and contribute to their loyalty.
- Value is context-dependent and depends on aligning intangible assets with the strategy.
- Value is potential. Transforming potential value into actual value requires appropriate internal processes. In the case of e-commerce, this particularly pertains to distribution and customer service processes.

Fig. 1. Digital customer relationship management process. Source: Own study.

The nature of functioning of internet-based businesses offering products requires the planning of an appropriate digital customer relationship management process. The digital customer relationship management process is presented in Fig. 1.

Taking into account the main elements of the value creation process for digital customers, specific components of this process can be identified in the case of Polish e-consumers. To do this, direct research conducted in 2020 on a sample of 1150 Polish online shoppers was used. The research had nationwide coverage and was carried out using an online survey method. The study included an equal number of women and men. The average age of the surveyed e-consumers was 39 years, with slightly over half of them having higher education. The majority of participants were employed (actively working).

The research focused on the characteristics of e-consumers, which formed the demographic and psychographic profile of internet users making purchases online. The study also provided insights into the product assortment structure of Polish e-consumers' shopping carts, their motivations for online shopping, methods of gathering information about e-commerce offerings, and identified factors influencing product selection and online purchasing conditions. The study examined e-consumers' post-purchase experiences, preferences regarding organizational forms of online commerce, as well as factors influencing their choice of shopping destination. It also identified internet users' attitudes towards change, obligations, trends, and environmental considerations. The full description of the methodology for studying Polish consumers is presented in Jaciow, Wolny (2011) and Jaciow, Wolny (2022).

Based on the obtained research results, an descriptive model of managing relationships with Polish e-consumers can be created (Fig. 2).

For digital consumers, the greatest values in the context of online shopping are:

1. Time savings
2. 24/7 availability of products
3. Lower prices compared to traditional retail
4. Ability to compare offerings from different manufacturers on websites or comparison platforms
5. Convenience of shopping

To ensure effective value creation, proper customer segmentation is necessary. Direct research indicates that the target group should consist of e-consumers (both women and men) with at least a secondary or higher education, actively employed, and with a monthly net income ranging from approximately 1730 to 7400 PLN.

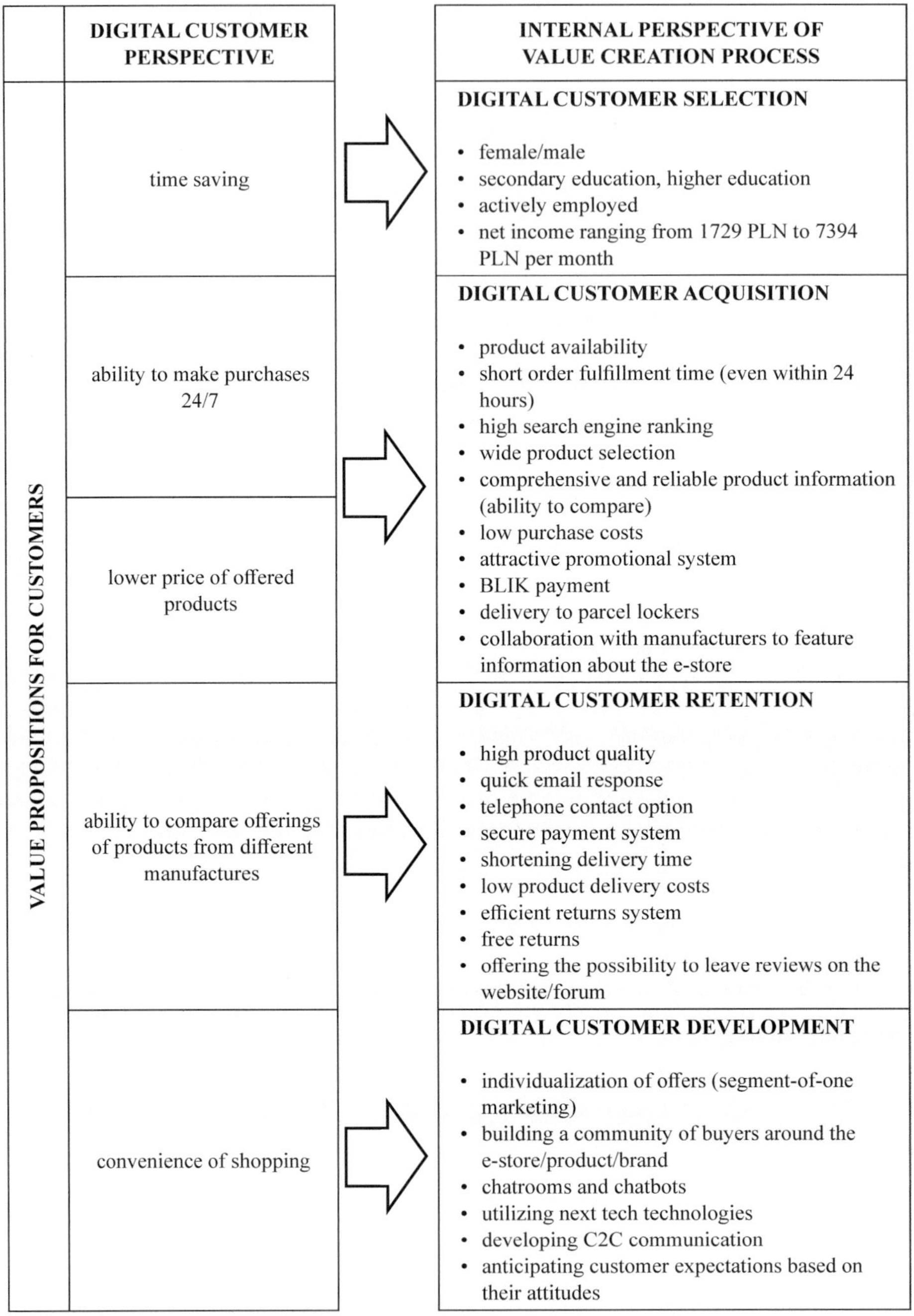

Fig. 2. Elements of managing relationships with Polish e-consumers. Source: adapted from (Kaplan, Norton, 2011, p. 132).

In the process of managing relationships with e-consumers, it is important to employ appropriate strategies to acquire digital customers. This includes ensuring product availability in the online store, offering a wide range of products with relatively low purchasing costs, and implementing an attractive promotional system.

Product offerings should be presented in a comprehensive and reliable manner, providing the ability to compare products based on various criteria. Collaboration with manufacturers is recommended to include information on where (in which e-stores) the product can be purchased. It is crucial to secure a high position for the e-store in search engine rankings. Order fulfillment time should be as short as possible (even within 24 hours), and digital customers should have the option of using BLIK payment and choosing delivery to parcel lockers.

In value creation, it is not only important to acquire customers (which is relatively easier) but also to retain them (which is more challenging). This involves offering high-quality products and ensuring consistent and prompt email communication with e-consumers, as well as providing the option for telephone contact. Customer retention is linked to secure payment systems, cost reduction, and shorter product delivery times. A seamless system for free returns should also be provided. Digital consumers should have the opportunity to share their opinions on the website/forum/social media profiles.

The most challenging aspect for businesses in managing relationships with digital consumers is developing customer relationships to transform them into "ambassadors" of the e-store. To achieve this, e-commerce companies should guarantee individualization of the purchasing process (segment-of-one marketing), build communities around the e-store/product/brand (e.g., on social media), utilize chatrooms and chatbots, as well as leverage technologies such as next-gen tech (including artificial intelligence, natural language processing, augmented and virtual reality, the Internet of Things, and blockchain).

E-commerce platforms should also foster C2C communication, allowing for mutual interactions not only between the e-store and the customer but also among customers themselves. Anticipating digital customer expectations resulting from their attitudes is also essential. For example, to address the growing environmental attitudes of e-consumers, a pro-environmental form of product delivery can be implemented, even if the customer does not currently expect or verbalize such an expectation (e.g., packaging-free products, reusable packaging, appropriately sized packaging, plastic-free packaging, electronic ticketing, etc.).

The presented ways of managing relationships with e-consumers are not a ready-made "recipe for success" for e-commerce companies, but they can help in attracting customers and building lasting relationships with them. As the experiences of many internet-based businesses have shown, simply existing online is no longer enough; it is necessary to skillfully manage the entire operation, including relationships with e-consumers.

Companies striving for market success must achieve a higher effectiveness than their competition in creating products desired by buyers (with high value for them), providing these products, and communicating the value they offer to selected target groups (digital customer types).

The sale of a product is a consequence of accepting an offer that digital customers perceive as best meeting their needs, preferences, and goals. For the buyer, the value of the offer matters, which includes its usefulness and the cost associated with accepting it.

Analyzing e-consumers' attitudes towards their environment, several characteristics of a product can be identified as valuable. Products that allow for social connections, are healthy (including low-calorie food), inexpensive yet high-quality, eco-friendly, trendy, time-saving, and cost-effective generate value for the buyer. From the analysis of e-consumers' needs satisfaction, it also becomes evident that desirable products are those that enable them to participate in culture, provide relaxation and recreation.

When conducting online sales, a company must constantly remind e-consumers of the benefits associated with this type of commerce. These benefits enhance the perceived value of the offer for e-buyers and include lower financial and time costs incurred during the purchase, as well as access to products and related information.

The value of the offer for e-consumers will be greater when there is a higher level of certainty regarding the seller's credibility, honesty, and reliability. Digital consumers expect to receive a product that matches the description provided by the seller in the online store, fulfills their order, and meets the conditions promised by the seller (such as delivery deadlines).

The risk that digital consumers fear is associated with the security of transactions. Sellers should minimize concerns about fraud related to e-payments and the disclosure of e-customer's personal data to third parties. The level of trust is also increased by the empathy and availability of sales personnel who are always open and willing to help, answer buyer's questions, handle complaints smoothly, or accept returns of purchased goods.

Digital consumers, in order to limit the risks associated with purchases, seek information. This information should relate to the product, its price, and technical specifications. Since the main source of information for e-consumers, as well as a factor they consider when choosing a product and a place of purchase, are the opinions of others, a trading company should provide the buyer with constant access to complete and honest information and reviews, even in situations where not all opinions are positive.

Taking a holistic view of how digital consumers make purchases: their motives, determinants of choices, sources of information they rely on, and the convenience offered by e-stores, it is possible to identify sources of competitive advantage for online sellers that generate value for customers. These include low prices, positive reviews, lower shipping costs, shorter order fulfillment times, offered promotions, secure payment systems, organizing online contests, providing product customization options, and price negotiation.

Knowledge of the main sources of competitive advantage for a company is the basis for building an effective communication strategy with the target group of e-consumers. The communication strategy involves implementing actions through which the company provides consumers with information about the product and/or the company. By undertaking communication activities, the company creates needs and stimulates purchasing behavior. With a range of marketing communication tools at their disposal, companies utilize the ones that are most effective in the target market.

For businesses operating online, actions related to creating opinion leaders are of particular importance. Opinion leaders are individuals whose behaviors and opinions are imitated by others due to their position, status, prestige, knowledge, etc. Consumers turn to opinion leaders for information, advice, or opinions. 60% of consumers make purchases under the influence of opinion leaders. The influence of opinion leaders involves consciously or unconsciously transmitting information to their surroundings about ways to meet needs, products, and places of purchase. The development of virtual communities has led to the emergence of virtual opinion leaders on the Internet, who have a real impact on the purchasing behavior of other internet users. From this perspective, reaching out to opinion leaders becomes particularly crucial for businesses.

Summary

The paramount values for digital consumers in online shopping encompass time savings, round-the-clock product availability, lower prices compared to traditional retail, the ability to contrast offerings from different manufacturers, and shopping convenience. To effectively create value, accurate customer segmentation is crucial, targeting e-consumers who possess at least a secondary education or higher, are actively employed, and have a monthly net income within a specific bracket.

Strategies for acquiring digital customers entail ensuring product availability, offering a broad product range at relatively low costs, and deploying an appealing promotional system. Product offerings should be presented in a comprehensive and reliable manner, facilitating product comparisons based on various criteria. Collaborations with manufacturers and securing a high search engine ranking are advised. Swift order fulfilment, flexible payment options, and delivery to parcel lockers are key for digital customers.

Customer retention is essential and can be achieved through offering high-quality products, regular and prompt email communication, telephone contact, secure payment systems, cost reduction, shorter delivery times, and a seamless free returns system. Providing platforms for customer opinions and feedback is also vital.

Transforming digital customers into "ambassadors" for the e-store entails strategies such as personalizing the purchasing process, fostering communities centred around the e-store/product/brand, utilizing chatrooms and chatbots, and leveraging cutting-edge technologies like artificial intelligence, augmented and virtual reality, and blockchain. Encouraging C2C communication and anticipating customer expectations, such as environmentally-friendly product delivery, are also recommended.

Companies should continuously remind e-consumers of the benefits associated with online shopping, amplify the perceived value of their offerings, and build trust by ensuring transaction credibility, honesty, reliability, and security. Providing complete and honest information, reviews, and opinions, and leveraging sources of competitive advantage, such as low prices, positive reviews, and secure payment systems, are pivotal for attracting and retaining digital customers.

Effective communication strategies with the target group of e-consumers encompass providing information, instigating needs, stimulating purchasing behavior, and reaching out to opinion leaders. Opinion leaders, including those present virtually on the internet, wield a substantial influence on the purchasing behavior of other consumers, making it imperative for businesses to engage with them.

References

Ameen, N. and Willis, R. 2015. *The effect of cultural values on technology adoption in the Arab countries.* NNGT International Journal of Information Systems and Prosumption. Sociology Compass, 2: 1–18.

Ardissono, L., Goy, A., Petrone, G. and Segnan, M. 2002. *Personalization in Business-to Consumer interaction.* Communications of the ACM, Special Issue. The Adaptive Web 45(5): 52–53.

Armstrong, G. Kotler, Ph. 2000. *Marketing: An Introduction*, Prentice Hall, pp. 112–113.

Bartneck, C., Suzuki, T., Kanda, T. and Nomura, T. 2007. *The influence of people's culture and prior experiences with Aibo on their attitude towards robots.* AI and Society 21: 217–230. DOI:10.1007/s00146-006-0052-7.

Belanche, D., Casaló, L. V., Flavián, C. and Schepers, J. 2020. *Service robot implementation: A theoretical framework and research agenda.* The Service Industries Journal. Available online: https://www.studeersnel.nl/nl/document/technische-universiteit-eindhoven/service-engineering-and-marketing/article-service-robot-implementation-a-theoretical-framework-and-research-agenda/14209106.

Berger, C. and Piller, F. 2003. *Customers as co-designers.* IEE Manufacturing Engineer (August/September): 42–45.

Błoński, K. and Witek, J. 2019. *Minimalism in consumption, Annales Universitatis Mariae Curie-Skłodowska*, sectio H – Oeconomia 53(2).

Chi, O. H., Chi, G. Ch., Gursoy, D. and Nunkoo, R. 2023. *Customers' acceptance of artificially intelligent service robots: The influence of trust and culture.* International Journal of Information Management, 70/102623, https://doi.org/10.1016/j.ijinfomgt.2023.102623.

Chi, O. H., Jia, Sh., Li, Y. and Gursoy, D. 2021. *Developing a formative scale to measure consumers' trust toward interaction with artificially intelligent (AI) social robots in service delivery. Computers in Human Behavior*, Elsevier, vo.118, 106700. DOI: https://doi.org/10.1016/j.chb.2021.106700.

Chmielarz, W. and Łuczak, K. 2016. *Mobile payment systems in poland – analysis of customer preferences.* Transformations in Business & Economics Vol. 15(2a).

Davies, P. and Ng, I. 2015. *Moving towards the incomplete: A research agenda for the development of future products in the digital economy.* Procedia Manufacturing, 3: 3368–3374. Elsevier. 6th International Conference on Applied Human Factors and Ergonomics (AHFE 2015) and the Affiliated Conferences, AHFE 2015.

Dennis, C., Merrilees, B., Jayawardhena, C. and Tiu Wright, L. 2009. *E-consumer behavior.* European Journal of Marketing 43 (9-10): 1121–1139.

Digital. 2022. Global Overview Report. https://datareportal.com/reports/digital-2022-global-overview-report.

Dobiegała-Korona, B. and Doligalski, T. 2010. *Zarządzanie wartością klienta. Pomiary i strategie.* Publisher: Poltext, Warszawa.

Doyle, P. 2000. *Value-based marketing.* John&Willey Sons.

Featherstone, M. 1991. Consumer Culture and Postmodernism, Sage, London.

G20 Digital Economy Task Force (DETF). 2016. G20 Digital economy development and cooperation initiative. https://www.mofa.go.jp/files/000185874.pdf, (Accessed on 23.07.2024).

Gajdzik, B., Grabowska, S. and Saniuk, S. 2021. *Key socio-economic megatrends and trends in the context of the Industry 4.0 framework.* Forum Scientiae Oeconomica, 9(3): 5–22. DOI: https://doi.org/10.23762/FSO_VOL9_NO3_1.

Gorschek, T. and Davis, A. 2008. *Requirements engineering: In search of the dependent variables.* Information and Software Technology 50: 67–75.

Goy, A., Ardissono, L. and Petrone, G. 2007. *Personalization in E-Commerce Applications.* Springer. https://citeseerx.ist.psu.edu/document?repid=rep1&type=pdf&doi=b2570605913b6dbeaffeecc4fdfacfd82916a2ad.

Grabowska, S., Saniuk, S. and Gajdzik, B. 2022. *Industry 5.0: improving humanization and sustainability of Industry 4.0.* Scientometrics. Springer; Akadémiai Kiadó 127(6): 3117–3144.

Grzywińska-Rąpca, M. and Grzybowska-Brzezińska, M. 2015. *The Level and Structure of Household Spending on E-shopping.* Konsumpcja i Rozwój 12(3).

Hill, N., Brierley, J. and MacDougall, R. 1999. *How to Measure Customer Satisfaction, Brookfield, Gower.* Aldershot.

Holbrook, M. 1999. *Consumer Value: A Framework for Analysis and Research, New York.* Routledge.

Humphreys, A. and Grayson, K. 2008. *The Intersecting Roles of Consumer and Producer: A Critical Perspective on Co-production, Co-creation.*

Jaciow, M. and Wolny, R. 2022. *Polski e-konsument. Dekada zmian.* Helion, Gliwice.

Jaciow, M., Wolny, R. and Stolecka-Makowska, A. 2013. *E-consumer in Europe. Comparative analysis of behaviors.* OnePress, Gliwice.

Jaciow, M. and Wolny, R. 2011. *Polski e-konsument. Typologia, zachowania.* Helion, Gliwice.

Kagermann, H., Wahlster, W., Helbig, J. (eds.). (April 2011). *Recommendations for implementing the strategic initiative Industrie 4.0: Final report of the Industrie 4.0. Working Group:* Industrie 4.0: Mit dem Internet der Dinge auf dem Weg zur 4. industriellen Revolution, VDI-Nachrichten, Acatech-National Academy of Science and Engineering: München, Germany, [online:] http://forschungsunion.de/pdf/industrie_4_0_final_report.pdf.

Kaplan, R. S. and Norton, D. P. 2011. *Mapy strategii w biznesie. Jak przełożyć wartości na mierzalne wyniki.* GWP, Gdańsk.

Kotler, Ph. 1991. *Principles of Marketing.* Prentice Hall, New York.

Kotler, Ph. and Keller, K. 2006. *Marketing Management. Ed. 13.* Prentice Hall, New Jersey, p. 6.

Kryvachuk, L. 2021. *Pokolenie iGeneration (Z) i Alfa. Analiza w kontekście sytuacji politycznej i zmian społecznych na Ukrainie. In:* Mikołajczyk, M. and Tasak, A. (eds.). Pokoleniowy potencjał polityki. Publisher: Instytut Wydawniczy Książka i Prasa, Warszawa.

Krzepicka, A. 2016. *Contemporary consumer – digital consumer Title in Polish: Współczesny konsument – konsument digitalny. Studia Ekonomiczne.* Zeszyty Naukowe Uniwersytetu Ekonomicznego w Katowicach, 255.

Kuksa, I., Fisher, T. and Kent, A. 2022. *Understanding Personalisation. New Aspects of Design and Consumption.* 1st Edition. Elsevier.

Lee, S. G., Trimi, S. and Kim, C. 2013. *The impact of cultural differences on technology adoption.* Journal of World Business.

Lehmann, D. R. and Winer, R. S. 2002. *Product management.* McGraw-Hill, Boston, 2002: 16–17.

Leodolter, W. 2017. *Digital Transformation Shaping the Subconscious Minds of Organizations.* Cham: Springer International Publishing.

Levitt, T. 1983. *The Marketing Imagination.* Free Press.

Ng, I. 2013. *Value and Worth: Creating Markets in the Digital Economy.* Cambridge: Innovorsa Press.

Ratajczyk, P. 2009. *Product as a value medium.* Zeszyty Naukowe Uniwersytetu Szczecińskiego, 559 Ekonomiczne Problemy Usług, 42, 2: 271:278.

Rau, P. P., Li, Y. and Li, D. 2009. *Effects of communication style and culture on ability to accept recommendations from robots.* Computers in Human Behavior 25(2): 587–595.

Saniuk, S., Grabowska, S. and Gajdzik, B. 2020. *Personalization of products in the Industry 4.0 concept and its impact on achieving a higher level of sustainable consumption.* Energies, 13: 5895. https://doi.org/10.3390/en13225895.

Schwab, K. 2016. *The Fourth Industrial Revolution.* World Economic forum, Cologny, Switzerland.

Śledziewska, K. and Włoch, R. 2020. *Gospodarka cyfrowa. Jak nowe technologie zmieniają świat.* Wydawnictwo Uniwersytetu Warszawskiego, Warszawa.

Solomon, M., Bamossy, G. and Askegaar, S. 1999. *Consumer Behavior.* A European Perspective, Prentice Hall Europe, Paris.

Tapscott, D. 1996. *The Digital Economy: Promise and Peril in the Age of Networked Intelligence.* McGraw-Hill, New York, NY.

Tkaczyk, J. 2016. *E-consumer in digital economy.* Kaminski Univeristy.

Tussyadiah, I. P., Zach, F. J. and Wang, J. 2020. *Do travelers trust intelligent servicerobots?* Annals of Tourism Research, 81: 102886.

Wolny, R. 2023. *Konsument i jego ślad w gospodarce cyfrowej. In*: Jaciow, M. and Wolny, R. (eds.). Cyfrowy ślad konsumenta. Uniwersytet Ekonomiczny w Katowicach, Katowice.

Yoo, Y., Henfridsson, O. and Lyytinen, K. 2010. *Research Commentary —The new organizing logic of digital innovation: An agenda for information systems research.* Information Systems Research 21(4): 724–735.

Yoon, Ch. 2009. *The effects of national culture values on consumer acceptance of e-commerce: Online shoppers in China Author links open overlay panel.* Information & Management 46(5): 294–301. https://doi.org/10.1016/j.im.2009.06.001. (accessed on 24.07.2024).

Zhang, J. and Mao, E. 2013. *The effects of consumption values on the use of location-based services on smartphones.* Strategy, Adoption, and Competitive Advantage of Mobile Services in the Global Economy, pp. 1–18.

Zupok, S. *Customer value and organization objectives. (Title in Polish: Wartość dla klienta a cele organizacji).* Studia i Prace WNEIZ US, 53/3. DOI: 10.18276/SIP.2018.53/3-07.

CHAPTER 6

Reflections on the Importance of Sustainability Management in Smart Cities

Normative Regulations using the Example of the German Sustainability Strategy

Christian Schachtner

Introduction

Due to the multidimensionality of the causes and the measures required that affect all people and that go beyond pure technological innovations, global changes are necessary. According to the IPCC (2021), this is referred to as a social transformation. When it comes to explaining what is meant by transformation, there are many explanations in the literature. To formulate a working definition, a transformation can be understood as a fundamental change that integrates cultural, social, technological, and economic aspects. Such a transformation requires the interaction of all actors as global competition and thus increases complexity.

Global governance is an international framework of principles, rules, laws, and processes for dealing with global problems. According to Grunwald and Kopfmüller (2022), this regulatory approach means understanding that globally active companies and organizations must take responsibility. The guiding principle of sustainable development is anchored worldwide at many global, national, regional, and local levels: at the political level, in the economy, in civil society and church groups as well as in citizens' initiatives.

Urbanization supports the globalization trend and is particularly noticeable in the emergence of so-called megacities. Megacities are cities in which more than 10 million people live. Due to the concentration of people, institutions, resources, goods, and

RheinMain University of Applied Sciences, Unter den Eichen 5, 65195 Wiesbaden.
Email: christian.schachtner@hs-rm.de, OCRID: 0000-0001-5332-628

financial flows, they play an important role in creating and at the same time remedying global changes. Sustainable urban development is one of the central fields of action of social transformation. These global, social, economic, and environmental challenges are summarized by the WBGU (2019) under the term global change. Comprehensive changes in infrastructures and regulatory systems in the interaction of politics, society, science, and business. According to Grißehammer and Brohmann (2015), these socially sustainable developments require smart implementation strategies.

Conceptual foundations

To develop a holistic strategy, several dimensions must be prepared so that the Sustainable Development Goals can unfold their impact in a networked form. On the way to a system of multifunctional sustainability integration, legal regulations are to be identified.

Regulatory foundations for conceptual frameworks

The main guideline competence in sustainability legislation is the so-called multi-level policy. This approach refers to the relationship structure of different horizontal and vertical political decision-making structures and stands for an interaction between different policy levels such as municipalities, regions, federal states, EU, UN, and non-state stakeholder groups (Panke, 2018). At the European level, sustainability aspects are included in the development of EU directives as part of so-called sustainability impact assessment processes.

Implementation of sustainability is complex because sustainability is not a legally clearly defined term. However, the demand for more binding definition is driven by the ongoing expansion of legal requirements. This results in several legal requirements for companies and organizations for the sustainable design of processes, structures, plants, and products that encompass the economic, ecological, and social aspects of sustainability. In addition to legal principles, many normative requirements, e.g., ISO standards, determine systematic standards for the development of management systems.

In the following, the framework for action for institutions will be presented based on various legal, political, and management-related regulations.

German Climate Protection Act (KSG)

The Climate Protection Act (KSG) sets national climate protection targets to ensure compliance with European targets. This must be continuously adapted to the current implementation situation and was already amended in 2021. The requirements and targets for greenhouse gas neutrality enshrined there have therefore been tightened. However, voluntary innovation efforts to reduce greenhouse gas emissions through institutional management systems must be consolidated in a collaborative manner with various actors from business, the public sector, civil society, and academia. The new target focuses on greenhouse gas neutrality by 2045, with emissions to be reduced by 65% by 2030 compared to 1990. This requirement for adaptation stems from the Paris Climate Agreement, which stipulates that global warming of more than 1.5°C must not be exceeded (European Union, 2016).

Other goals to be achieved in parallel are:

- By 2040, at least 88% of greenhouse gases must be reduced.
- In 2045, Germany will only be allowed to emit as many greenhouse gases as can be removed by incorporating carbon, e.g., into sinks
- Annual emissions are to be further reduced for all sectors by 2030.

For companies and institutions alike, the law means dealing with their own data on greenhouse gas emissions and working out potential savings. Currently, the requirement to record greenhouse gas emissions is regulated by the above-mentioned sustainability reporting obligation of the CSR-RUG.

EMAS "eco-management and audit scheme"

The European Regulation (EC) 1221/2009, also known as the EMAS Regulation, on the voluntary participation of organisations in a community eco-management and audit scheme has been in force since 2010 (European Parliament, 2019).

EMAS is a European instrument for the implementation of an environmental management system that, by registering in the EMAS database, shows that ecological values are responsibly implemented in its business activities.

In concrete terms, this means using resources efficiently and environmentally friendly for companies of all industries and sizes, implementing sustainability aspects and implementing climate protection measures. In addition, company-related environmental aspects can be dealt with in a legally compliant and transparent manner.

The German sustainability strategy

Nation-states represent an interface between global and local actors and drive national sustainability strategies at different paces. In 2002, the first national sustainability strategy in Germany was drawn up and updated every four years. The German Sustainable Development Strategy combines comprehensive areas such as energy, climate protection, waste management, housing, transport, food, and agriculture in the following six transformation areas to develop measures (German Government, 2021, 48–67):

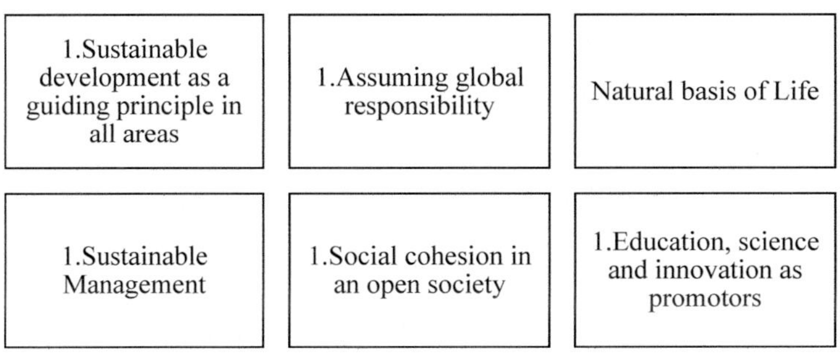

Fig. 1. Fields of action (Source: German Sustainability Strategy).

Examples of measures from the current sustainability strategy include the mobility transition, the energy transition, education and research funding, and health prevention.

The greatest challenges of implementation include the complexity of achieving goals, the interactions between causes and effects, and the impact of many different actors with diverse expectations (Grundwald and Kopfmüller, 2022, p. 47).

Digital transformation concept

Digital solutions can make a significant contribution to supporting the openness of innovation within the transformation process towards sustainability. However, since this also has a negative impact on sustainability, it is crucial to shape digitalization in a sustainable way. The challenges of the digital transformation lie in a complex design task, the coordination requirements in the federal approach and the involvement of many social actors. For the implementation, online communication of the participatory provision and participation of services and the formation of opinion through "e-democracy" and "e-participation" is important. As a result, digitalization is not only the subject of a scientific, but increasingly also a public debate.

Through the numerous interdependencies, the cooperation of these actors produces creative processes that must be designed on virtual platforms. At present, however, there is no nationwide obligation to disclose objectives, activities and sources of resources used or results achieved, so that the concept of open government is still needed to be completed on a large scale (Attard et al., 2015, p. 399-415.).

Concepts from environmental policy

A common basic understanding for all stakeholders means changing patterns of thought and action and making sustainability goals measurable. In addition, due to the lack of clear measurement indicators, the success of the engagement cannot be clearly depicted either qualitatively or quantitatively. And this would be important for strengthening the role of public organizations. According to Beltz et al., the success of the work depends on factors such as available information or sufficient representativeness of the groups involved (Beltz et al., 2020, 7–17).

These instruments include, for example, registration, information, and notification obligations. There are also economic instruments such as licenses, certificates, or subsidies (Ringel, 2021). The following categories comprise excerpts of instruments of governance based on:

- Environmental regulations as do's and don'ts.
- Environmental taxes as taxation or licences.
- Certificates as trading in pollution rights.
- Cooperation agreements as conditions between authorities and those affected.
- Informational messages as consumer information.

Can we rely on the fact that sustainable action is implemented voluntarily? History has shown that additional instruments are needed in the form of legal requirements to create incentives and liability. Rules are needed for the implementation of sustainability. Therefore, legal systems in the form of laws, ordinances and guidelines represent an important and necessary part of the framework conditions for enforcing sustainability (Kurhofer, 2022, p. 5-9).

However, due to its complexity, comprehensive long-term strategies and frameworks are also needed at both international and national levels. In addition, systematic action and implementation aids are needed that cover the broad spectrum according to sustainability criteria. In particular, the ISO 26000 standard, the international guideline for social responsibility, provides comprehensive support in the strategic planning and implementation of social responsibility. The guide, as well as all other standards, belong to non-legal systems.

Importance of municipalities in the context of sustainable development

Municipalities have a special significance in the context of sustainable development and there are already numerous measures that are being implemented at this level. Cities and municipalities are seen as the drivers of transformation processes (Grundwald and Kopfmüller, 2022, p. 225–230).

On the one hand, municipalities have a part in the global changes, on the other hand, they themselves are affected by the consequences of these changes. At the same time, they have the potential to help solve these global challenges and contribute to sustainable development. The role of municipalities in the context of sustainable development is:

- Municipalities are places and agents of economic, technical, social, political, and cultural change.
- Municipalities are centers of resource consumption, pollutant emissions and social inequality.
- Municipalities ensure the integration of newcomers from all regions, countries, and continents.
- Municipalities have a role to play in achieving global climate, development, and sustainability goals.
- Municipalities have the potential to shape the transformation towards sustainable development.
- Municipalities assume responsibility for services of general interest, ensuring the public good and the quality of life of their citizens (BMZ, 2022, 5).

For this reason, they are of great importance in the context of sustainable development. Cities and municipalities should create sustainable living spaces by acting as knowledge carriers and role models and offering a space for connecting people. Municipalities can be seen as pioneers and rehearsal spaces, so that successful concepts can be scaled from the local level to national or international entities. True to the motto "Acting locally, having a global impact", sustainable community development is an important field of action in the context of the transformation to a sustainable society (BMZ, 2022).

Evaluations can be carried out continuously or at different times. The prerequisite for any assessment is that you have clear and measurable goals or that the assessment can be carried out independently. Stakeholders in smart cities should also learn not only from their own experiences, but also from the experiences of other cities and other smart city initiatives. In this way, smart city actors can be innovative and future oriented. The development and initiatives of the smart city are supported by the smart city actors on the achievements inside and outside the city with tangible evidence (Ni and Liu, 2014).

Concept of sustainable citizens' commune and smart urban development

One of the challenges of sustainable transformation in municipalities is the tension between the legal framework, the financial strength of the municipalities, the expectations of the citizenry and trends such as urbanization, digitalization, and globalization. There are various international and national initiatives to support municipalities in their transformation towards sustainability. Examples include:

- United Nations Sustainable Cities Program (UNCHS/UNEP).
- Local Agenda 21-Initiative.
- ICLEI - International Council for Local Environmental Initiatives.

In general, municipal measures for sustainable development can be divided into three categories: firstly, those that directly affect municipalities, secondly, those that have an impact beyond national borders, and thirdly, those measures that have an impact in other municipalities around the world through international municipal partnerships. Cities and municipalities can participate by:

- commit to assessing the global impact of everyday local actions and adapting them for greater sustainability.
- make public procurement sustainable. To this end, there is a Competence Centre for Sustainable Procurement of the Procurement Office of the Federal Ministry of the Interior (BMI) in Germany, which supports decisions in the field of procurement.
- promote cultural and ethical diversity as well as diversity.
- Establishing sustainability and climate partnerships in developing countries and emerging economies.
- Be more involved in international negotiation processes on sustainable development.

Exemplary measures include climate-friendly mobility and energy supply, urban circular economy and agriculture, innovations in the context of digital technologies (keyword: smart city) The term smart city is used as a collective term for holistic development concepts for cities that are made more efficient, technologically advanced, greener, and more socially inclusive. The Institute of Urban Affairs (DIFU) reports on the implementation of sustainability in municipalities. The main message is that a successful socio-ecological transformation towards more sustainable municipalities requires a positive and motivating vision of the future that provides orientation. At the same time, the survey results show that the individual contribution of everyone is still small (Jossin, 2021).

The fields of action of a smart city usually consist of smart government, smart healthcare, smart building, smart mobility, smart energy, smart population, smart education, smart environment, smart infrastructure, smart technology, smart security, and smart agriculture.

The problems caused by increasing urbanization can be identified within the framework of the Sustainable Development Goals (SDGs), consisting of 17 main themes that are also the success factors of individual cities. Smart cities can indeed make a significant contribution to achieving the UN's SDGs. Smart city projects play a key role in how ecosystems and sustainable infrastructures for innovation are planned, built, operated, and financed. Private capital is crucial in both project investments and financial markets. The sustainability of smart city projects requires innovative approaches to the financing system. "Blended finance" refers to the strategic use of public funds to mobilize private capital flows. This financial system helps finance projects that would otherwise not receive private equity. The risk and return are distributed in such a way that the goals of the individual institutions are achieved. A major challenge, however, is how to finance the smart city infrastructure (Canas da Costa and Popović, 2020).

Status and challenges in the implementation of the German sustainable development strategy

Indicators are regularly used to review the success of sustainable action and the extent to which the Sustainable Development Goals have been achieved. There are different indicators. The indicator report of the Federal Statistical Office shows which indicators are used to measure the success of sustainable trade within the framework of the German Sustainable Development Strategy. The achievement of the individual SDGs is evaluated and presented in a uniform and structured manner over time based on different indicators. For example, the indicators used in the sustainability strategy to assess the achievement of the SDGs include:

1. Proportion of academically qualified and professionally more qualified.
2. Share of renewable energies in gross final energy consumption.
3. Total Raw Material Productivity.
4. Private and public expenditure on research and development.
5. Increase in settlement and traffic area.
6. Market share of products with government eco-labels.
7. Number of organizational sites with environmental management EMAS.

The status overview of individual indicators shows that Germany has so far been able to contribute to the achievement of the individual SDGs with varying degrees of success. Based on the indicators for sustainability goals and other structural characteristics of the municipalities, types of municipalities were identified.

This makes it possible to derive recommendations for action adapted to the individual requirements of the municipalities and to present practical examples from other municipalities. The indicators for municipalities are key figures that municipalities can use to map their contributions to achieving the SDGs (Peters et al., 2021).

In order to enable political decisions for sustainable development at the municipal level, assistance for monitoring the implementation of the SDGs, measures and assistance with reporting have been compiled on the website www.sdg-portal.de and are available to decision-makers at the municipal level. According to the Bertelsmann Stiftung (2022), the portal has the following purpose:

- enables the preparation of sustainability reports and provides each type of municipality with various measures as a basis for the implementation of sustainable development.
- can also be used by municipal decision-makers to map the current situation.
- supports the selection of appropriate indicators in line with local policy priorities.
- helps to identify and manage the need for action.
- helps to take the most effective measures to implement the SDGs.
- offers ideas and suggestions for municipal sustainability management.

To find suitable measures for municipalities, Peters et al. divide types of municipalities according to characteristics. Municipalities are assigned the respective type. The municipal types are formed from a combination of the urban and municipal or district types of the Federal Institute for Research on Building, Urban Affairs and Spatial Development (BBSR) as well as an extension or differentiation of this typology by the categories "growing", "stable" and "shrinking" cities and municipalities or districts, which were also determined by the BBSR. In total, two rough typifications have been made: city and municipality types as well as district types. The individual areas of action are mapped with specific indicators. These indicators focus on the following areas: poverty, education, labour market, housing market, land, and municipal finances. The portal either formulates how the specific challenge can be solved or how the challenge can be dealt with. In addition, the portal also offers impulses on what can be done to maintain or further expand a certain municipal advantage.

Smart governance, through its interaction between smart city technologies, people, policies, best practices, resources, social norms, and information, can effectively support city administration on the path to a smart city transformation. Smart governance is therefore at the heart of a smart city initiative. When implementing a smart city initiative, appropriate measurement methods, impact and performance indicators are required to monitor and evaluate the performance of the smart city. Methods for measuring the smart city initiatives include citizen surveys, dashboards, technical assessments of the action plan, and measuring the contribution to achieving the goals of the smart city program (Lopes, 2017).

Summary

Sustainable development, which considers economic, ecological, and social aspects in equal measure, requires a social transformation, especially because the necessary measures are multidimensional and global in scope. The numerous interdependencies between politics, the media and civil society are challenging. These can have a negative impact on both cooperation and the implementation of sustainable development measures.

Through their activities, companies contribute to social and climatic changes and have an influence on the availability of resources.

This participation is encouraged by regulatory instruments such as commandments, prohibitions, licences, subsidies, fees, charges, liability rules, etc. At the global level, it is usually the non-statutory but globally recognised targets, such as those of the 2030 Agenda, that require companies to design their production patterns responsibly.

For concrete implementation, companies can rely on recognized frameworks such as the ISO 26000 guide to social responsibility. Part of sustainable trade is regular sustainability reporting, some of which is required by law. Due to several advantages, it is worthwhile for companies to file reports even without legal pressure.

Due to the existing potential, cities and municipalities can also make an important contribution to sustainable development by offering a space for the participation of everyone. Through numerous national and international projects, they can promote sustainability beyond their borders. For example, the municipalities are involved to varying degrees, e.g., in the areas of education, mobility or health. As a matter of principle, each municipality must decide for itself, based on the specific framework conditions and priorities on the ground, which measures are relevant for management and can make the greatest contribution to achieving the SDGs.

References

Attard, J., Orlandi, F., Scerri, S. and Auer, S. 2015. *A systematic review of open government data initiatives*. Gov. Inform. Q. 32(4): 399–418.

Belz, J., Follmer, R., Hölscher, J., Stieß, I. and Sunderer, G. 2022. *Umweltbewusstsein in Deutschland 2020. Ergebnisse einer repräsentativen Bevölkerungsumfrage*. https://www.umweltbundesamt.de/sites/default/files/medien/479/publikationen/ubs_2020_0.pdf.

BMI 2022. *Die Kompetenzstelle für nachhaltige Beschaffung*. https://www.nachhaltige-beschaffung.info/DE/Allgemeines/1_1_KNB/1_1_Ueberuns_node.html.

BMZ 2022. Lokal handeln, global wirken. Kommunen in der Entwicklungspolitik. Bundesministerium für wirtschaftliche Zusammenarbeit und Entwicklung. https://www.bmz.de/resource/blob/23384/34d769164113856f508f1aea1eef5%202c4/lokal-handeln.pdf.

Canas da Costa, L. and Popović, T. 2020. *Financing sustainable infrastructures in a smart cities' context—innovative concepts, solutions and instruments*. pp. 229–243. *In*: Planing, P., Müller, P., Dehdari, P. and Bäumer, T. (eds.). Innovations for Metropolitan Areas. Springer.

European Parliament 2019. REGULATION (EC) No 1221/2009 OF THE EUROPEAN PARLIAMENT AND OF THE COUNCIL of 25 November 2009 on the voluntary participation by organisations in a Community eco-management and audit scheme (EMAS), repealing Regulation (EC) No 761/2001 and Commission Decisions 2001/681/EC and 2006/193/EC. https://eur-lex.europa.eu/legal-content/DE/TXT/PDF/?uri=CELEX:02009R1221-20190109&from=EN.

German Government 2021. Deutsche Nachhaltigkeitsstrategie. Weiterentwicklung 2021.https://www.bundesregierung.de/resource/blob/998194/1875176/3d3b15cd92d0261e7a0bcdc8f43b7839/deutsche-nachhaltigkeitsstrategie-2021-langfassung-download-bpa-data.pdf.

Glanze, E., Nüttgens, M. and Ritzrau, W. 2021. *Unternehmenserfolg durch Nachhaltigkeit – Reifegrad- und Vorgehensmodell zum Aufbau eines datenbasierten Nachhaltigkeitsmanagements*. HMD Praxis der Wirtschaftsinformatik. 58(1): 155–156.

Grißehammer, R. and Brohmann, B. 2015. *Wie Transformationen und gesellschaftliche Innovationen gelingen können*. https://www.umweltbundesamt.de/publikationen/wie-transformationen gesellschaftliche-innovationen.

Grunwald, A. and Kopfmüller, J. 2022. *Nachhaltigkeit*. 3. Edition, Campus Publishing.

Heyen, D. A. 2021. *Auf dem Weg zu einer nachhaltigen Wirtschaft. Den Strukturwandel erfolgreich gestalten*. Umweltbundesamt.

IPCC 2021. Climate Change 2021. The Physical Science Basis. Cambridge University Press.

Jossin, J. 2021. *Monitor Nachhaltige Kommune. Bericht 2021. Visionen zur Stadt der Zukunft. Kommunen in der sozial-ökologischen Transformation*. Bertelsmann Publishing.

Kurhofer, K. 2022. *Gesellschaftliche Verantwortung der Unternehmen und die Rolle der Unternehmensberichterstattung. Eine Untersuchung unter besonderer Berücksichtigung der Entwicklung in der EU und in Deutschland*. Springer Fachmedien Wiesbaden.

Lopes, N. V. 2017. *Smart governance: A key factor for smart cities implementation*. pp. 277–282. *In*: IEEE International Conference on Smart Grid and Smart Cities (ICSGSC).

Martens, J. 2018. *Zivilgesellschaft und Agenda 2030. Neue Allianzen für die sozial-ökologische Transformation*. Global Policy Forum. https://www.globaleslernen.de/sites/default/files/files/pages/zivilgesellschaft_und_agenda2030_online.pdf.

Ni, D. M. and Liu, R. H. 2014. *Study on the Enlightenment from EU smart city evaluation system*. Applied Mechanics and Materials 64(1): 624–628.

Panke, D. 2018. *Mehrebenenpolitik, Multi Level Governance*. *In*: Handbuch Staat. (R. Voigt, Hrsg.) Springer.

Peters, O., Jossin, J., Holz, P., Grabow, B., Floetig, H. and Scheller, H. 2021. *SDG-Maßnahmen für Kommunen. Kommunaltypen, Handlungsempfehlungen und Praxisbaispiele*. Bertelsmann Stiftung. https://www.bertelsmannstiftung.de/fileadmin/files/Projekte/Monitor_Nachhaltige_Kommune/SDG-MassnahmenfKommunen.pdf.

Ringel, M. 2021. *Instrumente der staatlichen Umweltökonomie: Auflagen, Steuern, Zertifikate*. pp. 55–84. *In*: Umweltökonomie, M. Ringel (eds.). Springer Fachmedien Wiesbaden.

Rothmund Insights 2021. Nachhaltigkeit im Fokus - Motive, Verhalten und Wünsche der Verbraucher. Trendstudie. https://www.presseportal.de/pm/152845/4829862.

WBGU 2019. Zusammenfassung. Unsere gemeinsame digitale Zukunft. Wissenschaftlicher Beirat der Bundesregierung Globale Umweltveränderungen (WBGU) https://www.wbgu.de/fileadmin/user_upload/wbgu/publikationen/hauptgutachten/hg2019/pdf/WBGU_HGD2019_Z.pdf.

Chapter 7

Creating New Values based on Assumptions Derived from the Climate Responsibility of Business and Society

Beata Sadowska,[1] *Nina Stępnicka*[2,*] and *Grzegorz Zimon*[3]

Introduction

Nowadays, business is moving away from single actions, whether environmental, charitable or social, to comprehensive, strategic thinking about corporate responsibility. Companies are developing internal growth documents aimed at transforming the entity into a just and prosperous company in line with the economics of sustainability.

The most important resource of a country is its society, the culture associated with it, and the cooperation between a country's citizens. The environment also plays a key role, as well as natural capital and international, global cooperation. The creation of new values based on assumptions derived from the climate responsibility of business and society is implied by the European Green Deal (EGD). These new values can be created using a variety of methods and tools, including the philosophy of foresight, understood as a process of ongoing inter-environmental cooperation to

[1] Faculty of Economics, Finance and Management, University of Szczecin, Mickiewicza 64, Szczecin 71-101, Poland.
Email: beata.sadowska@usz.edu.pl, ORCID: 0000-0003-4190-9440

[2] Department of Economics, Faculty of Economics and Finance, Casimir Pulawski University Radom Malczewskiego, 29, Radom 26-600, Poland.

[3] Department of Finance, Banking and Accounting, University of Technology Rzeszów, al. Powstańców Warszawy 12, Rzeszów 35-959, Poland.
Email: gzimon@prz.edu.pl, ORCID: 0000-0002-2040-4438

* Corresponding author: n.stepnicka@urad.edu.pl, ORCID: 0000-0002-3060-2876

make ongoing decisions and actions on the basis of a jointly developed vision for the development of the country or the world. Climate responsibility and understanding of the concept of "value" and the correlation of this definition with other concepts is reflected in the theory of economics. In light of such an outlined research problem, the chapter aims to: (1) deepen the theory in defining the new values of social responsibility in an environmental perspective; (2) identify the interaction occurring between the sustainable development of countries, corporate finance and social adaptation in the realization of the goals of the EGD by understanding the policy of decarbonisation of countries. The research objectives defined in this manner corresponds with the research hypothesis: H1: *International cooperation and dialogue with social partners, their awareness, access to information and knowledge determine the implementation of assumptions arising from the climate responsibility of business and society, thus creating new values.*

The study used the triangulation method, in particular: the method of literature analysis and criticism, the method of document research, the method of analysis and logical construction. The triangulation method ensures the reliability of the research approach and the acquisition of comprehensive and contextual knowledge of the phenomenon. Thanks to the possibility of using different research methods, triangulation increases the cognitive possibilities in relation to the studied phenomena (Zioło, 2020).

Study methodology

The analysis and critique of the literature was used as the first scientific method. Its purpose was to find out the originality of the issue taken up. This was followed by an examination of documents and materials in order to evaluate preliminary, descriptive as well as quantitative information about the issue under study. The second stage of empirical self-study was a general survey of business stakeholders on the decarbonisation of economies and aspects of climate protection. The level of statistical significance was examined. The third stage of scientific research was the study of experts' views (Delphi method).

As M. Remlein (2019) rightly notes, the Delphi method is one of the heuristic methods for creative problem solving. It is a survey method based on closed questions. In order to conduct the survey, a research sample was selected, i.e., experts. Due to the fact that the Delphi method research was preceded by surveys conducted among enterprises, it was considered necessary to include the opinions of both practitioners and theoreticians.

Delphi method research on the creation of new values based on assumptions derived from the climate responsibility of business and society was conducted based on the presented opinions of two groups of experts. The first group consisted of academics from public universities at home and abroad, and the second group consisted of representatives of the public, entrepreneurs, investors doing business in industries such as energy, chemicals, construction, clothing, transportation. The number of experts by group is shown in Table 1.

In order to conduct the study, a survey questionnaire was developed, which included the following questions:

Table 1. Number of experts in the Delphi method.

Group	Specification	Number of experts	Country
1st group	Academic staff of public universities	3	Poland
		2	Slovakia
		3	Ukraine
		1	Germany
		1	Czech Republic
2nd group	Different stakeholder groups	4	Poland
		1	Slovakia
		1	Ukraine
		2	Germany
		2	Czech Republic

Source: own elaboration based on survey, n = 20.

In your opinion:

(1) the basis of economic valuation is variously defined as "value", which is an inherently ambiguous concept, as it can appear as: a goal, a norm, a belief given by the valuator?

(2) in the economic sense, value is understood as a characteristic of a given good that is the sum of the benefits, quantified with money, that the buyer expects?

(3) psychologically, values are treated as individual phenomena related to people's needs or beliefs?

(4) "economic good" does not have to be material, it can mean, for example, the state of "being happy", "being safe", "being healthy"?

(5) it is values that determine the choice of specific behaviors and the evaluation of various types of events?

(6) climate responsibility of business and society will allow the creation of new values, i.e., significant improvements in our health and well-being?

(7) the most important values will be the energy security of the country and the problem of energy poverty will be solved?

(8) a sustainable forestry strategy that is based on the values of increasing and restoring forest resources and protecting areas of high biodiversity is key?

(9) the most important values will be a high quality of life in the city, taking into account "green transport" and "efficient housing"?

(10) new values should be sought at the global and international level and models should be drawn from there?

(11) the key to valuing phenomena and taking action will be broad education, information system and building awareness in society?

The survey was conducted in May and August 2023. Questions were answered using a Likert scale, which consists of a cafeteria of five responses arranged in order from total acceptance to total rejection. Variants of the scale were used in the survey:

- strongly agree - 5 points,
- rather agree - 4 points,
- have no opinion - 3 points,
- rather disagree - 2 points,
- strongly disagree - 1 point.

The Delphi method used required the survey to be conducted in two rounds, in which it was possible to obtain a relatively unified opinion on the area under study. The survey should be considered as a pilot study.

Results of literature research and documents and materials in the area of business and social climate responsibility, including values in the social sciences

The topic of climate responsibility of business and society, including values in the social sciences is not new. Climate changes are one of the most important global threats to the world today. Economically developed countries are primarily responsible for the state of the Earth, as they are the ones who brought about climate changes and have the means and capacity to introduce climate-neutral new technologies and practices in the economy (Wewerinke-Singh, 2018; Reid, 2015).

The Earth's climate is determined by number of factors over which people do not always have control. However, the actions of governments and enterprises should stimulate critical reflection on our own choices, on the condition of our environment. Every individual should have a stake in solving environmental issues, in conservation efforts. This is the climate responsibility of every member of society. This subject matter has been and continues to be of interest to researchers in Poland and around the world. It includes new business models, the sharing economy, changes in manufacturing technologies, transport, industry, digital transformation, changes in education.

More extensively, included in the studies: Stoczkiewicz (2009), Ciechanowicz-McLean (2017), Kaniewska (2015), Jamieson, (2010), Ciechanowicz-McLean (2021), Krot and others (2021), McKenzie (2023), Hirai, Comim (2022), Filho and others (2023), Jabłoński, Jabłoński (2020a), Jabłoński, Jabłoński (2021), Jabłoński, Jabłoński (2020b), Jabłoński and Jabłoński (2019), Przybojewska (2023).

A definition of "value" correlates with climate responsibility. Heraclitus of Ephesus, 6th and 5th centuries BC, distinguished between value relating to people and to goods and services. The value of people was measured by their morality, while the value of goods and services expressed their utility. The Greek philosopher Protagoras is considered the forerunner of the subjective theory of value, believing that value is the result of subjective sensations that depend on the relationship of someone or something (more: Hońko, 2013).

According to the author, "value is a subjective measure that depends on human desires, preferences, dreams, needs; value is assigned by the social individual, who may interpret the measurement of value differently; it is a direction of motivation in relation to human actions; an object, but also a criterion for positive evaluation." (Dońko, 2013, p. 15).

Read more about the issue of value in the social sciences in the works of: Dose (1997), Kowalik-Olubińska (2021), Antonowicz, Galiński (2020), Dutcher and others (2007), Elliot (1997), Stachowska (2016, pp. 1-20), Besser-Jones, Slote (2015), Przesławski (2020), Adler (1956), Maslow (1943).

An issue that combines climate responsibility and the understanding of values is the EGD. The European Commission on July 14, 2021 adopted a package of legislative proposals "Fit for 55" within the framework of the EGD, which aims to strengthen the EU's position as a global climate leader. The package aims to modernize existing legislation in line with the EU's 2030 climate target, which will help bring about the transformational changes needed in the economy, society and industry to achieve climate neutrality by 2050 and, to support this, reduce net emissions by at least 55% (compared to 1990) by 2030 (Śniegowski, 2022).

The EGD will not be unaffected by any sector of the economy, becoming a force for new business models, as well as dictating new obligations for businesses and communities. The impact of the EGD will be global. In the European Union and beyond, the EGD will force companies to reduce their carbon footprints, create business models that incorporate a circular economy framework, and make investments, including innovations in renewable energy and other clean technologies. In addition, the EGD will oblige companies to consider both environmental and social impacts in their entire supply chains (more: Ciechanowska, 2020; Nowak, 2021).

After that, documents and materials were examined in order to evaluate preliminary, descriptive as well as quantitative information about the issue under study. By analyzing the report prepared by J. Wajer, R. Hummel titled "Sustainable Value Study 2023" , it should be emphasized that climate change and the fight against it are becoming an inseparable part of the strategy of companies in Poland and around the world. This is required by numerous stakeholders, not only investors, but also employees, consumers or society. That is why all companies have publicly declared the fight against climate change. The creation of new values based on assumptions derived from the climate responsibility of business and society is reflected in the motivation of business units, as shown in Fig. 1.

For almost all of them, value creation is the main motive for their actions. The second most frequently cited reason is gaining a competitive advantage—globally, 9% of respondents indicated this as the most important reason, and in Poland as many as 17%. Respondents both in Poland and globally realize that investing in combating climate change is creating a value.

Business units are constantly developing their methods for measuring and managing activities in the fight against climate change, and then analyzing the adopted goals, using intermediate targets, milestones and scenarios to accelerate strategy implementation. The most common activities are those related to managing and measuring the implementation of strategies, which are those that require the least amount of money to create new value in climate responsibility (Fig. 2).

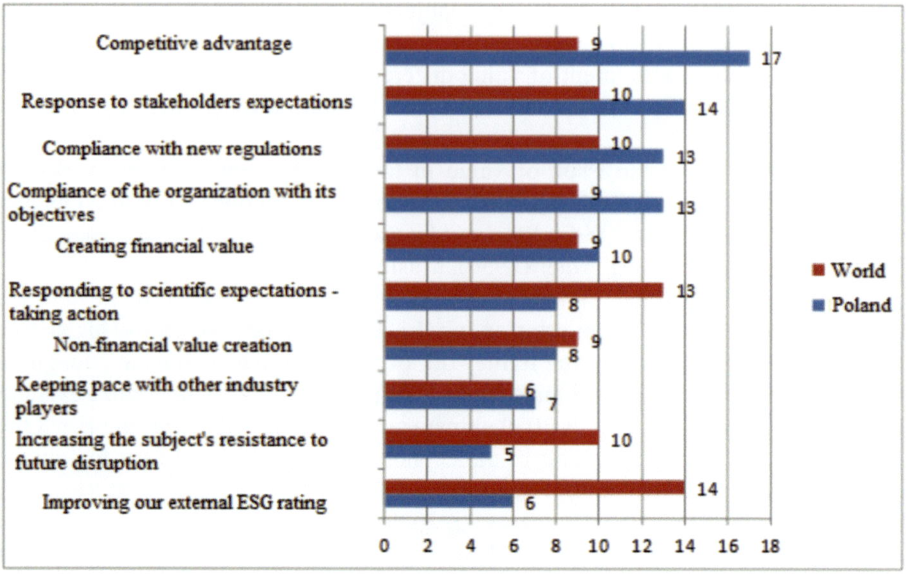

Fig. 1. Motivation to create new value vs. climate change initiatives (%). Source: J. Wajer, R. Hummel: *Badanie zrównoważonej wartości 2023*, https://www.ey.com/pl_pl/climate-change-sustainability-services/ey-sustainability-value-study-polska [access: 27.08.23r.].

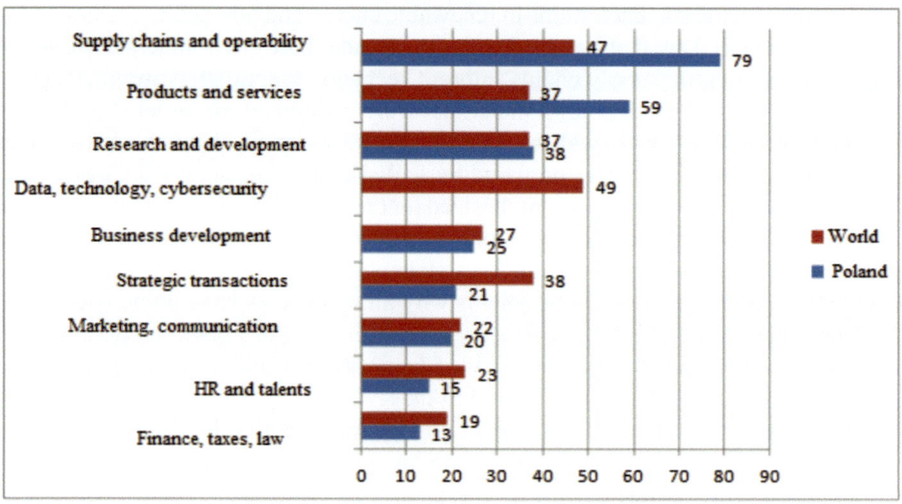

Fig. 2. Business areas of the organization in which the entity is investing the most to reduce greenhouse gas emissions and meet climate goals (%). Source: J. Wajer, R. Hummel: *Badanie zrównoważonej wartości 2023*, https://www.ey.com/pl_pl/climate-change-sustainability-services/ey-sustainability-value-study-polska [access: 27.08.23r.].

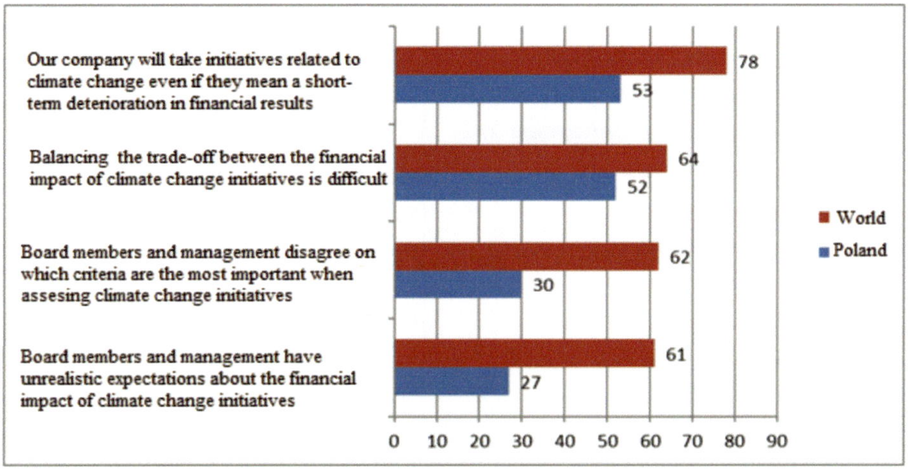

Fig. 3. Stakeholders' opinion on statements about the business entity's actions on climate change (%). Source: J. Wajer, R. Hummel: *Badanie zrównoważonej wartości 2023*, https://www.ey.com/pl_pl/climate-change-sustainability-services/ey-sustainability-value-study-polska [access: 27.08.23r.].

Poland, unlike the rest of the world, allocates financial outlays mostly to supply chains and its products and services. Unlike their global competitors, Polish companies have fewer internal problems related to managing the implementation of sustainability strategies. It is possible that the lack of internal conflicts is due to a weaker insistence on improving cooperation within the organization's management to more efficiently implement the strategy of creating new values based on assumptions derived from the climate responsibility of business and society (Fig. 3).

The global results are significantly better than the results obtained in Poland. "Sustainable Value Survey 2023" EY was conducted to understand what actions companies are taking to combat climate change. Among Polish respondents, the largest number of respondents represented manufacturing, trade, real estate and hotels and consumer products companies.

Results of empirical own research—survey of business stakeholders on decarbonisation of economies and aspects of climate protection

The second stage of empirical own research was a general survey of business stakeholders on the decarbonisation of economies and aspects of climate protection. The level of statistical significance was examined. The results of our own research are presented below (Figs. A1, B2, C3, D4, E5, Chart A1, B2, C3, D4, E5).

A. Voivodeship

Fig. A1. Voivodeship

	Number	Percentage
Warmińsko mazurskie	1	0,2%
Mazowieckie	1	0,2%
Opolskie	1	0,2%
Kujawsko pomorskie	2	0,3%
Dolnośląskie	2	0,3%
Pomorskie	4	1%
Śląskie	8	1%
Świętokrzyskie	8	1%
Lubuskie	19	3%
Lubelskie	25	4%
Małopolskie	90	14%
Zachodniopomorskie	233	37%
Podkarpackie	239	38%

Chart A1. Voivodeship

Source: own elaboration based on empirical research, n = 633.

As many as 38% of respondents are from Podkarpackie voivodeship, while only 0.2% of respondents each come from Opolskie, Mazowieckie and Warmińsko-Mazurskie voivodeship.

B. Indicate gender

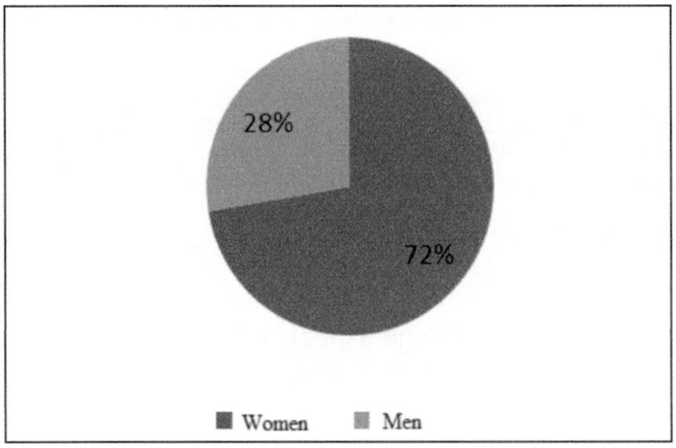

Fig. B2. Gender

	Number	Percentage
Women	458	72%
Men	175	28%

Chart B2. Gender

Source: own elaboration based on empirical research, n = 633.

The vast majority of respondents are women (72%).

C. In your opinion, which sectors of the economy are most affected by the decarbonisation policy?

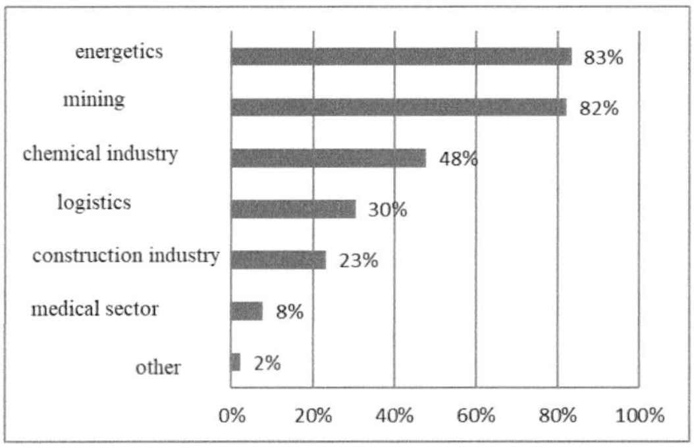

Fig. C3. Economic sectors most affected by decarbonisation policies

	Number	Percentage
other	15	2%
medical sector	50	8%
constructon industry	147	23%
logistics	193	30%
chemical industry	302	48%
mining	520	82%
energetics	527	83%

Chart C3. Economic sectors most affected by decarbonisation policies

Source: own elaboration based on empirical research, n = 633.

The largest number of respondents, 83%, said that energy is the most vulnerable to the impact of decarbonisation policies, 30% of respondents said that logistics is the most vulnerable to the impact of decarbonisation policies, while only 2% of respondents indicated a response that was “other”.

D. How do you think the decarbonisation policy can affect the course of individual socio-economic and environmental processes?

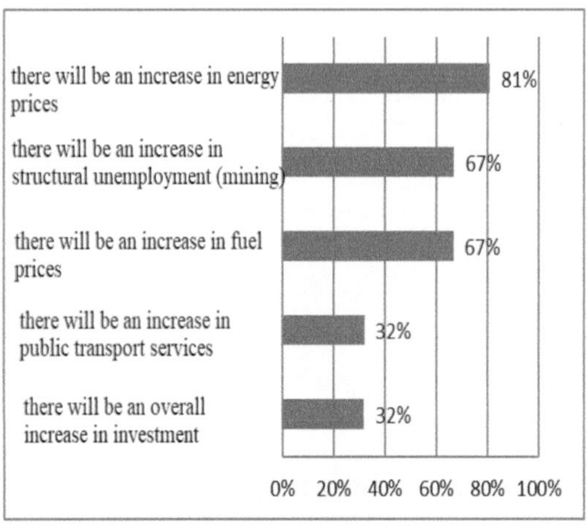

Fig. D4. The way decarbonisation policy can affect the course of individual socio-economic and environmental processes

	Number	Percentage
there will be an overall increase in investment	200	32%
there will be an increase in public transport services	202	32%
there will be an increase in fuel prices	421	67%
there will be an increase in structural unemployment (mining)	422	67%
there will be an increase in energy prices	511	81%

Chart D4. The way decarbonisation policy can affect the course of individual socio-economic and environmental processes

Source: own elaboration based on empirical research, n = 633.

The largest number of respondents, 81%, say there will be an increase in energy prices because of the decarbonisation policy, while 32% each say there will be an increase in public transportation services and a general increase in investment.

E. In your opinion, what is the biggest barrier to decarbonisation?

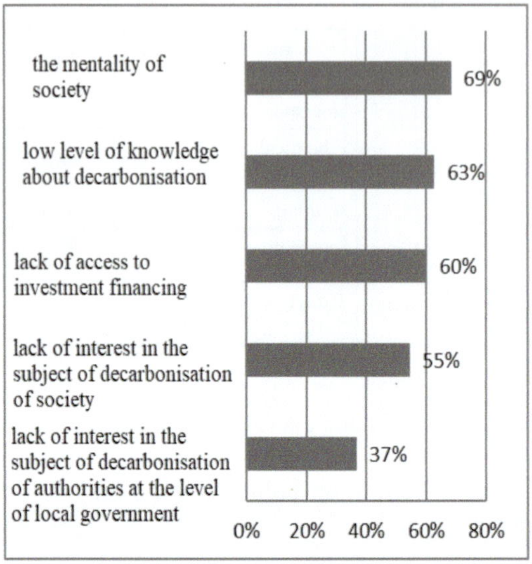

Fig. E5. The biggest barrier to decarbonisation

	Number	Percentage
lack of interest in the subject of decarbonisation of authorities at the level of local government	233	37%
lack of interest in the subject of decarbonisation of society	345	55%
lack of access to investment financing	382	60%
low level of knowledge about decarbonisation	398	63%
the mentality of society	434	69%

Chart E5. The biggest barrier to decarbonisation

Source: own elaboration based on empirical research, n = 633.

As many as 69% of respondents said that the biggest barrier to decarbonisation is the mentality of the society, 60% of respondents indicated a lack of access to sources of financing for investments, while only 37% of respondents indicated a lack of interest in the topic of decarbonisation of authorities at the local government level.

Correlationss:

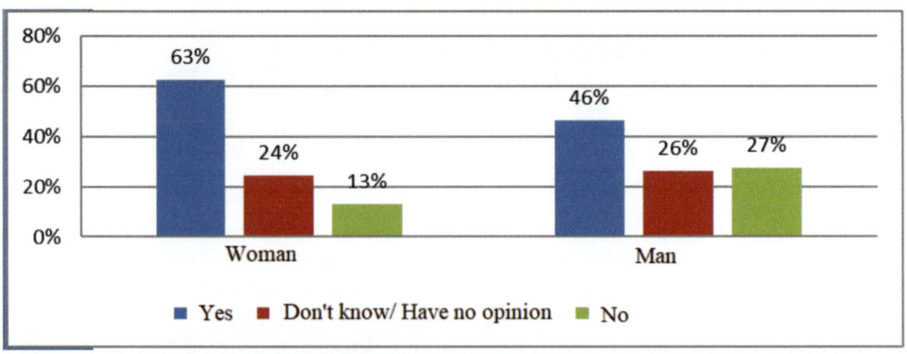

Fig. 4. Statistical dependencies. Source: own elaboration based on empirical research, n = 633.

Gender had an impact on whether Poland's decarbonisation policy would reduce global CO_2 emissions, or whether it would have no impact on the economy's global emissions (Fig. 4).
$P < \alpha$ ($p = 0{,}0002$).

Results of own empirical research—survey of experts' views (Delphi method)

The next stage of empirical own research was a survey of experts' views - using the Delphi method. The results of the survey obtained in the first round are presented in Table 2.

Table 2. Delphi test results – first round.

Question number	Experts																				Average points
	1	2	3	4	5	6	7	8	9	10	11	12	13	14	15	16	17	18	19	20	
1	5	4	5	5	5	4	5	5	5	5	5	5	5	4	5	5	5	5	5	4	**4,8**
2	4	5	5	4	4	5	5	5	5	5	4	4	3	3	5	5	5	5	4	4	**4,4**
3	4	4	4	5	5	5	5	5	5	3	3	5	5	5	5	5	5	5	5	5	**4,6**
4	2	3	5	5	5	5	5	5	5	5	5	5	5	5	4	4	4	5	5	2	**4,4**
5	2	4	4	4	4	4	5	5	5	3	5	5	5	5	5	5	5	5	5	2	**4,3**
6	4	5	5	5	5	5	5	5	5	4	4	5	5	5	5	5	4	4	5	4	**4,7**
7	4	5	5	5	5	5	5	5	5	3	5	5	5	5	5	5	5	5	5	3	**4,8**
8	1	3	3	3	4	4	4	5	5	2	5	5	3	3	5	5	5	5	5	1	**3,8**
9	2	5	5	5	5	4	4	5	5	4	4	5	5	5	5	5	5	5	5	3	**4,5**
10	4	4	4	4	4	4	4	5	5	4	4	5	5	5	5	5	5	5	5	4	**4,5**
11	5	5	5	5	5	5	5	5	5	5	5	5	5	5	5	5	5	5	5	5	**5**

Source: own elaboration based on empirical research, n = 20.

Due to the fact that there were extreme ratings in the responses of individual experts, a second round of the survey was conducted, during which the experts were presented with the average of all experts' ratings for each question. In the event of a significant variation from the average, the expert was asked to present his or her position and possibly revise the assigned rating. The result of the survey in the second round is presented in Table 3.

Based on the conducted study, it can be said that the results obtained are in line with literature studies and surveys. Environmental responsibility, including climate responsibility, and corporate social responsibility are crucial for modern economies. These economies operate on the principles of interdependence occurring between the sustainable development of countries, corporate finance and social adaptation in terms of achieving the goals of the economic unit itself, but in accordance with the objectives of the EGD.

Table 3. Delphi test results – second round.

Question number	Experts																				Average points
	1	**2**	**3**	**4**	**5**	**6**	**7**	**8**	**9**	**10**	**11**	**12**	**13**	**14**	**15**	**16**	**17**	**18**	**19**	**20**	
1	5	4	5	5	5	4	5	5	5	5	5	5	5	4	5	5	5	5	5	4	**4,8**
2	4	5	5	4	4	5	5	5	5	5	4	4	3	3	5	5	5	5	4	4	**4,4**
3	4	4	4	5	5	5	5	5	5	3	4	5	5	5	5	5	5	5	5	5	**4,7**
4	3	3	5	5	5	5	5	5	5	5	5	5	5	5	4	4	4	5	5	3	**4,5**
5	3	4	4	4	4	4	5	5	5	3	5	5	5	5	5	5	5	5	5	3	**4,4**
6	4	5	5	5	5	5	5	5	5	4	4	5	5	5	5	5	4	4	5	4	**4,7**
7	4	5	5	5	5	5	5	5	5	3	5	5	5	5	5	5	5	5	5	3	**4,8**
8	2	3	3	3	4	4	4	5	5	2	5	5	3	3	5	5	5	5	5	2	**3,9**
9	2	5	5	5	5	4	4	5	5	4	4	5	5	5	5	5	5	5	5	3	**4,5**
10	4	4	4	4	4	4	4	5	5	4	4	5	5	5	5	5	5	5	5	4	**4,5**
11	5	5	5	5	5	5	5	5	5	5	5	5	5	5	5	5	5	5	5	5	**5**

Source: own elaboration based on empirical research, n = 20.

Summary

The creation of new values based on assumptions derived from the climate responsibility of business and society is implied by the EGD. Values are concepts or beliefs, determine the choice of specific behaviours, relate to desired goals. New values can be created using diverse methods and tools.

The purpose of the chapter was to (1) deepen the theory in defining new values of social responsibility in an environmental perspective; (2) identify the interdependencies occurring between the sustainable development of countries, corporate finance and social adaptation in achieving the goals of the EGD by understanding the decarbonisation policies of countries. A triangulation method was used to achieve the goal of the chapter. Conducting literature and empirical research of its own, the research hypothesis that "international cooperation and dialogue with social partners, their awareness, access to information and knowledge determine the implementation of assumptions arising from the climate responsibility of business and society, thus creating new values" was proven. These new values include: life, health and happiness of individuals, well-being, restraint (primarily in over-consumption and over-consumption of resources), resource conservation, communitarianism (social solidarity), pride in "momentous decisions", environmental proactivity and high quality of urban life, maintenance of biodiversity of the plant and animal world.

References

Adler, F. 1956. *The Value Concept in Sociology.* The American Journal of Sociology 62(3): 272–279.

Antonowicz, P. and Galiński, P. 2020. *Społeczny, środowiskowy i jakościowy wymiar kreacji wartości organizacji*. Wydawnictwo Uniwersytetu Gdańskiego.

Cafaro, F. 2015. *Environmental virtue ethics*. pp. 427–444. *In*: Besser-Jones, L. and Slote, M. (eds.). The Routledge Companion to Virtue Ethics. Routledge.

Ciechanowicz-McLean, J. 2021. *Instrumenty prawne ochrony klimatu przed i w Europejskim Zielonym Ładzie.* Gdańskie Studia Prawnicze. 3(51): 9–20.
Ciechanowicz-McLean, J. 2017. *Węzłowe problemy prawa ochrony klimatu.* Studia Prawnoustrojowe. 37: 7–24.
Ciechanowska, M. 2020. *Europejski Zielony Ład wyzwaniem dla transformacji polskiego przemysłu naftowego i gazowniczego.* Nafta-Gaz. 10: 757–761. https://doi.org/ 10.18668/NG.2020.10.12.
Dose, J. J. 1997. *Work values: an integrative framework and illustrative application to organizational socialization.* J. Occup. Organ. Psych. 70: 219–240. https://doi.org/10.1111/j.2044-8325.1997.tb00645.x.
Dutcher, D. D., Finley, J. C., Luloff, A. E. and Johnson, J. B. 2007. *Connectivity with nature as a measure of environmental values.* Environ. Behav. 39(4): 474–493. https://doi.org/10.1177/0013916506298794.
Elliot, R. 1997. *Faking Nature: The Ethics of Environmental Restoration.* Routledge.
Filho, W. L., Yayeh Ayal, D., Wall, T., Shiel, Ch., Paco, A., Pace, P. et al. 2023. *An assessment of attitudes and perceptions of international university students on climate change.* Climate Risk Management. 39: 100486. https://doi.org/10.1016/j.crm.2023.100486.
Hirai, T. and Comim, F. 2022. *Measuring the sustainable development goals: A poset analysis.* Ecol. Indic. 145: 109605. https://doi.org/10.1016/j.ecolind.2022.109605.
Hońko, S. 2013. *Wycena w rachunkowości. Znaczenie, podstawy, parametry i zasady.* Przedsiębiorstwo Produkcyjno-Handlowe ZAPOL Dmochowski, Sobczyk, Szczecin.
Jabłoński, A. and Jabłoński, M. 2019. *Trust as a key factor in shaping the social business model of water supply companies.* Sustainability 11(20): 5805. https://doi.org/10.3390/su11205805.
Jabłoński, A. and Jabłoński, M. 2020a. *Social Business Models in the Digital Economy: New Concepts and Contemporary Challenges.* Palgrave Macmillan.
Jabłoński, A. and Jabłoński, M. 2020b. *Social perspectives in digital business models of railway enterprises.* Energies. 13(23): 6445. https://doi.org/10.3390/en13236445.
Jabłoński, A. and Jabłoński, M. 2021. *Shaping the safety culture of high reliability organizations through digital transformation.* Energies. 14(16): 4721. https://doi.org/10.3390/en14164721.
Jamieson, D. 2010. *Ethics, public policy and global warming,* pp. 77–86. *In*: Gardiner, S. M., Caney, S., Jamieson, D. and Sue, H. (eds.). Climate Ethics. Essential Readings. Oxford Univ Pr.
Kaniewska, M. 2015. *Zmiany klimatu jako wyzwanie do etycznego działania.* Journal of Modern Science. 27(4): 33–50.
Kowalik-Olubińska, M. 2021. *"Nie jesteś za młody, żeby zmieniać świat" – studium przypadku zjawiska dziecięcego aktywizmu klimatycznego.* Problemy Wczesnej Edukacji. 2(53): 165–177. https://doi.org/10.26881/pwe.2021.53.12.
Krot, M., Lech, E., Falkowski, P. and Polecki, K. 2021. *Strach, odpowiedzialność, nadzieja. Filozoficzno-społeczne aspekty globalnego ocieplenia.* Wydawnictwo Uniwersytetu w Białymstoku.
Leijten, I. 2019. *Human rights v. Insufficient climate action: The Urgenda case.* Neth. Q. Hum. Rights. 37(2): 115–116. https://doi.org/10.1177/0924051919844375.
Maslow, A. 1943. *A theory of human motivation.* Psychol. Rev. 7: 370–396.
McKenzie, M. 2023. *The geopolitics of climate change and education policy.* pp. 597–600. *In*: Tierney, R. J., Rizvi, F. and Ercikan, K. (eds.). International Encyclopedia of Education (Fourth Edition). Elsevier. https://doi.org/10.1016/B978-0-12-818630-5.01016-2.
Nowak, Z. 2021. *Europejski Zielony Ład–na drodze do neutralności klimatycznej UE.* Biuletyn PISM. 66(2264): 1-2.
Przesławski, T. (ed.). 2020. *W poszukiwaniu dobra w perspektywie jednostkowej i społecznej.* Wydawnictwo Instytutu Wymiaru Sprawiedliwości.
Przybojewska, I. 2023. *Lasy w kontekście prawnych unormowań ochrony klimatu.* Prawne Problemy Górnictwa i Ochrony Środowiska. 1: 1–29. https://doi.org/10.31261/PPGOS.2023.01.02.
Remlein, M. 2019. *Społecznie odpowiedzialne inwestycje w sprawozdawczości przedsiębiorstw.* Wydawnictwo Uniwersytetu Ekonomicznego w Poznaniu. https://doi.org/10.18559/978-83-66199-63-7.
Śniegowski, M. 2022. *Taksonomia-narzędzie wyznaczające kierunek transformacji w ciepłownictwie.* Instal. 1: 6–9. https://doi.org/10.36119/15.2022.1.1.
Stachowska, I. 2016. *Constraint as an ethical postulate in the context of ecological limits.* Ethics in Progress. 7(1): 1–20. https://doi.org/10.14746/eip.2016.1.1.

Stoczkiewicz, M. 2009. *The Polluter Pays Principle and State Aid for Environmental Protection.* Journal for European Environmental and Planning Law 6(2): 171–197.

Wewerinke-Singh, M. 2018. *State responsibility for human rights violations associated with climate change.* pp. 75–89. *In*: Duyck, S., Jodoin, S. and Johl, A. (eds.). Routledge Handbook of Human Rights and Climate Governance. Routledge.

Zioło, M. 2020. *Finanse zrównoważone. Rozwój. Ryzyko. Rynek.* Polskie Wydawnictwo Ekonomiczne. Warszawa-Szczecin.

Chapter 8

Sustainability in Football Clubs

Selected Experiences

Leszek Bohdanowicz[1,*] and *Rafał Jabłoński*[2]

Introduction

Awareness of *corporate social responsibility* and *sustainability* has increased in the twentieth century. Customers have begun to take them into account when making their purchasing decisions, and some investors have also used them as an investment criterion (Martinez-Ferrero et al., 2017; Lingnau et al., 2022). It is not surprising that companies across industries have turned their attention to corporate social responsibility and sustainability in their strategies, and some have even used it to differentiate themselves. As a result, there has also been research on the subject in various industries and organizations (Ali et al., 2017). Some were focused on sustainability reporting (Herzig and Schaltegger, 2006) or relationship between sustainability and performance (Magon et al., 2018). In particular, they concerned key sectors for economies and sectors under strong social pressure, such as the banking sector, energy sector or petroleum sector (Cerin, 2002; Guttiérrez-Ponce, 2023). Or sin sectors that are particularly sensitive to the legitimacy of their activities in the eyes of the public (Dhandhania and O'Higgins, 2022).

There have also been studies on corporate social responsibility and sustainability in sport management. After all, such organizations are important social institutions, both in terms of economic and social impact on society (Godfrey, 2009). In an economic sense, they are part of an increasingly important leisure industry, which accounts for growing customer spending. Perhaps it is not the largest sector of the

1 Department of Strategy and Value Based Management, Faculty of Management University of Lodz, Matejki Street 22/26, 90-237 Lodz, Poland.
2 Sportbm Ltd., Powstańców Warszawy Street 19, 81-718 Sopot, Poland.
Email: jablonski.privado@gmail.com, OCRID: 0009-0009-0646-3691
* Corresponding author: leszek.bohdanowicz@uni.lodz.pl, OCRID: 0000-0002-4456-070X

leisure industry but it is one of the sectors with the fastest growth rate (Gratton, 1998). The social impact of sport refers to its relevance to health, group membership and mutual support among group members as well as its impact on wider communities (Platow et al., 1999; Seippel, 2006).

The most important sport in the world in terms of popularity is football. Due to this popularity, football clubs started to professionalize and commercialize in the 1990s (Rohde and Breuer, 2017), and, as a result, began to generate increasing revenues from their activities. By expanding and diversifying their activities, clubs are not only committed to winning trophies and training young players in dedicated academies, but also managing commercial space in their stadiums, running insurance businesses, travel agencies or investing in start-ups. They are also constantly and creatively looking for new sources of revenue that can increase their budgets, resulting in the opportunity to contract better players and improve their sporting standing. In such an environment, in order not to lose the links with their communities, they are increasingly willing to turn to corporate social responsibility tools, which are also used by companies in other industries. An increasing number of clubs are also involved in activities that support environmental protection and sustainability (Fernández-Villarino, 2021). After all, little is still known about the reasons for implementation, the motives and the details of their sustainability strategies. The aim of this paper is to define the meaning and scope of sustainable development of professional football clubs, as well as the reasons for implementing sustainability strategies. Institutional theory has been used to explain these issues.

Sustainability as a business response to 21st century problems

In the second half of the 20th century, the prevailing approach was that the purpose of any company was to create value for its owners. Most often in the short term. This could have led to actions that did not take into account the interests of society and also to conflicts with various stakeholders and environmental degradation. In response to these threats, a number of different ideas arose that accommodated and promoted such interests. These can include, for example, consumerism, corporate social responsibility or sustainability (Carroll, 2008; Cravens and Hills, 1970; Ocasio et al., 2023).

These concepts have evolved over the years and have increasingly been incorporated into the strategies of today's companies and their business models. The importance of corporate performance has not been overlooked, which is crucial for any business. Today's companies are therefore expected to go beyond narrow, short-term financial focus and extend to economic, environmental and social sustainability (Haffar and Searcy, 2017) and will use their core competencies to create positive environmental, social (doing good) and economic (doing well) value by creating value networks with their stakeholders (Upward and Jones, 2015).

It is also worth emphasizing that both terms, i.e., corporate social responsibility and sustainable development (sustainability), refer to similar aspects and are often even used together. Bhagwat (2011) recognized that CSR is an integral part of sustainable development, and he recommended that CSR should be used as the social aspect of the concept of sustainable development, which is mainly based on a sensible approach to stakeholders. On the other hand, Ebner and Baumgartner (2008) pointed out that in many studies sustainable development is seen as an ethically justified basis for corporate social responsibility and often the two terms are used synonymously. It should also be added here that the concepts of sustainability and sustainable development have evolved since the very beginning of interest in them and their boundaries have changed. Hence their development may be difficult to understand and it may have different meaning. Many authors have argued that there is no single unanimous approach to sustainable development due to a variety of characteristics of different protection programs and different types of communities and institutions (Ciegis, et al., 2009; Radermacher, 1999).

However, direct interest in sustainable development increased with the publication in 1987 by the UN-sponsored World Commission on Environment and Development (WCED) Brundtland Commission's report "Our Common Future" (1987). This coherent report, produced in a global partnership, has become a turning point for the concept of sustainability. It indicated that "sustainable development is the kind of development, which satisfies the current needs without endangering the future generations to satisfy their own" and further specified that the essence of sustainability is fair distribution of natural resources both among different generations and among the present generation of people from the first, the second and the third world, and finding a positive consensus between the environmental, social, and economic dimensions of environment.

Since then, interest in the concept has gathered pace. In 1992 the World Bank defined sustainable development as "development that continues" (World Development Report, 1992). And in the same year the Rio de Janeiro declaration on Environment and Development described as "long-term continuous development of the society aimed at satisfaction of humanity's need at present and in the future via rational usage and replenishment of natural resources, preserving the Earth for future generations" (United Nations, 1992).

Similar aspects were included in the definitions of sustainable development and sustainability in scientific publications. Pearce, Markandya and Barbier (1989) concluded that it is the creation of the social and economic system that guarantees support for the following aims: increase in the real income, the improvement of the level of education, and the improvement in the populations' health and in the general quality of life. In turn, Munasinghe (1994) underlined that it is the process of increasing the spectrum of alternatives allowing individuals and communities to realize their aspirations and potential in the long perspective, at the same time maintaining the regeneration ability in economic, social, and ecological systems.

In all these considerations, it was also aptly noted that the idea of sustainability having three dimensions stems from the Triple Bottom Line concept (Elkington, 1994). According to this concept the conventional bottom line (profit) should be added care for the environment (the planet) as well as being good to people, for instance by providing facilities for the handicapped and hiring minorities (the social dimension) (Kuhlman and Farrington, 2010). And sustainability principles would aim to eliminate our contribution to:

a. Systematic increases in concentrations of substances from the Earth's crust.
b. Systematic increases in concentrations of substances produced by society.
c. Systematic physical degradation of nature.
d. Conditions that systematically undermine people's capacity to meet their needs (Johnston et al., 2007).

Institutionalization of the concept of sustainable development

The diffusion of the concept of sustainable development is most often described in terms of institutional theory (DiMaggio and Powell, 1983) and legitimacy theory (Deegan, 2002). These theories show elements of a complementary approach to each other and, as Suchman stated (1975), "legitimacy and institutionalization are virtually synonymous. Both phenomena empower organizations primarily by making them seem natural and meaningful".

Institutional theory provides strong arguments about why and how organizations do what they do (Berthod, 2016). No organization operates in a vacuum. Each is influenced by a number of external factors, such as legal and market requirements, cultural factors, or key stakeholder expectations. They all shape institutions, which are understood as beliefs, rules, norms and symbolic elements that create and cause the proliferation of organizational forms, their characteristics and various practices. These institutions influence changes that make organizations similar in many areas, create technical requirements and are of a different nature.

With these different natures in mind, DiMaggio and Powell (1983) identified three mechanisms that lead to institutional isomorphic change. These are coercive isomorphic, mimetic isomorphism and normative isomorphism. Coercive isomorphism is the result of political influence, or pressure from other organizations, which is linked to and from the cultural expectations of societies. The impact on uptake is therefore external. At the same time, it is linked to the problem of legitimacy. Through this kind of isomorphism, organizations are increasingly similar within a given domain and organized around rituals of conformity with wider institutions. Mimetic isomorphism is a result of standard responses to uncertainty. Uncertainty encourages imitation. Organizations copy the structures of other organizations believing that this is to their advantage. This type of isomorphism occurs when the objectives of the organization or the way in which these objectives are to be achieved is not clear. Mimetic isomorphism simply makes them feel safe. This type of isomorphism is also fostered by the migration of staff between organizations or consultancy operations. Normative isomorphism is linked to professionalization, the pressure of professions and the creation of inter-organizational networks. The norms developed during education are introduced into the organization. Socialization at work also reinforces conformity. People with similar educational backgrounds and similar experiences will prefer similar practices.

Scott (2013) lists three institutional pillars that influence organizational behavior. The first pillar is regulatory and enforces these behaviors through legislation. In football, for example, this is through the general application of joint-stock company rules and compliance with the resulting regulations (Commercial Law or accounting standards), or the need to comply with licensing regulations (maintaining youth teams). The second pillar is normative and stems from sharing common beliefs about what is right. This could be, for example, the expectation that a football club's elected board will take into account the club's history and the fans' perception of its values in its decisions. The third pillar is cultural-cognitive and refers to the taken for granted mental models created to explain how work should be done, as is the case with routine behavior in an organization. For example, in relation to the functioning of marketing, communication or the general organization of a football club.

In line with the approach described by legitimacy theory, companies must show that their actions are in line with public expectations. Responding to these expectations, companies have also started to use CSR and sustainable development as a marketing and branding tool (Fleming and Jones, 2013). It therefore happens that managers actually use them instrumentally (Aguilera et al., 2007). Suchman (1995) stated that "legitimacy is generalized perception or assumption that the actions of an entity are desirable, proper, or appropriate within some socially constructed system of norms, values beliefs, and definitions". In this context, the social contract between the organization and its stakeholders becomes central to legitimacy theory. Stakeholders exert influence on organizations and organizations strive to meet them. From this point of view, it is not only their CSR and sustainability strategies that are important, but also the transparency of their operations and their presentation to stakeholders, thus showing that the organization is fulfilling its social contract (Bachman and Ingenhoff, 2016).

Organizations go through different types of legitimacy. This is justified by the different approaches to viewing this mechanism according to the current interests of society and individuals and the importance that society and stakeholders attach to the organization. First and foremost, the organization must acquire cognitive legitimacy, which aims to extend its moral legitimacy that justifies social existence. Therefore, to ensure its survival (in terms of internal and external legitimacy), the organization is committed to building and developing its pragmatic legitimacy.

Football club as a vehicle for social ideas and the promotion of sustainability

Football clubs have always been a good vehicle for social ideas. They have evoked emotions and attracted people. They also conveyed different values. It gave the opportunity to compete and cooperate at the same time. This is also how clubs were formed. Sometimes close to the local community, as factory clubs (e.g., Arsenal or Manchester United), other times they were formed as vehicles for some idea. Like Celtic Glasgow, which was founded at a time when many poor Irish immigrants came to Scotland seeking a better life in its west. However, they encountered much mistrust and hostility and were often discriminated against because of their Catholic religion. Many of them lived in poverty. In 1888, a group of Irish businessmen decided to set up a charitable trust under the slogan 'Poor Children's Dinner Table' with the aim of feeding children from Irish poor families. They chose a football team as the vehicle to promote the campaign. In this way, Celtic from its inception was more of a social institution than just a football club (Donnelly et al., 2008).

Many other clubs have similarly fostered in local communities the ideas that today are the components of corporate social responsibility and sustainability. In addition, public trust in clubs as carriers of shared values has always been high. This is why they are keen to engage in them today. The rationale for this engagement can be summarized in a few points:

- Because sport is popular and reaches people all over the world, sport CSR activities attract media attention and provide access to audiences with their ability to communicate.
- CSR in sport appeals to young people. If a CSR activity is linked to a sports organization, team or personality, young people are more likely to get involved.
- Exercise provides a forum for organizing excellent programs and initiatives that can have a positive impact on health. CSR sport is also a great vehicle for this.
- CSR in sport requires constant participation in a group and therefore makes a strong contribution to social interaction. Cultural understanding, tolerance and integration is another powerful element characterizing CSR in sport.
- There are some sports that can lead their participants to environmental awareness and sustainability.
- Those who take part in sporting CSR activities also immediately experience their beneficial emotional effects (Ráthonyi-Ódor et al., 2020).

The CSR and sustainability activities undertaken by football clubs are quite extensive. Their activities include; charity donations (philanthropy), fundraising, athlete and employee participation in community programs, social media promotion, program development for causes (e.g., improving literacy, improving youth education, improving health), internal league training programs (diversity, violence prevention, life skills, etc.), internal safety programs, or implementing programmes and promoting environmental activities.

For many clubs, sustainable development is particularly important as a tool for shaping brand equity and fan perceptions of clubs. Many authors have even pointed out that incorporating sustainability into brand management is not only about communicating through advertising and various promotional materials, but also about the need to be rooted in values, to carry out process and attitude changes in the organization. The implementation of sustainability and practices is therefore a strategic decision by the company, which relates to all their dimensions (Kumar and Christodoulopoulou, 2014; Grubor and Milovanov, 2017). It is also pointed out that making sport in general more 'green' requires several conditions to be met, such as:

- Cooperation between sports representatives and those promoting nature conservation and environmental protection;
- Developing functional guidelines for sustainability in sport;
- Supporting and further developing sports that are compatible with nature and the environment;
- Building a more environmentally friendly sports-related infrastructure;

- Ensure that environmental standards are strictly adhered to by those funding sports facilities;
- Integrating environmental management into the activities of the sports administration of clubs, associations and commercial sports operators;
- Prioritizing voluntary action to protect the environment (Shiply, 2018).

This is the case in clubs from Europe's strongest leagues, such as the English, Spanish and German leagues. It is because of the impact on the brand that attitudes about sustainability in English football have changed. For example, Manchester City introduced an edible coffee mug and Forest Green Rovers introduced T-shirts made from recycled coffee bean waste and recycled plastic bottles. Aston Villa has been certified as a carbon neutral club. Liverpool and Southampton have introduced extensive sustainability strategies—The Red Way Liverpool and Southampton The Halo Effect. And Manchester United implemented the Reds Go Green initiative to improve waste management and educate fans about recycling. The aforementioned Forest Green Rovers, regarded as the greenest club in the world, seeks to distinguish itself on the basis of its approach to environmental protection.

Spanish clubs are also engaging in sustainability. In October 2020, Real Betis Balompié Seville presented the Forever Green programme, a global programme of Corporate Social Responsibility (CSR) that, through the club's foundation, enables the entity to position itself in areas of sustainable development and environment at a global level. Real Betis was the first football club to sign the United Nations' Climate Change Now initiative (Mora et al., 2021). RC Deportivo de la Coruña, like Forest Green Rovers, has incorporated recycled materials into its outfits. The Galician club, sponsored by Ecoalf, became one of the first clubs to wear a sustainable collection with fabrics made from plastic from the seabed. A different kind of environmental concern was displayed by Elche CF, who signed an agreement with Docuten to promote their digital transformation of administrative processes. Under it, the club aims to achieve sustainability in its daily operations by eliminating paper and reducing emissions when sending out documents. With the volume of the club's documentation, which was calculated to be around 7,000 sheets, Elche would avoid emitting 4.62 kg of CO_2, cutting 64 kg of wood and spending 70,000 liters of water used in the paper production process (all figures given on an annual basis). In this way, it will succeed in reducing its carbon footprint by becoming a more sustainable club, which is one of its main business objectives.

German clubs are also strongly involved in sustainability. S.C. Freiburg has already had solar panels installed on its roof since 1995 to reduce CO_2. Werder Bremen dedicates several hundred thousand euros a year to CSR activities, which involve working with schools and further educating young people about sport and healthy eating. And Hamburger SV, through its foundation and the Hamburger Way programme, implements various projects in the areas of education, sport and social issues. In one 2014/2015 season alone, 1,400 students and 130 teachers took part in educational activities (Grabowski, 2021).

Borussia Dortmund is also taking an active approach to sustainability with a number of solutions at its stadium - Signal Iduna Park. There was implemented DIN ISO 50001 energy management system. The stadium is supplied with 100% ecological electricity. Its roof is equipped with solar panels and all Borussia's buildings use green energy. The idea was to reduce CO_2 emissions. The club also developed nine charging stations at the stadium. The stadium is also a place of education where a nationwide project for children and youth is carried out in the form of workshops on such issues as: anti-mobbing, career counseling, social integration, intercultural dialogue, social inequalities, civil courage, teamwork, right-wing extremism, personal development, prevention violence, healthy lifestyle (Grabowski, 2021).

As these examples show, there are many opportunities for football clubs to incorporate into their sustainability strategies. They relate to: environmental conditions (e.g., biodiversity, ecosystem protection), land development and use, management of resources and energy use (e.g., use of renewable energy sources, LED lighting, energy saving, motion sensors; rainwater collection systems), waste management, environmental pollution (e.g., reducing emissions), protection of cultural heritage, as well as the impact on the environment of various sports-related activities (e.g., operation of facilities, transport, accommodation, sports tourism, meals, office work) (Ráthonyi-Ódor et al., 2020).

Sustainable football club strategies—case studies

1. Research method and sample

The development of the sustainability development concept in football clubs was analyzed through case studies in three football clubs. They all excelled in their activities. The clubs came from three different countries. The first one from Great Britain (Forest Green Rovers), the second from Norway (Odds BK), and the third from Poland (Warta Poznań). Information about their sustainability activities was collected from publicly available secondary data. They came from their websites, press articles and other materials such as unpublished presentations.

2. Case studies

Forest Green Rovers

Forest Green Rovers is an English club playing in the 2023/2024 season in League Two. The club is based in Nailsworth, Glocestershire, with a population of approximately 5,000. For years, he achieved only local successes. In 2010 it was on the verge of bankruptcy and was taken over by eccentric businessman Dale Vince, who lived in nearby Stroud.

Dale Vince is a New Age believer. In 1995, at the age of 34, he erected his first wind turbine on the Stroud hills, which was to power the military truck that was his home. As a follower of the New Age philosophy, freedom and the beautiful landscape of the surrounding hills were enough for him to be happy. The turbine idea turned out to be so successful that in 1996 he founded Ecotricity, a company operating in the renewable energy sources industry, and expanded his wind farm. Consistent building of the business meant that in 2009 his fortune was worth approximately £100 million.

After taking over Forest Green Rovers, Dale Vince first made sure that the club did not go bankrupt, and then he began to implement his vision, consistent with his own philosophy of life and business. This vision included both the stadium infrastructure, the organization of matches and the rules of team management. He installed photovoltaic panels on the stadium's roof, and a special solar-powered robot started mowing the grass on the pitch. It is maintained with natural fertilizers, without the use of chemicals. The pitch surface has been designed to ensure high retention. Rainwater is collected in a special tank and later used to water the pitch. After mowing, the grass goes to local farmers' composters. Oil used in cooking is made into fuel. Chargers for electric cars have appeared in the club's parking lot, and the players' bus is powered by electricity.

The club's strong focus on environmentalism has led to it being recognized by the United Nations for its work to protect the environment and halt climate change and receiving the 'Momentum for Change' award. Dale Vince stated: "We're pretty chuffed to have this recognition from the United Nations for our work in promoting sustainability through sport. Plenty of people doubted we could make this improbable combination of a football club and the environment work, but it's proven to be a powerful combination".

The changes that Dale Vince made also concerned matters fundamental to the fans, which must have affected the dissatisfaction of many of them. Before the 2011/2012 season, he changed the club's crest. The shield, which differed mainly in colours from that of FC Barcelona, was replaced by a coat of arms featuring a lion and a unicorn. As then team coach Dave Hockaday commented on the idea, "The lion signifies strength and the unicorn adds magical symbolism to the team". The colors of the costumes have also changed. The traditional white of the shirts has been replaced by bright green, which is the official color of Ecotricity, and the third set was designed in conjunction with Sea Shepherd, an organization working to protect the seas and oceans. The costumes are made from half recycled plastic and half bamboo charcoal.

In 2015, the club became fully vegan and in 2017 was recognized as a carbon-neutral institution. Meat sales have been banned in the stadium and burgers and hot dogs have disappeared from the stalls. The menu included vegan burgers, vegan fajitas, yam fries and Quorn cakes. On its website, the club explained that "Freshly made vegan food is much healthier than processed meats, with far less risk of heart disease." Football players have also started to be advised to limit meat, especially red meat. It has also been dispensed with during communal meals. Club nutritionist Tom Heulin praised veganism as follows: "Plant-based food is much faster absorbed by the human body and therefore better digested. This is crucial if you are a professional athlete."

Such drastic changes have discouraged some fans. Some have stopped identifying with him and are calling him Dale Vince F.C. To their accusations, the owner responded in an interview with CNN: "It seems to bother people when a vegan shows them that there is another way. But we're conscious not to wag our fingers at anyone. We don't want to be preachy. All we can do is live our lives and educate people who want to be educated. For every fan we lose, we've gained 10. Our attendances are at an all-time high".

The strategy employed by Dale Vince at Forest Green Rovers fits closely with that of his company. The owner himself stressed in an interview with CNN that he had thought along these lines: "What if we could use football as a new channel for communicating? We thought we could have some fun creating a green football club and speak to the wider world of sport. What if we could make football fans equally passionate about the environment? We couldn't do this without bringing our ethos and vision into it" (Borejza, 2019; Smoliński, 2020).

Odds BK

Odds BK presents itself as the most environmentally friendly club in Norway and tries to go green at every turn. Its Skagerak Arena has a number of solutions to prove it, t such as solar cells on the roof and a battery that captures excess energy. But not only—black granules (SBR) have been eliminated from the artificial turf and replaced with organic materials—sand and crushed olive stones. Stadium food outlets offer menus that lead to as little waste as possible, in line with the principles of the circular industry and the Zero Waste approach. This waste that is created is disposed of and recycled. The Broddrane Children's Club is run with a strong infiltration of ecology, including using less plastic, inviting green activities and shaping children's awareness. In addition, Odds BK organizes environmental conferences. A fast charger has been installed at the stadium for electric cars, which can additionally park for free on match day. The club is also a member of the Climate and Energy Network in the municipality of Vestfold and Telemark County, and undertakes a number of other activities, including: starting a partnership with environmental organizations in Greenland, building a bicycle parking area with a green roof, and encouraging people to come to matches by this mode of transport. It has introduced a vegetarian option in the stadium, uses bioenergy, holds environmental seminars for sponsors and has introduced e-ticketing. And these are just some of the solutions.

Warta Poznań

In Poland, a club that tries to act in a similar way to Forest Green Rovers is Warta Poznań. This club seeks to differentiate itself from other clubs managed like corporations, although at the same time it wants to strive to raise standards and professionalize. It was also accepted that, because of the colors (green and white, and the club refers to itself as 'Greens'), the club should be pro-environment and strongly socially committed. The action plan is based on five pillars: Sport, Infrastructure, Community, Finance and Organization. An important part of the development strategy is that of the sports division, which also has no shortage of CSR elements. It envisaged, in addition to the development of the first team, the launch of a reserve team, the development of a football academy, the creation of a women's team (initially a youth section after the merger with Leidis Luboń) and the launch of an AMP Football section.

Warta has also undertaken a number of other sustainability initiatives. It has undertaken actions such as bee protection, tree planting, fan education, reducing plastic consumption, joint environmental actions with the City of Poznań, neighborhood clean-ups, green gadgets, eco-friendly partners and an eco-friendly bus. Particularly noteworthy is the establishment of the 'Green Apiary' by the club. The beehives for the apiary were painted green by first-team and academy players. The players also autographed them, and the first frame with the bees was placed by the captain of the first team. By setting up the Green Apiary, Warta also wants to draw attention to the problem of protecting bees, which are threatened with extinction due to environmental degradation.

Not far from the apiary is a street named *Aleja Warciarzy*, where the club has planted trees to help clean up the city's air. But by the same token, they are to become a memorial to the most distinguished figures in the history of Warta Poznań, who have become patrons of the trees. In this way, young people were able to learn about the Warta and its history in an original, accessible and environmentally friendly way. The club did not want to erect granite monuments, but to do something that was in line with its new mission. This is how it was able to achieve it. Next to each lime tree is a wooden plaque with the patron's name and a QR code - scanning it will take you to the website www.alejawarciarzy.pl created for the project. It contains information about the entire initiative and short biographies of the patrons of the trees in the avenue (Aleja Warciarzy).

Summary

Corporate social responsibility and sustainable development have become an imperative for many businesses in recent years and a cornerstone of the business models of companies across a range of industries. Various coercive, mimetic and normative isomorphic mechanisms play a key role in their spread between organizations. The diffusion of sustainable development has not bypassed the world of sport, but the issue is not yet often addressed in academic studies. And yet, with the development of ESG policies in other industries and organizations, sustainable development measures have also been taken in clubs. Some of these have been successful and have helped to differentiate themselves from other clubs. Forest Green Rovers and Odds BK, for example, have done so. In Poland, for example, Warta Poznań is trying to position itself in the same way and is implementing green projects and striving to popularize green ideas. Also, by shaping the attitudes of children and young people or various social projects, such as planting trees or keeping bees. While of course, in all of these clubs, as in any other football club, the most important thing is to achieve sporting goals with an economic calculation, these clubs additionally try to behave in a pro-social and pro-environmental way.

These cases and the examples of many clubs from the English, Spanish and French leagues show what areas are covered by the sustainable development of football clubs. The first is the stadium infrastructure and its service. It includes, for example, measures such as installing solar panels, charging stations, rainwater tanks for watering the turf, avoiding chemicals in its care or using the cut grass as compost. The second area is technical equipment. This is where football clubs take measures such as electrical power for the club coach or lawnmowers. The third area is fan relations and fan service. As part of this, clubs encourage fans to come to matches on environmentally friendly means of transport, use recyclable tools such as drinks cups. The fourth is extensive pro-social activities, such as setting up bee hives or planting trees. The fifth activity is environmental education. Football clubs, thanks to their media presence, are good communicators of sustainability ideas by organizing, for example, environmental conferences. They also play an important educational role in relation to children and young people. They can also use their natural gambling abilities to enhance the appeal of such a message, e.g., by setting quizzes or enriching sports games. The use of new technologies can also be helpful here.

Football clubs undertake these various activities even though their main objectives are sporting in nature. However, they are also increasingly part of today's common behavior to legitimize their action in the eyes of their stakeholders. In this case, by changing their operating models in a pro-environmental direction. The institutionalization of these behaviors comes from changing cultural expectations of societies, the behavior of other clubs, or businesses in other industries. Club behavior is therefore linked to coercive isomorphism. Although the creation of norms in society as a result of environmental promotion and education, normative isomorphism is also gaining strength. Smaller clubs, such as those described in the case study, can instead diversify through sustainable business models to build a brand and attract new fan groups. Thus reduce their uncertainty resulting from inferior financial potential. The substrate of their functioning becomes mimetic isomorphism.

This article is one of the few publications on the sustainable development of football clubs at the moment, but it certainly does not exhaust the issue of changing the business models of these organizations and becoming environmentally oriented. It provides a basis for further research on football clubs and sustainability. It could be important to identify how sustainable development affects their performance, including, in particular, the ability to increase budgets by growing audiences and merchandising revenues. Another direction for further research could be the impact of football clubs on raising awareness of sustainability. Football clubs and football players are at the center of public interest. Research can show the effectiveness of their educational role and the possibilities of its application. And finally, new technologies in football are growing in importance in management, marketing, communication, game analysis and training. New technologies also support sustainable development. An important area of analysis is their further development and adaptation. Including technologies that support sustainable development in football clubs.

References

Aguilera, R. V., Rupp, D. E., Williams, C. A. and Ganapathi, J. 2007. *Putting the S back in corporate social responsibility: A multi-level theory of social change in organizations*. Acad. Manage. Rev. 32: 836–863.

Ali, W., Frynas, J. G. and Mahmood, Z. 2017. *Determinants of corporate social responsibility (CSR) disclosure in developed and developing countries: A literature review*. Corp. Soc. Resp. Env. Ma. 24: 273–294.

Bachman, P. and Ingenhoff, D. 2016. *Legitimacy through CSR disclosures? The advantage ouweights the disadventages*. Public Relat. Rev. 42: 386–394.

Bebbington, J., Larrinaga, C. and Moneva, J. M. 2008. *Corporate social reporting and reputation risk management.* Account. Audit. Accoun. 21: 337–361.

Berthod, O. 2016. *Institutional Theory of Organizations. In:* Farazmand, A. (eds.). Global Encyclopedia of Public Administration, Public Policy, and Governance. Springer, Cham.

Bhagwat, P. 2011. *Corporate social responsibility and sustainable development.* Conference on Inclusive & Sustainable Growth. Role of Industry Government and Society Conference Proceedings.

Borejza, T. 2019. *Klub z angielskiej czwartej ligi ma stadion, który inspiruje świat. "Najbardziej zielony klub świata".* https://smoglab.pl/klub-pilkarski-przeszedl-na-100-energii-ze-slonca-i-wiatru-od-tego-czasu-awansowal-i-oszczedzil/ [14.11.2023].

Brundtland, G. 1987. Report of the World Commission on Environment and Development: Our Common Future. United Nations General Assembly Document A/42/427.

Carroll, A. 2008. *A history of corporate social responsibility: Concepts and practices*. pp. 19–46. *In:* Crane, A., Matten, D., McWilliams, A., Moon, J. and Siegel, D. (eds.). The Oxford Handbook of Corporate Social Responsibility. Oxford University Press.

Cerin, P. 2002. *Communication in corporate environmental reports.* Corp. Soc. Resp. Env. Ma. 9(1): 46–55.

Ciegis, R., Ramanauskiene, J. and Martinkus, B. 2009. *The concept of sustainable development and its use for sustainability scenarios.* Eng. Econ. 62(2): 28–37.

Cravens, D. and Hills, G. E. 1970. *Consumerism: A perspective for business.* Bus. Horizons. 13(4): 21–28.

Deegan, C. 2002. *Introduction: The ligitimizing effect of social and environmental disclosure - A theoretical foundation.* Account. Audit. Accoun. J. 15(3): 282–311.

Dhandhania, A. and O'Higgins, E. 2022. *Can "sin industries" prove their legitimacy through CSR reporting? A study of UK tobacco and gambling companies.* Account. Audit. Accoun. J. 35(4): 1009–1034.

DiMaggio, P. and Powell, W. W. 1983. *The iron cage revisited: Institutional isomorphism and collective rationality in organizational fields.* Am. Sociol. Rev. 88(2): 147–160.

Donnelly, T., Donnelly, M. and Donnelly, T. 2008. *Take-over and turnaround at Celtic: The McCann years 1994–1999.* International Journal of Sport Management and Marketing. 4(1): 49–61.

Ebner, D. and Baumgartner, R. J. 2006. The relationship between Sustainable Development and Corporate Social Responsibility. Corporate Responsibility Research Conference, 4th-5th September, Dublin.

Elkington, J. 1994. *Towards the sustainable corporation: Win-win-win business strategies for sustainable development.* Calif. Manage. Rev. 36(2): 90–100.

Fernández-Villarino, R. 2021. *Sustainability in the football industry: An approach to the gap between theoretical formulation and practical application, through the results of the social fair play project.* Heliyon. 7(6): e07318.

Fleming, P. and Jones, M. T. 2013. *The End of Corporate Social Responsibility.* Crisis and Critique. London: Sage Publication.

Godfrey, P. C. 2009. *Corporate social responsibility in sport: An overview and key issues.* Journal of Sport Management. 23(6): 698–716.

Grabowski, A. 2021. *Implementation of sustainable development in Borussia Dortmund Gmbh&CoKgaA.* J. of Phis. Education and Sport 21(2): 1094–1090.

Grubor, A. and Milovanov, O. 2017. *Brand Strategies in the Era of Sustainability.* Interdisciplinary Description of Complex System. 15(1): 78–88.

Guttiérrez-Ponce, H. 2023. *Sustainability as a strategy base in Spanish firms: Sustainability reports and performance on the sustainable development goals.* Sustain. Dev. 31(4): 3008–3023.

Haffar, M. and Searcy, C. 2017. *Classification of trade-offs encountered in the practice of corporate sustainability.* J. Bus. Ethics. 140: 495–522.

Herzig, Ch. and Schaltegger, S. 2006. *Corporate sustainability reporting: An overview.* pp. 301–324. *In:* Schaltegger, S., Bennett, M. and Burritt, R. (eds.). Sustainability Accounting and Reporting. 21. Springer, Dordrecht.

Johnston, P., Everard, P., Santillo, D. and Robert, K.-H. 2007. *Reclaiming the definition of sustainability.* Environ. Sci. Pollut. R. 14(1): 60–66.

Kuhlman, T. and Farrington, J. 2010. *What is sustainability?* Sustainability 2(10): 3436–3448.

Kumar, V. and Christodoulopoulou, A. 2014. *Sustainability and branding: An integrated perspective.* Ind. Market. Manag. 43(1): 6–15.

Lingnau, V., Fuchs, F. and Beham, F. 2022. *The link between corporate sustainability and willingness to invest: new evidence from the field of ethical investments.* Journal of Management Control 33(4): 335–369.

Magon, R. B., Thome, A., Ferrer, A. and Scavarda, L. 2018. *Sustainability and performance in operations management research.* J. Clean. Prod. 190: 104–117.

Martinez-Ferrero, J., Villaron-Peramato, O. and García-Sánchez, I. M. 2017. *Can investors identify managerial discretion in corporate social responsibility practices? The moderate role of investor protection.* Aust. Account. Rev. 27(1): 4–16.

Mora, G., Ginesta, X. and Vela, J. 2021. *Corporate social responsibility and football clubs: The value of environmental sustainability as a basis for the rebranding of Real Betis Balompié in Spain.* Sustainability 13(24): 13689.

Munasinghe, M. 1994. *Sustainomics: A transdisciplinary framework for sustainable development.* Keynote Paper. Proceedings of the 50th Anniversary Sessions of the Sri Lanka Association for the Advantages of Science (SLAAS), Colombo, Sri Lanka.

Ocasio, W., Kraatz, M. and Chandler, D. 2023. *Making Sense of Corporate Purpose.* Strategy Science 8(2): 123–138.

Pearce, D., Markandya, A. and Barbier, E. 1989. *Blueprint 1: For a Green Economy.* Routledge.

Platow, M., Durante, M., Williams, N., Garrett, M., Walshe, J., Cincotta, S. et al. 1999. *The contribution of sport fan social identity to the production of prosocial behavior.* Group Dyn.-Theor. Res. 3(2): 161–169.

Radermacher, W. 1999. *Indicators, green accounting and environment statistics-information requirements for sustainable development.* International Statistics Review 67(3): 339–354.

Ráthonyi-Ódor, K., Bába, E., Müller, A., Bács, Z. and Ráthonyi, G. 2020. *How successful are the teams of the European football elite off the field? – CSR activities of the Premier League and the Primera División.* Int. J. Env. Res. Pub. He. 17(20): 1–31.

Rohde, M. and Breuer, C. 2017. *The market for football club investors: A review of theory and empirical evidence from professional European football.* Eur. Sport. Manag. Q. 17(3): 265–289.

Scott, W. 2013. *Institutions and Organizations: Ideas, Interests, Identities*. Sage, Thousand Oaks.

Shiply, M. 2018. *Sport and Environment.* https://www.progressiveteacher.in/sport-andenvironment/.

Smoliński, P. 2020. *Stadion o imieniu Kevin, weganizm i New Age. Poznajcie Forest Green Rovers.* https://sport.tvp.pl/51486119/forest-green-rovers-pierwszy-weganski-klub-na-swiecie-stadion-o-imieniu-kevin-weganizm-i-new-age. [15.11.2023]

Suchman, M. C. 1995. *Managing legitimacy: Strategic and institutional approaches*. Acad. Manage. J. 20(3): 571–610.

United Nations. Rio Declaration on Environment and Development. 1992. https://www.un.org/en/development/desa/population/migration/generalassembly/docs/globalcompact/A_CONF.151_26_Vol.I_Declaration.pdf [15.11.2023].

Upward, A. and Jones, P. 2015. *An ontology for strongly sustainable business models*. Organ. Environ. 29(1): 97–123.

World Bank 1992. World Development Report 1992: Development and the Environment, Oxford University Press (Published for the World Bank), New York.

Chapter 9

The Challenges of Sustainability and Strategic Awareness

Marcin Budziński, Yurii Vitkovskyi,[a] Aleksander Ostenda,[b] Małgorzata Mańka-Szulik[c] and Agnieszka Szostak[d]*

Introduction

Strategic perspectives in climate changing processes refer also to the new challenges, which faced organizations nowadays. It might be interpreted in many ways, but the paper focus on three key issues:

- process of participation in creation local development strategies related to strategic awareness and the level of strategic knowledge among citizens,
- prioritization of UN SDG importance and implementation in the context of quality of life in the municipality,
- practical understanding of sustainable local development.

All three key issues above might be also understood as the way of sustainable local management process and its decomposition, what was shown on Fig. 1 below. Although this approach is focused on public organizations it might be useful in all types of organizations—business, NGO's and public ones.

Worth noting that in modern municipalities many theoretical and practical development concepts are getting more popular nowadays. On one hand in local and regional development management sustainability challenges are observed, but on

Faculty of Social Sciences and Humanities, Academy of Silesia, Poland.
[a] Email: yurii.vitkovskyi@akademiaslaska.pl, ORCID: 0000-0001-5806-8671
[b] Email: aleksander.ostenda@wst.pl, ORCID: 0000-0002-3467-157X
[c] Email: m.szulik@wp.pl, ORCID: 0000-0002-5328-8736
[d] Email: agnieszka.szostak@akademiaslaska.pl, ORCID: 0009-0001-1084-1837
* Corresponding author: marcin.budzinski@akademiaslaska.pl, ORCID: 0000-0002-6383-5369

Fig. 1. Decomposition of sustainable local development. Source: authors' own elaboration (Budziński et al., 2024).

the other hand the idea of smart cities spreads rapidly. Both approaches to local and regional development should be treated complementary.

Regarding this conception four stages of smart city evolution were diagnosed (Cohen, 2015). The first, basic one is the city inspired by available technologies (technology driven), second one is the city with a decisive role for public administration (technology enabled, city-led) and next, the third one is the city based on creative involvement of its inhabitants (citizen co-creation). The highest, fourth stage in smart cities evolution is a city that takes advantage of the opportunities offered by sustainable development (Makieła et al., 2022, p. 2). This idea is also based on 3T's of economic development, which consist of main factors: technology, talent, tolerance (Florida, 2003, p. 3-19). Richard Florida's idea was further developed and researched into the concept of 4T capitals–talent, tolerance, technology, trust. According to this approach the stakeholders' participation in creation of local development policies, general strategic awareness as well as improving quality and accessibility to public services are very important issues (Budziński, 2022, p. 21).

Research questions and hypothesis

Taking into consideration all above three main research questions were asked:

- Q1: How the concept of "sustainable local development" is practically understood in Poland and in particular by Metropolis GZM inhabitants?
- Q2: Which of The United Nations Sustainable Development Goals are the most important in Poland and in particular for Metropolis GZM inhabitants from the point of view of the quality of life in the municipality?

- Q3: What is the level of strategic awareness in Poland and among three researched areas: Metropolis GZM, Gdańsk-Gdynia-Sopot Metropolitan Area and The Ruhr Metropolitan Area in Germany?

Furthermore the study set out three main hypotheses:

- H1: The concept of "sustainable local development" is mostly understood both—in Poland and in particular in Metropolis GZM as development that harmoniously takes into account social, economic and environmental aspects.
- H2: Good health and well-being is the most important goal in Poland as well as among Metropolis GZM inhabitants from the point of view of the quality of life in the municipality among all seventeen United Nations Sustainable Development Goals.
- H3. At least 2/3 of respondents in Poland and also in each of researched metropolitan areas do not have any knowledge and interest about their municipal strategy or have basic knowledge only that the city has a strategy.

There additional hypotheses were created regarding strategic awareness:

- H4: There are no significant differences in the level of strategic awareness between all the Poland and GZM Metropolis.
- H5: There are no significant differences in the level of strategic awareness between all the Poland and Gdańsk-Gdynia-Sopot Metropolitan Area.
- H6: According to the strategic awareness indicator the situation in The Ruhr Area in Germany is better than in Poland and polish metropoles.

Theoretical background

Sustainable local development can be defined in many ways and this concept corresponds to environmental sciences, agriculture and social sciences such as economics. The diversity of topics with which this concept is linked is so great that it demonstrates its multidisciplinary nature, which manifests itself in a holistic vision of knowledge in favour of the sustainable evolution of society (Milán-García et al., 2019, p. 14). Sustainable development (SD) might be defined among others as a process of changes which ensures that the needs of the present generation are met without diminishing the development opportunities of future generations, including through integrated economic, social and environmental development activities. With more emphasis on the social factor, social sustainability can also be defined as a process of changes which ensures, that the needs of society as a whole are met without diminishing the development opportunities of any of its groups now and in the future (Korneluk et al., 2019, p. 5-7).

When considering the definition of SD it is also important to present, that the notion that development equals growth is one of the leading causes of the current climate change crisis. The American ecological economist and Nobel Laureate Herman Daly proposed a steady-state economy model as the only way for sustainable

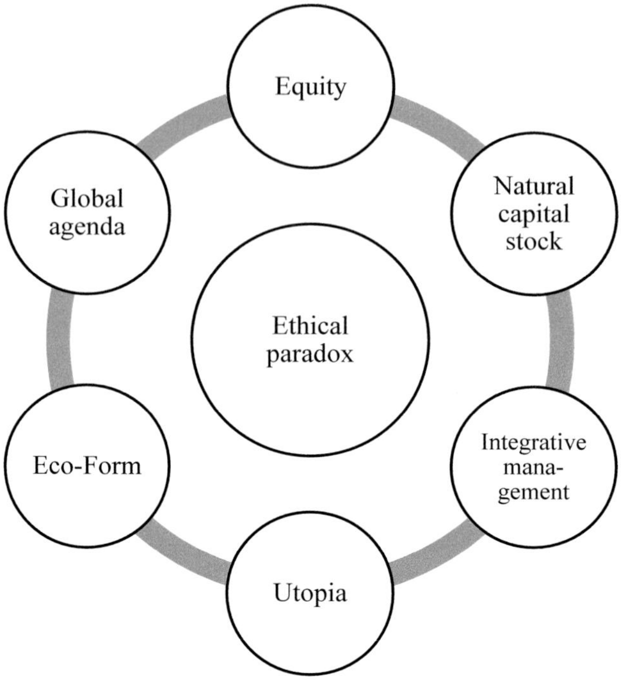

Fig. 2. Conceptual framework for sustainable development. Source: Jabareen Y. (2008) A new conceptual framework for sustainable development, p. 179–192.

development, where the economy is treated as a subsystem of the environment (Daly, 2007). This is aligned with the vernacular worldview that the human community shares an ethic of mutual-reciprocal relationship and responsivity toward one another and the natural world (Cajete, 2020). Daly's theory of SD challenges the traditional economic growth paradigm, which assumes that unlimited economic growth is both possible and desirable. While Daly's theory of sustainable development does not explicitly reference vernacular knowledge, the principles and values inherent in vernacular solutions for example in architecture can be seen as compatible and complementary to his framework (Hu et al., 2023, p. 3).

Additionally the conceptual analysis made by Yosef Jabareen identifies seven concepts which together synthesize and assemble the theoretical framework of SD. (Jabareen, 2008, p. 178-192). This framework is presented on Figure 2 below.

The conceptual framework was based on the fragmented multidisciplinary literature and different bodies of knowledge focusing on SD. The wider explanation of each concepts are as follows (Jabareen, 2008, p. 178-192):

- the paradox between 'sustainability' and 'development' is articulated in terms of ethics. SD tolerates diverse interpretations and practices that range between 'light ecology', which allows intensive interventions, and 'deep ecology', which allows minor interventions in nature,

- natural capital represents the environmental and natural resource assets of development and preservation; the theoretical framework of sustainability advocates keeping the natural capital constant for the benefit of future generations,
- equity represents the social aspects of SD about sharing the capacity for well-being between current and future generations,
- eco-form refers to the ecologically-desired form of urban spaces and communities and refers to desired spatial form of human habitats to create eco-forms, which are energy efficient and designed for long life,
- integrative management represents the holistic view and the integration of environmental, social, and economic concerns in planning and management for SD is essential,
- utopianism represents visions for the human habitats based on SD. Generally, such utopias envision a perfect society in which justice prevails, the people are perfectly content, the people live and flourish in harmony with nature, and life moves along smoothly, without abuses or shortages,
- political global agenda represents new worldwide political environmental discourse reconstituted around the ideas of sustainability, starting since the Rio Summit.

This political global agenda concept was practically developed by the Transforming Our World declaration: The 2030 Agenda For Sustainable Development. It was decomposed into UN SDG and the implementation process, almost worldwide is still in progress. The key issue is, that on the one hand the responsibility of the implementation is on the national and governmental level, but on the other hand each organization and even single person can contribute in achieving UN SDG. In Poland the current progress towards achieving SDGs in the framework of the Voluntary National Reviews on national level is presented in the report "Polish SDG statistics in a nutshell" (2023).

Moreover the growing pressure to implement SD and environmental, social and governance factors (ESG) to measure non-financial impacts of investments and organizations in all types of organization are well seen. The Synergist report (Trends and anti-trends in the implementation of sustainable transformation of organizations in 2024) present main pressure factors of sustainability. They are presented of Fig. 3 below.

Neverminded the type of organization—business, NGO's or public one the sustainability pressure is well seen, even if there are some specific differences and the pace of implementation. In all types of organizations there are some formal and legal regulations, finance institutions deals with all types of organizations and the importance of employees sustainable attitudes do not have organizational borders. The conscious change and sustainable transformation among leaders, owners or managers might be also in all types of organizations as well as sustainable aware customers or wider, product or services recipients.

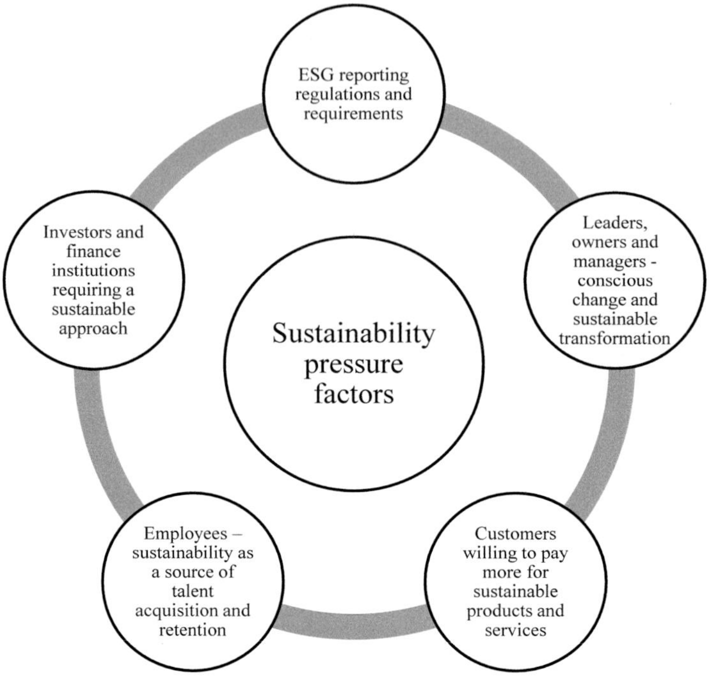

Fig. 3. Main sustainability pressure factors. Source: authors' own elaboration based on: Synergist report: Trends and anti-trends in the implementation of sustainable transformation of organizations in 2024, p. 4.

Another key, theoretical issue worth explaining is strategic awareness. It plays a critical role in the process of decision-making in small enterprises and it is considered a skill for entrepreneurs that assist them in the strategies formulation stage and determining the best strategies path to execute the strategy (Haraisa et al., 2022, p. 42-55; Pencarelli et al., 2009). In relation to public organizations it may be defined as a level of municipal strategy knowledge and involvement in the process of creating or consulting a strategy among citizens. This level of municipal strategy knowledge among stakeholders/inhabitants was decomposed into four groups presented as a percentage of all the population (Budziński et al., 2024):

- LK—lack of knowledge and interest in a strategy (%),
- BK—basic knowledge, only that the city has a strategy (%),
- IK—intermediate knowledge—reading some parts of a strategy (%),
- ICC—involvement in the process of creating or consulting a strategy (%).

It is worth to mention, that to analyse strategic awareness in any municipalities new strategic awareness indicator (SAI) was proposed:

$$SAI = (LK+BK) - (IK+ICC)$$

Thanks to the indicator it is possible to rank the cities. On the other hand it shows the strategical knowledge gap, because empirically (LK+BK) are usually higher then (IK+ICC). It is presented in percentage and interpretation of SAI is: the lowest value it has the better it is or the lowest value it has the smaller strategical knowledge gap it is (Budziński et al., 2024). It can be also evaluated, that values over 50% seems to be high, between 30–50% as the medium level and under 30% as the low ones.

It is also possible to use strategic awareness indicator as the tool to measure the level of strategic awareness of any type of organization, not only the municipality or the public one. In that situation the meaning of stakeholders groups is wider:

- LK—lack of knowledge and interest in organization's strategy (%),
- BK—basic knowledge, only that the organization has a strategy (%),
- IK—intermediate knowledge—reading some parts of the organization's strategy (%),
- ICC—involvement in the process of creating or consulting the organization's strategy (%).

The main challenge is still similar—the practical way of collecting data among all or representative members or organization stakeholders, which usually need dedicated researches to be done.

Materials and methods

The study was conducted on the basis of a survey questionnaire, using the Computer Assisted Website Interview method with two selected and representative research samples of almost 8500 respondents. In all cases the data were collected by the Ariadna panel and all respondents were adults—18 years old or more. First part of the data collection refers to 3301 representative respondents, who were Metropolis GZM inhabitants. The Metropolis GZM, which is located in southern Poland in the central part of Silesian Voivodship consist of 41 cities and communes and respondents came from all the municipalities of Metropolis GZM. Basic data collection took place in June 2023, after those basic statistical analyses were made (Budziński et al., 2024). Second part of the data collection refers to 2707 representative respondents from all the Poland and data collection took place in May and June 2024. Third data collection refers to 2450 representative respondents which consist of 824 respondents in 41 cities in Metropolis GZM, 824 respondents in Gdańsk-Gdynia-Sopot Metropolitan Area (GGSMA) (*Obszar Metropolitalny Gdańsk-Gdynia-Sopot*) and 802 respondents form the Ruhr Area in Germany. In GGSMA research was focused in main cities: Gdańsk, Gdynia, Sopot, Pruszcz Gdański, Reda, Rumnia, Tczew. In the Ruhr Area main cities were selected to the research were Bochum, Bottrop, Dortmund, Duisburg, Essen, Gelsenkirchen, Hagen, Hamm, Herne, Mülheim an der Ruhr, Oberhausen. This data collection took place in July and August 2024. The study protocols were approved by the University Research Committee at the Academy of Silesia, Katowice, Poland. The study followed the ethical requirements of anonymity and voluntary participation. Written informed consent was obtained from each participant before inclusion. The costs of conducting this research were co-financed by three sources:

- Metropolis GZM under the "Metropolitan Science and Education Support Fund" program in 2022–2024 within two granted projects: "Challenges of Public Space and Social Cohesion of the Metropolis GZM in Poland—an interdisciplinary approach", "Challenges and recommendations for the management of social inclusion in the context of the internationalization of metropolises—a comparative analysis of GZM with metropolitan areas in Poland and abroad",

- Ministry of Education and Science under the "Science for Society II" program within the granted project "Urbanization and health in the context of sustainable development—an international prospective study",
- Academy of Silesia own funds.

The research results were presented in a comparative approach, both for the entire representative population of Poland and the Metropolis GZM and in cross-sectional approaches, which include specifics by gender, age, place of residence or diagnosed level of life satisfaction. To measure life satisfaction understood as the result of comparing one's own situation with self-established standards and a key factor of well-being, the SWLS Life Satisfaction Scale (Diener et al. 1985) in the Polish adaptation (Jurczyński, 2009) was used. The reliability of the scale in this study was high, and Cronbach's α index was 0.911 (Budziński et al., 2024). Table 1 below presents detail information.

According to this approach it is also important to present, that in first research related to Metropolis GZM 809 respondents (24,5%) declared low life satisfaction, 1306 respondents (39,6%) had medium life satisfaction and 1186 respondents (35,9%) declared high life satisfaction. In second research related to the whole population of Poland 604 respondents (22,3%) declared low life satisfaction, 1133 respondents (41,9%) had medium life satisfaction and 970 respondents (35,8%) declared high life satisfaction.

Table 1. Life Satisfaction Scale with polish interpretation SWLS: temporary Polish standards (N = 555).

Result	Sten	Interpretation
31–**35**	10	High scores: 7–10 sten (24–35 points) (high life satisfaction)
29–30	9	
27–28	8	
24–26	7	
21–**23**	6	Medium/average scores: 5–6 sten (18–23 points) (medium/average life satisfaction)
18–20	5	
15–17	4	Low scores: 1–4 sten (5–17 points) (low satisfaction with life)
12–14	3	
10–11	2	
5–9	1	

Source: Juczyński, Z. (2009). *Narzędzia pomiaru w promocji i psychologii zdrowia* (Measurement instruments in the promotion and psychology of health) Warszawa: Pracownia Testów Psychologicznych PTP

Results

The results of the research were presented each time referring to the total number of representative respondents in Metropolis GZM (first research) in comparison with the total number of representative respondents in Poland (second research) It is also presented with their division by gender, age and level of life satisfaction which was low, medium or high. In comparison to the theoretical research Table 2 and Table 3 below show practical understanding of the concept of "sustainable local development" among the inhabitants of Poland and Metropolis GZM in comparative perspective.

Analyzing the data in the Table 2, it should be noted that the greatest gap in understanding the concept of "sustainable local development" between the inhabitants of Poland and Metropolis GZM is observed in understanding

Table 2. Understanding the concept of "sustainable local development" among the inhabitants of Poland and Metropolis GZM—comparative perspective in total, by gender and level of life satisfaction.

Understanding sustainability in Poland and Metropolis GZM	Respondents in Poland (PL) and Metropolis GZM (GZM) (%)											
	total		level of life satisfaction						gender			
			low		medium		high		women		men	
	GZM	PL	GZM	PL	GZM	PL	GZM	PL	GZM	PL	GZM	PL
development that harmoniously takes into account social, economic and environmental aspects	45,2	48,7	46,1	47,0	47,2	49,4	42,3	48,9	43,0	48,4	47,5	49,1
development that respects current needs without overusing resources for future generations	26,1	23,8	24,0	25,8	24,6	23,1	29,4	23,4	28,3	24,6	23,8	23,0
development based on responsible management of resources	16,3	15,8	16,6	14,3	16,8	16,9	15,5	16,3	14,7	15,1	18,0	16,5
development based on environmental and ecological values	12,4	11,7	13,3	12,9	11,5	10,6	12,8	11,4	14,0	12,0	10,7	11,4

Source: own elaboration based on researches results

Table 3. Understanding the concept of "sustainable local development" among the inhabitants of Poland and Metropolis GZM—comparative perspective by age.

Understanding sustainability in Poland and Metropolis GZM	Respondents in Poland (PL) and Metropolis GZM (GZM) by age in years (%)									
	18–24		25–34		35–44		45–54		55+	
	GZM	PL	GZM	PL	GZM	PL	GZM	PL	GZM	PL
development that harmoniously takes into account social, economic and environmental aspects	40,0	50,4	44,5	51,1	49,1	48,3	48,8	46,8	44,2	48,1
development that respects current needs without overusing resources for future generations	29,2	28,6	25,4	24,2	21,9	22,8	24,6	24,1	27,9	22,5
development based on responsible management of resources	16,0	11,7	21,5	15,6	16,9	16,5	14,8	18,5	14,3	15,3
development based on environmental and ecological values	14,8	9,3	8,6	9,1	12,1	12,4	11,8	10,6	13,6	14,1

Source: own elaboration based on researches results

sustainability as development that harmoniously takes into account social, economic and environmental aspects (+3,5%). At the same time, the nature of this gap in understanding is interesting, as it significantly increases among respondents with high level of life satisfaction (+6,6%). And most importantly, this difference is mainly formed in the female part of the population (+5.4%), while for men it is not so big (+1.6%). Moreover, by analyzing the data from the research, it can be seen that for the inhabitants of the Metropolis, the understanding of sustainability as a development that respects current needs without overusing resources for future generations is becoming increasingly important (–2,3%). And again, this gap in the indicators arises among the group of respondents with high level of life satisfaction (–6,0%), as well as due to the female part of the respondents (–3,7%). Thus, it can be concluded that for the population of Metropolis GZM comparing to Poland (mostly for respondents with high level of life satisfaction), the overall understanding of sustainable local development as a development that harmoniously takes into account social, economic and environmental aspects decreases, while the understanding of it as a development that respects current needs without overusing resources for future generations increases.

To see the full picture, an analysis of understanding by age groups was also conducted, the data of which is presented in Table 3. And here, the difference in results was also quite interesting. Analyzing the obtained data, it can be said that for the inhabitants of Metropolis GZM and Poland aged 35–54, the understanding of the concept of "sustainable local development" is very similar. The biggest difference in understanding the concept is observed among young people aged 18–24. It can be confidently stated here that for the residents of the Metropolis at this age, compared to Poland, the balance of understanding the category of sustainability has significantly shifted towards responsible management of resources and development based on environmental and ecological values. This result may be caused by various reasons, but first and foremost, it may indicate educational initiatives of educational institutions as well as the Metropolis GZM administration's efforts in promoting the concept of "sustainable local development".

It is also wort underline, that in all categories of life satisfaction, gender or age as well as totally the understanding sustainable local development as development that harmoniously takes into account social, economic and environmental aspects is the most popular one both in Metropolis GZM and in all the Poland. At least 40% of respondents and sometimes even more than 50% declared so.

Respondents were also asked about UN SDG prioritization. Table 4 and Table 5 below shows importance of UN SDG goals from the point of view of the quality of life in the municipality among the inhabitants of Poland and in comparison with Metropolis GZM inhabitants.

More than half of respondents in Metropolis GZM have chosen four out of seventeen UN SDG—almost 56% in total, but for all the Poland it was less than 50%. The most important goal was "good health and well-being" with 21,9%. In total as well as in all genders and levels of life satisfaction for more than 21% of respondents in Metropolis GZM it was the most important UN SDG in comparison to the all country, where this goal also was most important, but 3–4% lower levels. Second most important goal in GZM Metropolis was "decent work and economic growth" with total value 12,9%. For people with low life satisfaction it was even more important (15,8%), for those with high life satisfaction over 4% less (11,6%). For respondents in all the Poland this second most important goal was chosen 2–3% often with the total value 14,3%. Differences can be observed in third, fourth and fifth places. The goal "No poverty" in total was third most important for Metropolis GZM inhabitants (11,6%) but only fifth (7,6%) in all the country respondents' answer. Poland's prioritization in third place rank "Zero hunger" and "Peace, justice and strong institutions" as the fourth one with almost 9%.

It should also be pointed out that 6 respondents in the nationwide survey, referring to gender, indicated that they did not want to answer about their gender or indicated a gender other than female or male. Therefore the answers and percentages in this case refer to the sum of 2701, not 2707 respondents.

Quite big differences are shown in analysing the goal "good health and well-being" regarding the age in Metropolis GZM. The youngest respondents declared no more than 18%, but on the other hand for the oldest ones it was 26%. In countrywide research this difference was smaller—only more than 3%. Regarding the goal "decent work and economic growth" more than 8% difference was in Metropolis GZM also between the youngest respondents (9,4%) and people in the age 45–54 years (17,5%). In Poland the biggest difference almost 7% was between the youngest (9,3%) and the people in the age 34–45 ears (16,2%). Third goal "no poverty" with

Table 4. United Nations Sustainable Development Goals (UN SDG) prioritization—importance of goals from the point of view of the quality of life in the municipality in Poland and Metropolis GZM—comparative perspective in total, by gender and level of life satisfaction.

UN SDG prioritization	Respondents in Poland (PL) and Metropolis GZM (GZM) (%)											
	total		level of life satisfaction						gender			
			low		medium		high		women		men	
	GZM	PL	GZM	PL	GZM	PL	GZM	PL	GZM	PL	GZM	PL
good health and well-being	21,9	18,1	22,5	17,9	22,0	19,3	21,3	18,7	22,1	17,8	21,6	18,3
decent work and economic growth	12,9	14,3	15,8	14,7	12,3	12,5	11,6	14,0	13,0	14,5	12,9	14,1
no poverty	11,6	7,6	13,6	10,3	10,6	8,0	11,5	5,5	10,7	6,4	12,6	8,9
zero hunger	9,5	9,1	7,0	9,3	10,8	8,6	9,6	9,6	8,3	8,8	10,7	9,4
clean water and sanitation	5,5	6,6	5,6	6,5	5,2	6,4	5,8	7,0	5,5	7,6	5,5	5,6
peace, justice and strong institutions	5,4	8,6	4,3	9,1	5,5	8,5	6,0	8,4	5,6	8,6	5,1	8,6
quality education	4,7	4,5	4,1	3,0	4,3	4,7	5,5	5,3	4,7	5,1	4,6	3,9
affordable and clean energy	4,5	5,4	4,4	3,1	4,2	5,5	5,0	6,7	3,9	4,1	5,3	6,8
climate action	4,3	5,1	3,8	6,0	4,1	4,9	4,7	4,6	4,8	5,3	3,7	4,6
industry, innovation and infrastructure	4,0	4,3	4,3	5,5	4,1	3,4	3,7	4,5	4,4	5,3	3,6	3,3
sustainable cities and communities	3,9	3,2	4,1	2,8	4,5	3,3	3,1	3,3	4,2	3,3	3,6	3,1
responsible consumption & production	3,6	2,5	4,1	2,3	3,4	2,2	3,5	3,1	4,1	2,9	3,1	2,2
gender equality	3,0	3,2	1,6	2,2	3,1	3,5	4,0	3,5	3,6	3,8	2,4	2,6
reduced inequality	2,5	3,4	3,0	4,5	2,6	3,4	1,9	2,6	2,4	3,4	2,5	3,3
partnership for the goals	1,1	2,4	0,7	1,3	1,5	3,2	1,0	2,3	1,4	2,0	0,8	3,0
life on land	0,9	1,1	0,7	1,2	1,0	1,5	0,8	0,6	0,9	0,8	0,9	1,4
life below water	0,7	0,7	0,2	0,5	0,8	1,0	0,8	0,4	0,4	0,4	1,0	1,0

Source: own elaboration based on researches results

11,6 % in total was the most important for respondents in the age 43–45 years and the less important for the oldest one 9,7%. Fourth goal was "zero hunger" with total value 9,5%.

Eleven UN SGD in Metropolis GZM and 9 in national perspective received in total no more than 5%, but is some age groups answers were sometimes higher. For example the goal "industry, innovation and infrastructure" was indicated by 7,2% respondents in the age 35–44 in Metropolis GZM and by 6,5 % respondents in the age 25–34 in Poland. Additionally 6,2% the youngest respondents in Metropolis and 7,3% in the age 25–34 in all the country voted for the goal "quality education".

Table 5. United Nations Sustainable Development Goals (UN SDG) prioritization—importance of goals from the point of view of the quality of life in the municipality in Poland and Metropolis GZM—comparative perspective by age.

UN SDG prioritization	**Respondents in Poland (PL) and Metropolis GZM (GZM) by age in years (%)**									
	18–24		**25–34**		**35–44**		**45–54**		**55+**	
	GZM	**PL**	**GZM**	**PL**	**GZM**	**PL**	**GZM**	**PL**	**GZM**	**PL**
good health and well-being	17,9	18,3	20,8	15,4	18,6	17,1	21,4	15,3	26,0	21,6
decent work and economic growth	9,4	9,3	13,9	13,7	10,6	16,2	17,5	15,3	12,9	14,4
no poverty	11,5	7,2	11,1	8,9	16,0	9,2	12,0	6,8	9,7	6,4
zero hunger	10,7	9,0	10,6	9,9	10,4	9,4	9,9	10,2	7,7	7,9
clean water and sanitation	5,5	7,6	5,5	6,3	5,0	8,0	5,7	8,7	5,7	4,6
peace, justice and strong institutions	5,8	6,6	3,6	4,8	3,5	7,3	5,3	6,6	7,0	13,2
quality education	6,2	5,9	5,3	7,3	5,8	6,1	2,5	3,2	4,2	2,2
affordable and clean energy	4,9	3,8	5,1	4,4	4,3	5,9	3,4	5,3	4,8	6,2
climate action	4,1	4,8	4,2	4,0	3,3	3,7	2,7	6,0	5,6	6,2
industry, innovation and infrastructure	3,9	5,2	2,9	6,5	7,2	3,5	4,4	5,3	2,9	2,7
sustainable cities and communities	3,5	3,1	3,5	4,2	4,1	1,9	4,1	3,4	4,1	3,3
responsible consumption & production	3,1	1,4	3,3	1,6	3,2	3,0	4,9	2,6	3,5	3,2
gender equality	4,9	7,6	3,3	3,6	3,9	2,6	2,5	1,7	1,9	2,7
reduced inequality	3,9	5,2	2,9	3,2	1,7	2,3	1,9	4,5	2,2	3,0
partnership for the goals	1,6	3,1	1,6	3,6	0,7	1,6	1,1	2,8	0,9	1,9
life on land	1,2	1,0	1,6	1,6	0,9	1,2	0,5	1,7	0,5	0,5
life below water	1,9	1,0	0,7	0,8	0,7	1,0	0,4	0,6	0,3	0,2

Source: own elaboration based on researches results

Last important study approach was practical recognition of strategic awareness. Detail information about respondents' answers on strategic awareness understood as a level of knowledge about municipality's development strategy in comparative approach was presented below in Table 6. The comparison was made between three metropolitan areas—two in Poland Metropolis GZM and Gdańsk-Gdynia-Sopot Metropolitan Area and one in Germany—The Ruhr Metropolitan Area. Additionally research data were collected for Metropolis GZM twice—in 2023 and 2024. Moreover research among inhabitants in all the Poland was also made in the year 2024.

There are no significant differences between Poland and Metropolis GZM in 2023 and in 2024. Analyzing the obtained data, it can be said that around 26–30% of all respondents do not have any knowledge and interest in a strategy. Additionally

Table 6. Strategic awareness—knowledge about the development strategy of municipality—comparative perspective in total.

Strategic awareness – level of municipal strategy knowledge	Respondents (%)				
	Poland 2024	Metropolis GZM 2023	Metropolis GZM 2024	Gdańsk-Gdynia-Sopot Metropolitan Area 2024	The Ruhr Area (Germany) 2024
lack of knowledge and interest in a strategy (LK)	28,8	30,3	26,3	17,2	18,8
basic knowledge, only that the city has a strategy (BK)	43,3	44,8	48,6	49,7	57,5
intermediate knowledge - reading some parts of a strategy (IK)	24,9	21,5	21,8	29,1	16,5
involvement in the process of creating or consulting a strategy (ICC)	3,0	3,4	3,3	4,0	7,2

Source: own elaboration based on researches results

less than half of them (43–49%) have only basic knowledge, 21–25% respondents have intermediate knowledge and only 3% were involved in creation or consultation process. In Gdańsk-Gdynia-Sopot Metropolitan Area situation looks slightly different. Only 17,2% respondents do not have any knowledge, and the basic level refers to almost half of all the researched population (49,7%). It is also very good to observe, that almost 30% of respondents knows at least any parts of municipal strategy and 4% were involved in creation process. On the other hand respondents in The Ruhr Area in Germany answered in different way. Although over 7% were involved in strategy's creation process only 16,5% have intermediate knowledge. More than 57% have basic knowledge, and only less than 19% do not have any knowledge in strategy. Thanks to the data above strategic awareness indicator (SAI) is possible to be calculated. The value of SAI is presented in comparative perspective in the Table 7 below.

The interpretation of strategic awareness indicator (SAI) allows to evaluate each of the researched groups. Generally it is worth to remind, that the lowest indicator value it has the better situation it is, and the smallest strategical knowledge gap it is. Although The Ruhr Area has over 7% of inhabitants involved in the process of creating or consulting a strategy (overt twice better than in Poland) the total SAI value is the highest – 52,6%. It is because over 76% of all respondents do not have any strategical knowledge, or have only the basic one. According to the data above the best situation is in Gdańsk-Gdynia-Sopot Metropolitan Area 2024, where SAI index is the lowest – 33,8%. It is mainly because of the fact, that over 33% have

Table 7. Comparative perspective of strategic awareness indicator.

Strategic awareness – level of municipal strategy knowledge	Respondents (%)				
	Poland 2024	Metropolis GZM 2023	Metropolis GZM 2024	Gdańsk-Gdynia-Sopot Metro-politan Area 2024	The Ruhr Area (Germany) 2024
Strategic Awareness Indicator (LK+BK) - (IK+ICC)	44,2	50,2	49,8	33,8	52,6

Source: own elaboration based on researches results

intermediate strategical knowledge or was involved in creation or consultation process. The indicator for all the Poland is on the middle level 44,2% and because the SAI was measured twice in Metropolis GZM small progress form high (50,2%) to the medium level (49,8%) is observed between years 2023 and 2024.

Discussion and conclusion

The results above allowed answering all research questions and to prove or deny each of the hypotheses:

- H1: The concept of "sustainable local development" is mostly understood both—in Poland and in particular in Metropolis GZM as development that harmoniously takes into account social, economic and environmental aspects—was **proved**; at least 45% of respondents in total follow this way of understanding,
- H2: Good health and well-being is the most important goal in Poland as well as among Metropolis GZM inhabitants from the point of view of the quality of life in the municipality among all seventeen United Nations Sustainable Development Goals—was **proved;** in total as well as in all genders and levels of life satisfaction for more than 21% of respondents in Metropolis GZM it was the most important UN SDG—in Poland this goal also was most important, but with 3–4% lower levels,
- H3: At least 2/3 of respondents in Poland and also in each of researched metropolitan areas do not have any knowledge and interest about their municipal strategy or have basic knowledge only that the city has a strategy—**was proved;** in all researched cases over 2/3 of respondents have basic knowledge or do not have any knowledge, but for example in Gdańsk-Gdynia-Sopot Metropolitan Area it was just a little bit above 2/3 (0,2%), and in The Ruhr Area in Germany it was almost 10% more than 2/3,
- H4: There are no significant differences in the level of strategic awareness between all the Poland and GZM Metropolis—**was proved,** each four stages of knowledge was similar—no more than 3% differences in comparison between Poland and Metropolis GZM in 2023, and no more than 5,3% differences in comparison to Metropolis GZM in 2024,

- H5: There are no significant differences in the level of strategic awareness between all the Poland and Gdańsk-Gdynia-Sopot Metropolitan Area—was **denied;** there are quite a big differences in particular stages of knowledge, especially the basic level was differ more than 11,5%,
- H6: According to the strategic awareness indicator (SAI) the situation in The Ruhr Area in Germany is better than in Poland and polish metropoles—was **denied**; the value of SAI in the Ruhr Area was the highest among all researched areas, so it means, that the strategic gap was the biggest.

To make main conclusions more practical there were transformed into recommendations for better answering sustainable challenges and strategic awareness:

- because the most popular way of understanding sustainable local development means that it harmoniously takes into account social, economic and environmental aspects, this approach should be also present in public debate and in local and regional documents, especially in the strategical ones; it is also important to take into consideration this sustainability approach in implementation processes, in projects or other activities,
- prioritization of all seventeen United Nations Sustainable Development Goals on one hand should correspond with local and regional development priorities and on the other hand should be an inspiration to updating development strategies into sustainable development strategies related also to UN SDG implementation,
- because less than only 1/3 of all 8458 respondents have intermediate knowledge about their municipal strategy or took part in strategy's creation/consultation process new and efficient ways of community involvement into local activities should be implemented as well as new, well-targeted ways of communication process related to strategy to inhabitants and other stakeholders; additionally good practices in that areas should be promoted,
- develop social capital and cross-sectoral cooperation as a multidimensional support for activities aimed at strengthening and sometimes rebuilding social capital at the local, communal, inter-municipal and metropolitan levels and development of cross-sectoral cooperation with the use of tools such as urban labs, multifunctional dialogue platforms, formal and informal meetings leading to the creation of partnership projects to implement strategy (Budziński et al., 2022, p 189),
- together with other researchers develop the theoretical idea of strategic awareness indicator and treat the results as the basis for further in-depth research, taking into account, among other, comparative possibilities with other domestic and foreign metropolitan areas and the evolution of the studied phenomena over time not only to public, but also business and NGO's organizations,
- spread the idea of strategic awareness indicator in practices and using it to measure the strategic awareness gap; promote this knowledge among all the Metropolis GZM municipalities and outside the metropolis to other cities and municipalities and other institutions in Poland and abroad.

References

Budziński, M., Kinelski, G., Raczek, M. and Wrana, K. 2022., Wdrażanie koncepcji Smart City w miastach Górnośląsko-Zagłębiowskiej Metropolii – Identyfikacja przejawów współpracy miast Górnośląsko-Zagłębiowskiej Metropolii w zakresie wdrażania koncepcji Smart City i rozwijania kapitałów 4T, in: Koncepcja Smart City i potencjały 4T. Inteligentne Zarządzanie Miastami Górnośląsko-Zagłębiowskiej Metropolii / Makieła Z. Mucha-Kuś K., Kinelski Gr. (red.), Akademia WSB, p. 189.

Budziński, M., Raczek, M. and Wrana, K. 2022. Koncepcja Smart City i kapitały 4T w politykach rozwoju miast Górnośląsko-Zagłębiowskiej Metropolii, in: Koncepcja Smart City i potencjały 4T. Inteligentne Zarządzanie Miastami Górnośląsko-Zagłębiowskiej Metropolii/Makieła Z., Mucha-Kuś, K. and Kinelski, G. (red.), Akademia WSB, p. 21–42.

Budziński, M., Vitkovskyi, Y., Ochnik, D., Buława, B., Gachowski, M., Nagel, P. et al. 2024. *Sustainable development management and strategic awareness of the Metropolis GZM inhabitants*. European Research Studies Journal, Volume XXVII, Special Issue B, 17-32, DOI: 10.35808/ersj/3474.

Cajete, G. A. (2020). *Indigenous science, climate change, and indigenous community building: a framework of foundational perspectives for indigenous community resilience and revitalization*. Sustainability 12(22) https://doi.org/10. 3390/su12229569, p. 9569.

Cohen, B. 2015. *The 3 Generations Of Smart Cities*. IMPACT, https://www.fastcompany.com/3047795/the-3-generations-of-smart-cities.

Daly, H. E. 2007. Ecological Economics and Sustainable Development: Selected Essays of Herman Daly, Edward Elgar.

Diener, E., Emmons, R. A., Larsen, R. J. and Griffin, S. (1985). *The Satisfaction With Life Scale*. Journal of Personality Assessment nr 49, p. 71–74.

Florida, R. 2003. *City and the creative class*. City & Community 2(1) March 2003, p. 3–19.

Haraisa, Y. E. Al. 2022. *The impact of strategic alignment and strategic awareness on strategic performance: Evidence from Jordan*. International Journal of Academic Research in Accounting Finance and Management Sciences 12(4): 42–55.

Hu, M., Świerzawski, J., Kleszcz, J. and Kmiecik, P. 2023. *What are the concerns with New European Bauhaus initiative? Vernacular knowledge as the primary driver toward a sustainable future*. Next Sustainability 1, 100004, p. 3.

Jabareen, Y. 2008. *A new conceptual framework for sustainable development*. Environ. Dev. Sustain. 10: DOI 10.1007/s10668-006-9058-z, Springer Science+Business Media B.V. 2006, p. 179–192.

Juczyński, Z. 2009. *Narzędzia pomiaru w promocji i psychologii zdrowia [Measurement instruments in the promotion and psychology of health]*. Warszawa: Pracownia Testów Psychologicznych PTP.

Korneluk, K., Bielawska, M., Zygadło, S., Dominiak, B. and Kruczek, A. 2019. Human Smart City przewodnik dla samorządów; Ministerstwo Inwestycji i Rozwoju: Warszawa, p. 5–7.

Makieła, Z., Stuss, M., Mucha-Kuś, K., Kinelski, G., Budziński, M. and Michałek J. 2022. *Smart City 4.0: Sustainable Urban Development in the Metropolis GZM*. Sustainability, 14, nr 6, DOI:10.3390/su14063516, p.2.

Milán-García, J., Uribe-Toril, J., Luis Ruiz-Real, J. L. and Valenciano, JdP. 2019. *Sustainable Local Development: An Overview of the State of Knowledge*. Resources 8(31): 14.

Pencarelli, T., Savelli, E. and Splendiani, S. 2009. *Strategic awareness and growth strategies in small enterprises*. The International Journal of Business & Economics 8(1).

Polish SDG statistics in a nutshell (2023), Statistics Poland, Warsaw.

Transforming Our World: The 2030 Agenda For Sustainable Development sustainabledevelopment.un.org A/RES/70/1 https://www.unic.un.org.pl/files/164/Agenda%202030_pl_2016_ostateczna.pdf.

Trendy i anty-trendy we wdrażaniu zrównoważonej transformacji organizacji w 2024, Synergist, Trends and anti-trends in the implementation of sustainable transformation of organizations in 2024 synergist.eu.com/wp-content/uploads/2024/02/synergist-raport-2024.pdf.

Chapter 10

Eco-Innovation as a Determinant of the Development of Contemporary Organizations

Ecolabnet Eco-Innovation Network

Waldemar Jędrzejczyk[1,*] and *Miia Lammi*[2]

Introduction

The problem of environmental pollution and over-exploitation of natural resources continues to exist. The scale of the impact of human activity on nature, and indirectly on economic systems, is increasing—it is becoming more and more visible and poses a growing threat to humanity. Anthropogenic factors throwing ecosystems out of balance are translating into increasing pressure on economic systems from a changing environment, with ever more dynamic phenomena, such as the effects of climate change (global warming) in the form of tornadoes, violent storms, torrential rains, and extremely high temperatures, which are causing increasing damage to the Earth. Humankind has already realised the seriousness of this problem. However, the measures taken are not yet sufficient—the problem is still growing. Some "respite" for the Earth was the global lockdown in 2019–2020, caused by the COVID-19 pandemic. It was not a good time for the worldwide economy, but it was a good time for the environment.

Actions aimed at reducing harmful human activity on the environment should be undertaken at all levels of management: (1) macro—from the point of view of global, community, and national economy, (2) meso—from the point of view of the sector,

[1] Czestochowa University of Technology, Faculty of Management, Poland.
[2] Vaasa University of Applied Sciences, Design Centre MUOVA, Finland.
Email: Miia.Lammi@muova.fi, ORCID: 0009-0006-4150-205X
* Corresponding author: waldemar.jedrzejczyk@pcz.pl, OCRID: 0000-0001-7820-8352

supply chain, service system, product system and (3) micro—from the point of view of the enterprise, process, product, service. This process should involve national governments, consortia and R&D units, corporations, and large enterprises, as well as entities from the SME sector, which aim to find and create ways to reduce negative environmental impact. A significant trend is the development and promotion of eco-innovation, understood as the production and application of new products, services, processes, systems, and procedures to meet human needs and provide a better quality of life while minimising the consumption of natural resources and emission of pollutants to the environment.

Unfortunately, the level of eco-innovation in all world economies is still low (Sobczak et al., 2022, p. 17), with significant differences between regions or countries depending on their level of development, industrialisation, and economic policy (EIO, 2013, s. 19). Therefore, there is a constant need for projects that stimulate eco-innovative behaviour in the economy. Such a project is the Network of Service Providers for Eco-innovations in Manufacturing SMEs (Ecolabnet), which aims to create a network to increase access to expertise, new eco-innovative products and services, and to support their implementation in small and medium-sized enterprises.

The chapter's main objective is to identify the potential of the created eco-innovation network Ecolabnet enabling the development of eco-innovation in small and medium-sized enterprises in the Baltic Sea Region countries.

Materials and methods

The chapter consists of two main parts, the theoretical and the empirical one. In the theoretical part, a synthetic characterisation of the concept of eco-innovation and its importance in the modern economy was made. Explaining the concept of eco-innovation was necessary from the point of view of the chapter's primary objective. However, no in-depth analysis was carried out to determine:

- the differences between the different types of pro-environmental innovations,
- the benefits of eco-innovation, broken down into economic, environmental, and social benefits, while identifying the primary beneficiaries of those benefits,
- the primary motivators and drivers for eco-innovation,
- the criteria for grouping eco-innovations and their categories.

The aspects indicated are essential from the point of view of the issue of eco-innovation in the economy but not relevant to the purpose of the chapter.

The theoretical part also identifies the main determinants of the development and implementation of eco-innovation, stressing that activities in this area require a holistic view of a particular solution, taking into account not only the direct consequences of its application but also the indirect effects.

The theoretical part was developed using the critical literature analysis method, also referred to as document analysis and criticism, or literature studies. The analysed works were selected as follows: (1) Internet resources were searched for publications, both books and scientific articles, which had the following keywords in their titles: eco-innovation, environmental innovation and green innovation. (2) The set of analysed studies was expanded to include documents published by institutions promoting the concept of sustainable development and corporate social responsibility, such as the European Commission (EC), the Organisation for Economic Co-operation and Development (OECD), the World Commission on Environment and Development (WCED), which are also oriented towards supporting pro-environmental and eco-innovative activities. (3) Due to the subject matter, it was assumed that publications published in 2000–2022 would be considered. In contrast, it was assumed in advance that the majority of publications would be those published within the last five years. (4) Publications were analysed in chronological order, from the oldest to the newest, so as not only to clarify the issues under consideration but also to distinguish emerging trends.

The second part of the chapter presents fragmentary research results conducted within the Network of Service Providers for Eco-innovations in Manufacturing SMEs (Ecolabnet) project. In the presented research, an attempt was made to answer the following problematic question: Is it possible to identify the categories of the services which will be adapted to the contemporary needs of SME enterprises in the area of eco-innovation?

Finding an answer to such a question required preceding finding answers to the following problem questions:

1. Do small and medium-sized enterprises have similar needs and expectations in the area of eco-innovation?
2. Do small and medium-sized enterprises have a similar level of knowledge about eco-innovation and its importance in business?

The results of the research in this area are described in detail in the publication of Jędrzejczyk (2021), and in this study they are presented briefly.

The problem question posed in the chapter is correlated with the specific objectives defined in the project, which are presented in Subsection 5.2 of this chapter.

To carry out the empirical part of the chapter, the inductive method was used. The starting point were the results of deductive reasoning in which answers to problem questions 1 and 2 were searched for.

Eco-innovation—concept and importance in contemporary economy

Taking environmental aspects into account in production processes and creating new, innovative processes and product solutions is called eco-innovation. The concept of eco-innovation emerged in the 1990s. Two phenomena contributed to its emergence: (1) the increasing importance of innovation in the economy, which is treated as a critical determinant of competitiveness and economic development (Castellacci et al., 2017; Bierwisch et al., 2021), both of individual enterprises and countries, and (2) the increase in people's awareness of the threats of civilisation to the environment. The notion of eco-innovation is often identified with environmental innovation and green innovation, but they are not entirely identical (Karakaya et al., 2014).

Eco-innovations are a particular type of innovation. Their characteristic feature is that they contribute directly or indirectly to improving the state of the natural environment—they improve a company's relationship with the environment. Eco-innovation is often combined with the concept of sustainable development, meaning development that makes it possible to satisfy the needs of the present generation in a way that does not reduce the possibility of future generations satisfying theirs needs (WCED, 1987; Sobczyk, 2014, p. 119). The concept of sustainable development should consider both the economic, ecological, and social dimensions (Jones et al., 2001, p. 16; Dudek et al., 2019, p. 14). Eco-innovations should therefore be interpreted as solutions that will be economically viable, will bring benefits for the natural environment, and which will not cause social costs. This is reflected in numerous definitions of the term, e.g., the European Commission defines eco-innovation as all forms of activities aiming at significant and visible progress towards sustainable development objectives by reducing negative environmental impact or achieving greater efficiency and responsibility in resource use (EC, 2006; EC, 2011, p. 2). In turn, R. Kemp and P. Pearson (2007, p. 7) understand eco-innovation as products, production methods, procedures for exploiting resources, ways of providing services and management methods that are new to the organisation and that, over their entire life cycle, ensure lower environmental risk, emit less pollution, consume fewer raw materials and cause less harmful effects to the environment than alternative solutions. This understanding of eco-innovation can be found in many field studies (Jones et al., 2001; Peiró-Signes and Segarra-Oña, 2018).

Based on the analysis of the cited definitions, as well as the definitions contained in other works, i.e., Rennings (2000), Sinclair-Desgagne (2003), Daddi et al. (2012), Albort-Morant et al. (2017), Tamayo-Orbegozo et al. (2017), Pecorari, Camello Lima (2020), Šūmakaris, Korsakienė (2021), it can be stated that eco-innovations are innovations that improve the efficiency of the use of natural resources in the economy, reduce the negative impact of human activity on the environment and strengthen the resistance of the economy to environmental pressures. This definition completely captures the essence of eco-innovation. It indicates that, in addition to reducing the harmful impact of economic processes on the environment, it is also vital to make productive use of natural resources. Therefore, the economic and safety dimensions are also critical apart from the ecological and health dimensions.

The concept of eco-innovation is multidimensional. It can be analysed cross-sectionally, taking into account various criteria, such as, among others: the scope concerning the life cycle, the scale of implementation, the method of development. Several basic types of eco-innovation can be distinguished, most frequently: product, process, marketing and organisational (EIO, 2013; OECD, 2005). Eco-innovation is no longer limited to product and process only. According to Oslo Manual 2018, they are extended to all business processes, e.g., logistics and distribution, marketing and sales, ICT, administration and management (OECD, 2019).

Determinants of eco-innovation development and implementation

Environmental regulations are the primary determinant of the demand for eco-innovations by enterprises, particularly from the SME sector. Tightening legal regulations and emission standards force entrepreneurs to implement new pro-ecological solutions. Market incentives are also gaining importance, encouraging enterprises to improve the efficiency of resource use and image issues, forcing them to conduct business in line with the concept of corporate social responsibility (CSR). Activities in this area depend primarily on the competence of the management, their knowledge of the available pro-efficiency solutions and their ability to assess the long-term benefits of their implementation (Xavier et al., 2020). Since the level of expertise in eco-innovation is usually low, the field literature more and more often asserts that when companies do not directly benefit from the introduced eco-innovations, the state's supply-side policy, instead of supporting the existing incentives, has to create new ones through regulation (Arimura et al., 2007; Mickwitz et al., 2007; Kesidou and Demirel, 2010). These can take the form of standards, bans, orders, as well as the establishment of price incentives that lead to the internalisation of negative externalities of environmentally harmful economic activities (Meade, 1952).

The low level of managerial knowledge in eco-innovation is not the only barrier to the introduction of eco-innovation in organisations. There are also many other barriers. The primary categories of barriers include legal barriers, economic barriers, demand barriers, technological barriers, R&D barriers, personnel barriers, and cooperation barriers (Shah et al., 2022). Detailed explanations of the distinguished categories of barriers to eco-innovation implementation can be found in various studies, e.g., by the European Commission and the OECD.

The indicated categories of barriers are not prescriptive. Different barriers can be identified for different types of eco-innovation (Iraldo et al., 2009; Dangelico and Pujari 2010; Horbach et al., 2011). The heterogeneity of barriers may result from various implementation incentives for specific types of eco-innovation (cost reduction, consumer demand, government standards) in different areas (e.g., energy efficiency vs water or air pollution) and different levels of maturity of specific technologies (conceptual stage, prototyping, product/service ready for implementation).

Public support schemes for eco-innovation can help reduce barriers to eco-innovation within organisations. Direct and indirect support for the development and implementation of eco-innovation is one of the current priorities of EU enterprise policy (Nitkiewicz, 2012; Ociepa-Kubicka, 2015). Examples of the use of EU funds in supporting enterprises in innovation activities, which can also be used for the implementation of eco-innovation, addressed primarily to enterprises in the SME sector, are regional programmes—e.g., in Poland in the form of Regional Operational Programmes (ROP).

The development and implementation of eco-innovation requires a comprehensive view of a given solution, taking into account the direct and indirect effects of its application. Otherwise, there is a risk of transferring environmental problems from one area of economic activity to others, e.g., it might seem that replacing traditional cars with electric ones is more environmentally friendly. The reality is not so obvious. Electric vehicles certainly consume less energy (an electric car about 20 kWh per 100 km, a petrol car about 70 kWh per 100 km) and do not emit exhaust fumes while driving, which in turn leads to a reduction in the adverse phenomenon of low emissions. However, the fact that an electric car does not emit exhaust fumes into the atmosphere does not mean that the technology used is "clean".

The electricity used to charge the batteries has to be produced somewhere. If it is the energy generated by burning coal (e.g., in Poland 90% of electricity is produced in conventional power plants), then driving an electric car for 100 km generates about 20 kg of CO_2, which is more or less the same as generated by a medium-sized off-road car with a petrol engine. However, these are not the only adverse side effects. High greenhouse gas emissions are caused by battery production. Each kilowatt-hour of capacity corresponds to 150–200 kg of CO_2 release. This means that an electric car equipped with a 100-kWh battery leaves a carbon footprint of 17.5 tonnes of CO_2 already at the production stage—as much carbon dioxide is released into the atmosphere during 8 years of using a petrol car (Ernst, 2019; Melin, 2019; Kulik, 2022).

Therefore, each newly created eco-innovative solution, especially at the design stage, must consider multidimensional technological, ecological, social and economic aspects.

The potential of Ecolabnet—key results from project activities

1. What is Ecolabnet?

Ecolabnet (Ecolabnet, 2024) [access: 26.09.2024] is a transnational cooperation network between: Research and Development Institutes (RDI), Intermediary Organization (IO) and enterprises from the SME sector (Small and Medium Enterprises), in the area of the development of eco-products for small and medium-sized enterprises in the Baltic Sea region. The aim of the network is to increase access to specialist knowledge, new eco-innovative products and services and to support their implementation by small and medium-sized enterprises. Ecolabnet increases the potential for commercialization of various eco-innovations from scientific and research institutions.

The Ecolabnet eco-innovation network was developed as part of the following project: Network of Service Providers for Eco-innovations in Manufacturing SMEs (ECOLABNET), financed by the Interreg Program of the Baltic Sea Region 2014–2020 and co-financed by the program of the Polish Minister of Science and Higher Education PMW 2019–2021; agreement No. 5006/INTERREG BSR/2019/2. The total budget of the project is EUR 2.25 million. The project was implemented in the period from January 2019 to December 2021. The project leader was Design Center MUOVA from Finland, and the main consortium of partners implementing the project consisted of scientific and research and development institutions from six Baltic countries: Denmark – VIA University College, Estonia – Estrotech Ltd, University of Tartu; Finland – Centria University of Technology, Lithuania – Kaunas University of Technology, Labsamera MB, Lithuanian Business Confederation, Vilnius University; Poland – Czestochowa University of Technology and Sweden – Sustainable Innovation. The authors of this chapter were the main contractors in the project teams from the Czestochowa University of Technology and Design Center MUOVA.

2. Research method

The main objective of the project was to create a cooperation network for the provision of consulting services in the area of eco-product development and eco-services for small and medium-sized enterprises in the Baltic Sea region. The operationalisation of the objective required an understanding of the SME needs, vision, and challenges related to eco-innovation and how, and through which services, Ecolabnet can meet these needs and contribute to business development. Therefore, specific objectives were identified under the primary goal - only those related to the issues discussed in the chapter were given:

1. Identification of the needs of enterprises from the SME sector in the area of eco-innovation and assessment of the degree of their eco-innovation awareness;
2. Defining the basic types of eco-identity of enterprises;
3. Development of eco-innovation service packages;
4. Development of a Digital Collaboration Tool (DCT) system (DTC Ecolabnet, 2024) [access: 26.09.2024].

The results of the study showed that the needs and expectations of enterprises in the area of eco-innovation are diverse, ranging from no need for external support, due to extensive experience in this field, to the need for appropriate support in all aspects related to the implementation of eco-innovative solutions—in terms of financing sources for eco-innovative projects, legal regulations and new eco-innovative solutions, especially in terms of materials, technologies, services, and products. The study results also showed that in the studied population of enterprises, there is a significant variation in the level of knowledge about eco-innovation and its importance in business. The results of project research in the field of the needs and expectations of enterprises from the SME sector in the area of eco-innovation are presented in more detail in the study of Jędrzejczyk (2021, pp. 2821–2822).

The determination of the needs and expectations of enterprises operating in the SME sector in the area of eco-innovation and the assessment of the degree of their eco-innovation awareness were used for the following purposes:

- Categorization of users to better adapt the network offer to customer expectations,
- Developing packages of eco-innovative services provided by the ecolabnet network,
- Developing a DCT system enabling unlimited access to Ecolabnet resources.

The identified needs of enterprises and levels of knowledge about eco-innovation made it possible to develop a categorisation of SME enterprises, mapping their eco-innovative nature. Six types of eco-innovative attitudes so called eco-identity have been distinguished: Eco-Opportunist, Eco-Booster, Eco-Developer, Eco-Optimizer, Eco-Cautious and Eco-Laggard. The first three types of eco-identity are the most advanced enterprises in terms of eco-innovation, and the last three are enterprises with a much lower level of advancement, which pay attention primarily to compliance with the legal requirements in terms of eco-innovation. The results of project research in the field of eco-identity of enterprises are presented in more detail in the study of Jędrzejczyk (2021, pp. 2821–2822).

This chapter presents the main results of the project research that involve developed packages of eco-innovative services provided by the ecolabnet network—the result specific objective 3.

The concept of the created DCT system, which enables the collection and presentation of eco-innovative products and services developed by website users with the possibility of searching for connections between entities, services and products, will be discussed in the next papers.

The chapter's main objective is to determine the potential of the created eco-innovation network Ecolabnet.

3. Eco-innovation service packages

Based on the results of the research on identified gaps and eco-innovation needs of SMEs, 8 packages of eco-innovation services were developed at Ecolabnet: (1) Business strategy, (2) Eco-innovation management, (3) Bio-based materials, (4) Product design and development, (5) 3D printing, (6) Environmental assessment, (7) Marketing, (8) Other eco-innovation expertise.

3.1 Business strategy

The services in the package relate to consulting in buyer-supplier relations with the scope of sustainable development and the circular economy, generating ideas, adapting solutions and accelerating business model transformation. The package also offers services related to partner search, networking and cooperation between relevant parties, design of products and services using 3D models and planning innovative solutions.

3.2 Eco-innovation management

The services in the package are primarily related to expert training on eco-innovation as a source of competitive advantage. The proposed training and advisory services focus on the practical implementation of eco-innovation and the benefits arising from such implementation. The package also includes services for planning project activities and developing and implementing projects.

3.3 Bio-based materials

The package includes testing materials and products, determining properties, and characterising biopolymers and polymer biocomposites. Chemical analysis services of various materials are also offered in the package.

3.4 Product design and development

The services in the package relate to the testing of biomaterials and bioproducts, production of prototypes and serial tests, research and development activities, partner search and networking and collaboration through the provision of advisory, mentoring and training services. The package is completed by services related to the design of products and services (collection of basic information, idea generation, creation of concepts and 3D models) and provision of theoretical and practical knowledge for designing prototypes in a Virtual Reality environment.

3.5 3D printing

The bundled services relate to testing the suitability of photo-curable materials for optical 3D micro/nano printing, prototype production, material and product testing, and the development of plastics and composite materials for 3D printing.

3.6 Environmental assessment

The services in the package relate to the analysis of the impact and assessment of the effects of investments on the environment, the determination of ways to prevent, reduce or minimise the adverse impacts of implemented projects, testing of materials and products, as well as research on end-of-life solutions. The package is designed to support activities in line with the concept of sustainable development.

3.7 Marketing

The services in the package are related to consultancy in conducting marketing research. They cover research design and conception, consumer behaviour, branding, strategic and operational branding, prototype development and co-development, testing and experimentation, evaluation, and decision-making in marketing activities.

3.8 Other eco-innovation expertise

The services in the package relate to the analysis of waste heat potential by auditing the sources, quantity and quality of waste heat generated and analysing the possibilities to recover and use waste heat to minimise energy consumption. The package also offers services on materials testing, chemical analysis of materials, partner search, networking opportunities, innovation funding opportunities and promotion of innovative products and services through technology transfer.

Selected eco-innovative services specified in individual packages are presented in Table 1.

Each package has been assigned a specific set of services, consisting of services developed and offered in the first instance by the project partners. Each service is described in detail with the following components: Name of service, Offeror's logo, Offeror of product, Category of service, Type of service, Description of service, Areas of interest/Trade, Related services and Status of service. It has a specific purpose and a described infrastructure of the service provider.

Service providers from research institutions, intermediary organisations, and other entities, have appropriately qualified and competent advisory and training staff to deliver the proposed services. They are experts, advisors, and trainers who have experience providing such services to the SME sector. They also have the necessary infrastructure for training and service delivery, especially in laboratory testing essential software, e.g., LCA specialised software engineering tools. The service providers also have the appropriate specialised equipment, e.g., test equipment, optical 3D printers and equipment available in the indicated laboratories.

Table 1. List of selected eco-innovative services offered in the Ecolabnet network.

Package name	Selected eco-innovative services specified in package
Business strategy	Business development for sustainability EU support and investments Innovation funding opportunities Private financing
Eco-innovation management	Training for eco-innovation and implementation Eco-innovations as a source of competitive advantage Project planning Project preparation and implementation
Bio-based materials	Synthesis of custom made ionic liquids and development of biofriendly ionic liqudis Chemical analysis of various materials Design and synthesis of biopolymers and polymeric biocomposites Characterization of biopolymers and polymer biocomposites and investigation of their properties Material and product testing
Product design and development	Preparation and characterization of various polymer (including biopolymer) composites Product design Service design Service prototyping Prototype and small test series manufacturing Creating, testing and integrating 3D models and visual effects into film footage
3D printing	Additive manufacturing employing optical 3D micro/nano-printing esting suitability of photo-curable materials for optical 3D micro/nano-printing Development of plastic and composite materials for thermal 3D printing Creating props using 3D printing technology
Environmental assessment	Analysis of compostability of plastics Environmental impact assessment R&D on end-of-life solutions to improve sustainability Analysis of the impact of investment on the environment
Marketing	Advisory in the scope of conducting marketing research Marketing research and advisory Branding
Other eco-innovation expertise	Analysis of the potential of waste heat Analysis of the possibility of recovery and utilisation of waste heat Utilisation of waste heat to minimise energy consumption Promotion for innovative services, products and knowledge (technology transfer) Determination and measurement of exact denominations of radio electronic components

Source: own study

The developed service packages are not a closed set. They can be created on an ongoing basis as part of competence improvement by existing service providers, or completely new ones. The resulting packages of services may meet the needs of potential recipients—enterprises from the SME sector to an ever-greater extent, contributing to reducing identified gaps. SMEs are a possible direct group of recipients. Intermediary organisations can also use the network's resources to connect SMEs with service providers.

The service packages describe the different types of services that Ecolabnet members offer to companies. The service packages are used to categorise the services in the DCT tool.

Discussion and conclusions

Interest in eco-innovation is constantly growing, particularly on the part of researchers and public authorities, as a result of the environmental problems which have been growing in recent years and the search for a new, more sustainable paradigm of economic development. Businesses, including small and medium-sized enterprises, are also increasingly interested in the issue of eco-innovation, but their capacities in this field are limited. There are still many barriers to developing and implementing eco-innovative solutions in economic practice.

Companies in the SME sector are forced to acquire knowledge of new solutions from external sources. The conducted research and analyses have shown that SMEs in the Baltic States have problems accessing R&D facilities, consulting services and expertise. Therefore, they should be supported in this process by other organisations, especially R&D units and intermediary organisations. There are many examples of clusters operating in different areas and industries in practice.

An example is the Ecolabnet project, which aims to develop and promote eco-innovation. The project integrates research and development units, intermediary organisations, and small and medium-sized enterprises, which should be considered a good strategy. Numerous results show that the success of eco-innovation projects depends on the integration and interaction developed between the companies and the institutional and external partners (Biscione, 2021, s. 1–17).

Ecolabnet targets the SME sector, i.e., enterprises for which the barriers to implementing eco-innovation are significantly higher than those for large and very large enterprises. It aims to stimulate and support SMEs in implementing eco-innovative solutions. In the paper an attempt was made to answer the research question: Is it possible to identify the categories of the services which will be adapted to the contemporary needs of SME enterprises in the area of eco-innovation?

The answer to this question is affirmative. The identified needs of enterprises in the area of eco-innovation contributed to the development of packages of eco-innovation services. Eight packages of eco-innovation services were distinguished in the project: Business strategy, Eco-innovation management, Bio-based materials, Product design and development, 3D printing, Environmental assessment, Marketing, Other eco-innovation expertise. Service packages are used to categorize services in DCT system. They describe the different types of services Ecolabnet offers to businesses. These packages enable SMEs to access the latest expertise at a high level.

Ecolabnet contributes to the different dimensions of eco-innovation by offering products and services to entrepreneurs, meeting the declared eco-innovation needs, or helping in implementing actions to reducing environmental impacts. The offered expert services and the ongoing research in the area of designing and implementing eco-innovations mainly relate to the following topics: designing eco-products, designing eco-innovative services, eco-branding and developing business models, biocomposite materials and prototyping products based on 3D printing.

The considerations presented in the chapter do not exhaust the issues and require further research. The main limitations of the study are as follows: (1) Research population size—the research was conducted in six Baltic Sea countries, but on a relatively small research population. Carrying out the research in more countries and a larger sample size could give a better generalization of the results. Currently, in order to identify the appropriate service package for a given type of eco-identity of enterprise, additional questions should be asked, such as: What kind of support does the enterprise need? What knowledge can contribute to increasing the level of eco-innovation of the enterprise? What are the company's needs in terms of external expert support? (2) A relatively small number of services offered so far in the Ecolabnet network. The DCT system was implemented in September 2021. The database of products and services is systematically growing, but it is still relatively small. The main bidders are the project partners. Increasing the number of bidders and the number of eco-innovative services and products offered in the Ecolabnet network will certainly translate into an increase in its potential.

References

Albort-Morant, G., Henseler, J., Leal-Millán, A. and Cepeda-Carrión, G. 2017. *Mapping the field: A bibliometric analysis of green innovation*. Sustainability (Switzerland) 9(6): 1–15.

Arimura, T. H., Hibiki, A. and Johnstone, N. 2007. *An empirical analysis of environmental R&D: What encourages facilities to be environmentally innovative?* pp. 142–173. *In*: Johnstone, N. (red.). *Environmental Policy and Corporate Behaviour*. Edward Elgar, Cheltenham.

Bierwisch, A., Huter, L., Pattermann, J. and Som, O. 2021. *Taking eco-innovation to the road—a design-based workshop concept for the development of eco-innovative business models*. Sustainability 13(16): 8811.

Biscione, A., de Felice, A., Gallucci, T. and Lagioia, G. 2021. *Four types of eco-innovation for Baltic firms*, Economic Research, pp. 1–17.

Castellacci, F. and Lie, C.M. 2017. *A taxonomy of green innovators: Empirical evidence from South Korea*. Journal of Cleaner Production 143: 1036–1047.

Daddi, T., Tessitore, S. and Frey, M. 2012. *Eco-innovation and competitiveness in industrial clusters*, International Journal of Technology Management 58(1/2): 49–63.

Dangelico, R. M. and Pujari, D. 2010. *Mainstreaming green product innovation: Why and how companies integrate environmental sustainability*. Journal of Business Ethics 95(3): 471–486.

DCT, https://dct-ecolabnet.pcz.pl.

Dudek, M., Prandecki, K., Wrzaszcz, W. and Żekało, M. 2019. *Jak powstają innowacje ekologiczne w gospodarstwach rolnych? Analiza i przykłady*, IERiGŻ-PIB, Warszawa.

EC. 2006. *Competitiveness and Innovation Framework Programme (2007–2013)*, European Commission, Brussels.

EC. 2011. *Communication from the Commission to the European Parliament, the Council, the European Economic and Social Committee and the Committee of the Regions, Innovation for a sustainable Future – The Eco-Innovation Action Plan (Eco-AP)*. European Commission, Brussels, 15.12.2011, COM(2011) 899 final.

ECOLABNET, https://ecolabnet.org.

EIO. 2013. *Europe in transition: Paving the way to a green economy through eco-innovation*. Eco-Innovation Observatory, Funded by the European Commission, DG Environment, Brussels.

Ernst, D. 2019. *Electric car: 697,612 km to become green! True or false?* Available online: http://blogs.ulg.ac.be/damien-ernst/electric-697612-km-to-become-green-true-or-false/ (accessed on 12 January 2022).

Horbach, J., Rammer, C. and Rennings, K. 2011. *Determinants of eco-innovations by type of environmental impact. The role of regulatory push/pull, technology push and market pull*, ZEW Discussion Papers 11-027, ZEW - Zentrum für Europäische Wirtschaftsforschung. Center for European Economic Research.

Iraldo, F., Testa, F., Oikonomou, V., Melis, M., Frey, M. and Spijker, E. 2009. *A literature review on the links between environmental regulation and competitiveness.* Working Papers 200904, Scuola Superiore Sant'Anna of Pisa, Istituto di Management.

Jędrzejczyk, W. 2021. *Managing customer relations and value in organizations with the use of it tools: Customer segmentation on the market of eco-innovative services*. Procedia Computer Science, ELSEVIER 192: 2816–2825.

Jones, E., Harrison, D. and McLaren, J. 2001. *Managing creative eco-innovation. Structuring outputs from ecoinnovation projects*. The Journal of Sustainable Project Design 1(1): 27–39.

Karakaya, E., Hidalgo, A. and Nuur, C. 2014. *Diffusion of eco-innovations: A review.* Renewable & Sustainable Energy Reviews 33: 392–399.

Kemp, R. and Pearson, P. 2007. *Final report MEI project about measuring eco-innovation*. Um-Merit, Maastricht.

Kesidou, E. and Demirel, P. 2010. *On the drivers of Eco-innovations: Empirical evidence from the UK*, NUBS Research Paper Series.

Kulik, R. *Czy samochód elektryczny jest bardziej ekologiczny*, Available online: https://katowice.eu/SiteAssets/dla-mieszka%C5%84ca/eko-artyku%C5%82y/Czy%20samoch%C3%B3d%20elektryczny%20jest%20bardziej%20ekologiczny%20%E2%80%93%20katowice%20dla%20odmiany%20klimatu.pdf (accessed on 11 January 2022).

Meade, J. 1952. *External economies and diseconomies in a competitive situation*. Economic Journal.

Melin, H. E. 2019. *Analysis of the climate impact of lithium-ion batteries and how to measure it.* Circular Energy Storage, Available online: https://www.transportenvironment.org/wp-content/uploads/2021/07/2019_11_Analysis_CO2_footprint_lithium-ion_batteries.pdf (accessed on 10 January 2022).

Mickwitz, P., Hyvättinen, H. and Kivimaa, P. 2007. *The role of policy instruments in the innovation and diffusion of environmentally friendlier technologies: popular claims versus case study experiences.* Journal of Cleaner Production 16: 62–70.

Nitkiewicz, T. 2012. *Fostering eco-innovation development and implementation in polish companies through operational program innovative economy*. *In*: Knosala, R. (red.). *Innovations in Management and Production Engineering*. Oficyna Wydawnicza Pol-skiego Towarzystwa Zarządzania Produkcją, Opole.

Ociepa-Kubicka, A. 2015. *EMAS – a Tool Supporting Eco-Innovations*. LAP LAMBERT Academic Publishing, Saarbrucken.

OECD. 2005. *Oslo Manual 2005: Guidelines for Collecting and Interpreting Innovation, Data*, 3rd Edition, OECD, Eurostat.

OECD. 2019. *Oslo Manual 2018: Guidelines for Collecting, Reporting and Using Data on Innovation*, 4th Edition, OECD, Eurostat.

Pecorari, P. M. and Camello Lima, C. R. 2020. *Analysis of eco-innovation from a business perspective*. Revista Produção Online. Florianópolis, SC 20(3).

Peiró-Signes, Á. and Segarra-Oña, M. 2018. *How past decisions affect future behavior on eco-innovation: An empirical study*. Business Strategy and The Environment 27: 1233–1244.

Rennings, K. 2000. *Redefining innovation—eco-innovation research and the contribution from ecological economics*. Ecological Economics 32(2): 319–332.

Fahad, S., Alnori, F., Su, F. and Deng, J. 2022. *Adoption of green innovation practices in SMEs sector: Evidence from an emerging economy*. Economic Research-Ekonomska Istraživanja.

Sinclair-Desgagne, B., Feigenbaum, D. and Pawlak, É. 2003. *The Integrated Product Policy and the Innovation Process: An Overview*, Scientific Series, CIRANO, Montreal, pp. 112.

Sobczak, E. and Głuszczuk, D. 2022. *Diversification of eco-innovation and innovation activity of small and medium-sized enterprises in the european union countries*. Sustainability, Vol. 14.

Sobczyk, W. 2014. *Sustainable development of rural areas*. Problems of Sustainable Development 9(1): 119.

Šūmakaris, P. and Korsakienė, R. 2021. *Mapping the field of eco-innovation strategies: A review*. International scientific conference contemporary issues in business. Management and Economics Engineering.

Szpor, A. and Śniegocki, A. 2012. *Ekoinnowacje w Polsce. Stan obecny, bariery rozwoju, możliwości wsparcia*, Instytut Badań Strukturalnych, Warszawa.

Tamayo-Orbegozo, U., Vicente-Molina, M.-A. and Villarreal-Larrinaga, O. 2017. *Eco-innovation strategic model. A multiple-case study from a highly eco-innovative European region*. Journal of Cleaner Production 142(4).

WCED. 1987. *Our Common Future*. World Commission on Environment and Development, Oxford University Press, Oxford, New York.

Xavier, A., Reyes, T., Aoussat, A., Luiz, L. O. and Souza, L. 2020. *Eco-Innovation maturity model: A framework to support the evolution of eco-innova-tion integration in companies*. Sustainability 12(9): Art. 3773.

CHAPTER 11

Sustainable Development in Urban and Metropolitan Areas

International Comparative Approach

Marcin Budziński, Yurii Vitkovskyi,*[a] *Aleksander Ostenda,*[b] *Agnieszka Szostak*[c] and *Ewa Palarczyk*[d]

Introduction

In modern world, the ideas of sustainable urban development began to spread widely at the end of the 20th century: in 1990, the UN program for the creation of sustainable cities (United Nations. Sustainable Cities Programme 1990–2000) was launched, and in the early 2000s, the concept of sustainable development began to dominate municipal strategic planning in accordance with Agenda 21 (United Nations Conference on Environment & Development 1992). Today, sustainable urban development is a separate area in the list of the UN Sustainable Development Goals (hereinafter - SDGs). SDG No. 11 focuses, in particular, reduction of the negative environmental impact of cities (target 11.6), development of public spaces (target 11.7) and implementation of strategic planning (target 11.b). In wider context sustainable development in urban and metropolitan areas is also related to almost all other SDG and refers all types of organizations—public, private and non-governmental/social ones.

The purpose of our research is also to analyse existing approaches to assessing sustainable development, identify their advantages and areas of improvement and propose the international comparative approach to measure the sustainable

Faculty of Social Sciences and Humanities, Academy of Silesia, Poland.
[a] Email: yurii.vitkovskyi@akademiaslaska.pl, ORCID: 0000-0001-5806-8671
[b] Email: aleksander.ostenda@wst.pl, ORCID: 0000-0002-3467-157X
[c] Email: agnieszka.szostak@akademiaslaska.pl, ORCID: 0009-0001-1084-1837
[d] Email: epalarczyk@synergist.eu.com, ORCID: 0009-0008-4399-5112
* Corresponding author: marcin.budzinski@akademiaslaska.pl, ORCID: 0000-0002-6383-5369

development focusing on implementation in urban and metropolitan areas. Additionally the study presents main challenges in sustainability implementation as well as challenges of managing social inclusion in metropolis. Key fields of the study are presented on Fig. 1 below:

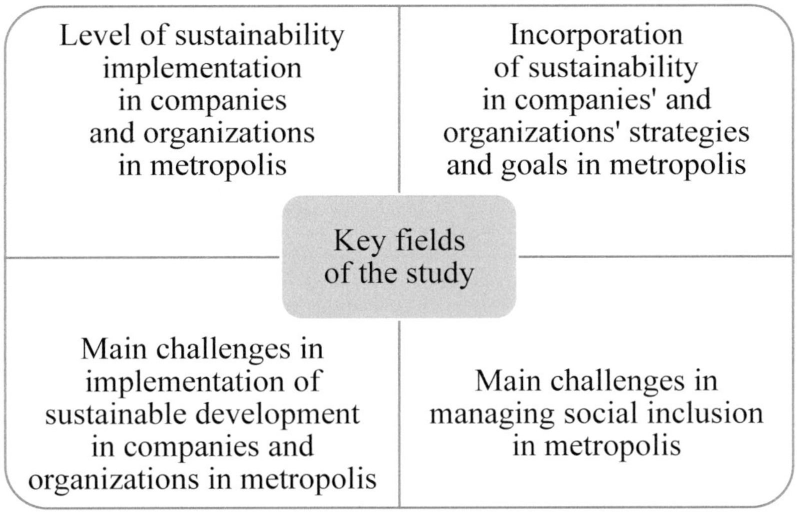

Fig. 1. Key fields of study regarding sustainable development in urban and metropolitan areas in international comparative approach. Source: Authors' own elaboration

Research questions and hypothesis

Taking into consideration all above four main research questions were asked:

- Q1: What is the level of sustainability implementation in companies and organizations in metropolitan areas?
- Q2: What are the main challenges in implementation of sustainable development managing in companies and organizations in metropolitan areas?
- Q3: What is the level of incorporation of sustainability in companies' and organizations' strategies and goals?
- Q4: What are the main challenges in managing social inclusion in three metropolitan areas?

All questions refers always to comparison between three metropolitan areas, which are the subject of the study: Metropolis GZM in Poland, Gdańsk-Gdynia-Sopot Metropolitan Area in Poland and The Ruhr Metropolitan Area in Germany. Moreover regarding this research questions above additional important issue was to present main similarities and differences among three metropolitan areas as well as practical recommendation.

Main hypothesis of the study are presented on Fig. 2.

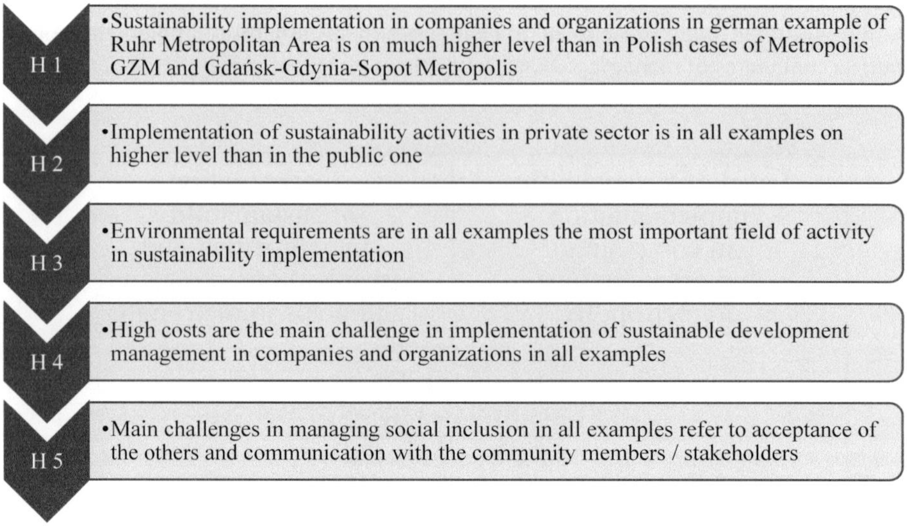

Fig. 2. The main hypothesis of the research. Source: Authors' own elaboration.

Theoretical background

In scientific literature, as a rule, a sustainable city is a city that achieves the UN Sustainable Development Goals: it is safe, green, comfortable and wealthy (Simon, 2016) or has economic, social and environmental sustainability (Vavulin and Malaya, 2020). Often SDG-based dimensions of sustainable development complement other dimensions. For example, a sustainable city should have goods, services and opportunities available to residents and be socially just (Simon, 2016); have a creative urban environment and architectural uniqueness (Vavulin and Malaya, 2020); have developed social capital; be characterized by growth in the average size of pensions, capacity of polyclinics, retail trade turnover or become a smart city.

In practice, definitions developed by international organizations are often used. For example, the Association of Local Governments for Sustainable Development, which unites more than 2,500 local and regional governments, identifies the following characteristics of a sustainable city: low greenhouse gas emissions, development based on proximity to nature, circular economy, crisis and disaster resilience, social justice and people-centered development. The International Telecommunication Union considers sustainability as the ability of a city to apply modern technologies to improve the quality of life, efficiency of urban management and services, and ensure competitiveness on the world stage, and the World Urban Forum proposes to consider as sustainable a "properly" managed city that has implemented innovative financing mechanisms, innovative urban solutions in the field of housing, mobility, planning and management, modern technologies, open investment platforms, etc.

The concept of a sustainable city is based on key contemporary theoretical urban planning approaches, which generally also aim to balance economic and social development and ecology The main types of approaches are as follows:

- *Creative Cities* (Landry, 2000); creativity as a strategic factor of urban management and socio-economic development, environmental protection.
- *Ecological economics* (Daly and Farley, 2004; Daly, 2007). Economy of sustainable state, harmony of socio-economic and ecological development,
- *Circular economy* (Geissdoerfer et al., 2017) A closed-loop economy based on resource renewal, an alternative to the traditional linear economy (create, use, landfill),
- *Urban metabolism* (Kennedy et al., 2007; Understanding Urban Metabolism, 2014) The city as a living organism that generates, consumes, releases, accumulates and consumes resource flows; the need to control resource and waste flows.
- *A city for people* (Gehl, 2010); creating a human-centered urban environment, compact, green, liveable cities with a developed public transportation system.
- *Compact city* (Conticelli, 2019; Dempsey and Jenks, 2010); regulating population density, size and layout to enhance urban development and achieve an optimal balance between the positive and negative externalities of concentration.
- *Sustainable Mobility* (Schiller and Kenworthy, 2017); The introduction of modes of transportation, transportation systems, regulatory measures, and urban planning solutions that have positive economic, environmental, and social impacts simultaneously.
- *Sustainable urban planning* (Cervero et al., 2017), transit-oriented design (Calthorpe, 1993) Projects with integrated efficiency (social, environmental and economic); internalization of negative externalities from transport; urban development along the lines of an urban transport framework that includes a system of rapid public transport lines.
- *Sociocultural approach to urban design* (Building Sustainable Cities, 2020) creating a place for recreation, sports and people's life, their entertainment and enjoyment of life. Environmental, social and economic aspects of sustainable urban development for the realization of SDG #11.
- *Smart Cities* (Smart Cities, 2013) The application of ICT and other innovative developments to improve the quality of life and effective governance, environmental protection, economic and social development.

There are also approaches which develop or combine earlier existing ones. For example in conception of Smart City, the highest, fourth stage in development of smart cities is a City that takes adventage of the opportunities offered by sustainable development (Makieła et al., 2022, p. 2). This approach is also related to the search for new models and tools for shaping development by city authorities. Based on the ideas provided by the Smart City concept and the concept of Creative Class and Creative City developed approach of 4T capitals (talent, tolerance, technology, trust) was researched in particular issues related to increasing the participation of residents in shaping local development policies and the comprehensive use of modern technologies—both to improve the accessibility of residents to urban services as well as to increase the influence of residents on the future of their city (Budziński et al., 2022, p. 21; Budziński et al., 2022; Budziński et al., 2024, p. 17–32).

Next approaches focus on measuring sustainable urban development. To measure the sustainability of a city or metropolis, different systems of indicators have been proposed in the world, which can be conditionally divided into three groups:

- ready-made set of indicators based on the SDGs (based on the UN ideas);
- selection of indicators according to the "correct" algorithm;
- integral indicators for individual areas of sustainable development.

Most approaches use a system of indicators reflecting SDG No11 and other SDGs. For example, UN-Habitat suggests using indicators such as (Recommendation Y.4900/L.1600. 2016):- "proportion of urban population living in slums or poor housing", "proportion of population with easy access to public transportation" (corresponding to SDG No11);- "proportion of population living in households with access to basic utilities", "proportion of total adult population with secure land tenure" (SDG No1);- "proportion of wastewater treated adequately" (SDG No6), etc.

The International Telecommunication Union and UNECE (United Nations Economic Commission for Europe) have developed 91 key performance indicators (KPIs) for smart sustainable cities that reflect the economic, environmental, social and cultural impacts of modern technologies in order to realize SDG No. 11 under the United for Smart Sustainable Cities initiative. For example, KPIs measure: in the economic sphere—the level of e-commerce development and the number of wireless broadband connections per 100,000 inhabitants; in the environmental sphere—the use of energy from renewable sources, reducing greenhouse gas emissions; in the social sphere—the use of ICT, increasing social inclusiveness, etc.

SDG indicators are also the basis for sustainable development indices of European Union, USA and China. In the scientific literature, approaches based on "completing" SDG No11 indicators with a set of additional indicators and expanding the list of "sustainable development dimensions" are widely presented. For example, it is proposed to supplement the indicators of SDG No11 with: indicators of building density, infrastructure and green spaces, social justice (Simon, 2016, p. 11-144) or indicators that take into account the age and gender composition of the population, availability of fixed assets and their degree of wear and tear, environmental protection costs.

The approaches described above suggest a universal "right" set of indicators; a more flexible approach assumes that there is no "right" set of indicators, as all cities are unique, and indicators should be selected according to the "right" algorithm. The "right" algorithm includes three steps: compiling an initial list of indicators, selecting indicators from this list according to certain rules, and, if necessary, discussing the results and correcting the resulting set of indicators. To compile the initial list, it is proposed to either include indicators of 7 different types (Tanguay et al., 2010), for which there is a consensus in the scientific literature and for which there is a consensus in the scientific literature. For example, it has been suggested that the initial list should include 7 different types of indicators (Tanguay et al., 2010), for which there is consensus in the scientific literature, and 20 of their subcategories 16, namely:

- indicators from the three main spheres of sustainable development: environmental, social and economic;
- additional indicators lying at the intersection of the three main spheres: these are indicators of Liveable (intersection of environmental and social), Equitable (economic and social), Viable (environmental and economic) and Sustainable (intersection of all three "dimensions of sustainable development").

Liveability indicators are the amount of household waste sent to landfills, traffic fatalities and injuries per 1,000 inhabitants; equity is the number of households with income less than $10,000 and the percentage of the population aged 18 and older without a high school diploma; viability is the percentage of businesses with environmental certification; sustainability is the presence of policy initiatives that support sustainable development, etc. At the second stage, indicators are selected from the initial list according to the following principles: the selected indicators should cover all 7 types and 20 subcategories of sustainable development, and the share of additional indicators measuring the intersection of the three main spheres of sustainable development should be increased; indicators should not be numerous, they should be understandable and have practical relevance. A similar approach is proposed for measuring the "smart sustainable city": the initial set includes 304 indicators, which are grouped into blocks: smart sustainable economy, population, engineering infrastructure, social infrastructure, intelligent management and mobility, "digital platforms and data". Further, available indicators (collected by statistical services) reflecting the degree of transition to the concept of "smart city" were selected from them.

The calculation of aggregate indicators is carried out for individual "directions of sustainable development", and the main directions—environmental, social and economic—can be supplemented by other directions. Thus, a methodology has been developed to assess cities using a composite index for six "sustainable dimensions"—sustainability of human resources, information space, production, natural, institutional and organizational environment, environmental, economic, social and "smart" priorities, subsystems of the economy, social sphere, infrastructure and environment.

The ratings of cities by A.T. Kearney, Mercer, Mori Memorial Foundation Global Power City Index, Economist Intelligence Unit, Arcadis, Resonance Consultancy, etc., can also be referred to the assessment of urban development sustainability on the basis of integrated indicators. As a rule, the rating calculates a number of integrated indicators that cover the economy, environment, social sphere and a number of additional "areas of sustainable development". Thus, there are various approaches to the definition of sustainable urban development and its measurement, which can be conditionally called "classical".

The main advantage of "classical" approaches is the possibility of international comparisons, which is necessary to understand the limitations and advantages of the city under study, its unique features and prospects of development on a global scale, the development of strategies for tourism and export development, personnel attraction program, etc. The advantages of "classical" approaches are also: ease of implementation in practice, consensus on the applicability of indicators, availability of time series of indicator values to track the dynamics, etc. However, "classical" approaches are not without a number of limitations.

- First, the SDGs (and SDG-based indicators) were originally developed for the global and national level and do not fully reflect the specifics of urban development. Consequently, SDG-based approaches either do not include indicators of urban environmental quality at all or contain a very limited set of such indicators, which makes it very difficult to reflect the unique features and challenges of urban development, including urban environmental quality.
- Secondly, sustainable urban development is understood as simultaneous progress in all three areas (economy, ecology, social sphere). However, the development strategies of a modern city are often focused on a breakthrough, a radical change in the urban environment, economy, positioning of the city or its development trajectory; it is an ambitious, breakthrough strategy that can provide the city with the necessary resources for the development of conditionally "lagging behind" areas. Such strategies should include projects with integrated efficiency "3-in-1"—the development of one area without prejudice to other areas of sustainable development, the effectiveness of which is poorly quantifiable for all three components.
- Third, a significant disadvantage of the considered approaches is the use of a limited list of quantitative indicators. A set of quantitative indicators was relevant in the second half of the XX century, but not today: data on the life of a modern city are multidimensional, can be considered in space and time, in macro- and microscale. For example, the number of green areas within walking distance (on a map), traffic congestion (on a map, in real time, by days of the week, months, years), the number of offenses in space and time, etc. The limitations of "classical" approaches also include their subjectivity: reflection of the specifics of the activity of the international organization-developer of the methodology or the author's methodology.

Existing approaches to sustainable development assessment based on SDGs were initially developed for the global and national level and do not fully reflect the specifics of urban development, are subjective, difficult to apply for the purposes of comparing a city with a narrow range of its real competitors, do not take into account the unique features and objectives of a particular city, and also contain indicators, the monitoring of which for individual cities has no value. In addition, the development strategies of a modern city are often focused on a breakthrough, radical changes in the urban environment, economy, positioning of the city or its development trajectory. At the same time, a set of typical SDG-based indicators cannot reflect a unique creative urban development strategy. Thus, the transition to sustainable urban development implies the realization of a breakthrough, creative and unique development strategy, which should provide resources for the main directions of sustainable development. The strategy should be centered on the person, resident and guest of the city and their needs with an emphasis on comfort and environmentally friendly solutions—green buildings, multi-format development, pedestrian zones, green paths and open public spaces, the use of environmentally friendly transport. The needs of residents of all ages and social groups, including pensioners, children, youth, immobile citizens, as well as tourists, should be taken into account.

That is why it is necessary to take into account the process of social inclusion of the population in a metropolis. Until recently, the metropolis was considered more as a functional centre in the global economic system. However, in the second half of the twentieth century, ideas about urban development expanded their subject matter. The emphasis on the active role of members of society, individually and collectively participating in the life of society, is primarily associated with the social inclusion. In this case, metropolises not only adapt the structural features of society to local conditions, but also form social structures. The role of a city dweller is rethought: he is perceived not as a consumer of resources, but as an active subject of urbanization, participating in the creation of urban environment. One of the characteristics of the urban environment is the ability to unite (integrate) heterogeneous elements into a holistic phenomenon. Such inclusion occurs not only on the material (physical encounters of citizens in public spaces), but also on the social (formation of self-identification, sense of belonging) and institutional (formation of new social structures) levels. And, of course, there is no constant proportion between inclusion and interaction.

Another important aspect of sustainable development of the metropolis is the implementation of SDGs by enterprises and organizations of all types of ownership, so it is worth considering this issue in more detail. Modern companies around the world are aligning their development strategies with the Sustainable Development Goals developed by the United Nations General Assembly. The directions specified in the Sustainable Development Goals dictate the direction of development of large companies in the period up to 2030.

In the process of building development strategies, companies take into account ESG (Environmental, Social, Governance) factors. These factors reflect how closely the company monitors such important aspects of its activities as:

- environmental friendliness of production through such indicators as greenhouse gas emissions, environmental pollution, resource depletion, as well as other similar factors;
- social development by monitoring the working conditions of employees (labour safety, working conditions, gender composition), investing in social projects and supporting the education and professional development of its employees;
- corporate governance by curbing corruption within the company's operations;
- corporate governance by preventing corruption within the company's operations;
- corporate social responsibility by ensuring that the company's employees are aware of the environmental impact of its activities; and
- corporate governance by preventing corruption within the company's operations.

The concept of sustainable development originated at the turn of the 60s–70s of the twentieth century and has been significantly transformed several times since then. This evolution was caused by a regular shift of focus towards one of the components (social or environmental dimension) depending on the demands of society in a particular historical period. At the initial stage of the concept's development, an ecologically centered approach prevailed. Although the social and economic aspects were not rejected by the followers. Although the social and economic aspects were not rejected by the followers of this approach, they were seen as rather secondary and often even as a threat to the planet's environmental sustainability. However, it was then, and more precisely since the 1990s, that the three-pronged approach became more popular, in which all factors were given equal attention and sustainability was seen as a reasonable balance between three equally important components (the so-called three-pronged approach).

At the same time, analysis of recent international conferences and non-financial reports of companies shows that in practice the environmental dimension remains the most developed. The majority of recent events are related to climate change, energy efficiency and carbon footprint reduction. Moreover, even in the years when the triune approach was dominant, the environmental dimension received considerably more attention. It seems that it was the active development of business that contributed to the "renaissance" of the environmental priority. It is obvious that the problems of green economy are closer to business. Firstly, it is much easier for management to justify to the Board of Directors and shareholders the subsequent financial benefits from financing environmental innovations than from social ones. Secondly, environmental results are much easier to measure with econometric tools. As an intermediate conclusion, let us formulate the following thesis: in the normal course of life, the concept of sustainable development without the influence of supranational structures tends to return to the environmental agenda. However, the current situation after COVID-19 can hardly be called normal. It is clear that in the current situation both national governments and private companies are more concerned with the social sphere: from protecting the health of workers to preserving consumer demand.

To measure the sustainability of urban development for the purposes of strategic planning in this interpretation, a broad set of indicators is required, measuring both the breakthrough direction and other traditional directions of sustainable development; the selected set of indicators should combine both classical numerical indicators and indicators displayed with the help of modern technologies. On the other hand it is also possible to measure sustainability with using the percentage level of implementation of sustainable activities, incorporation of sustainability in companies and organisations strategies and goals or define key challenges in sustainability implementation and social inclusion.

Materials and methods

The study was conducted on the basis of a survey questionnaire, using the Computer Assisted Website Interview method with selected and representative research sample of totally 2900 respondents. It consist of 1274 respondents in 41 cities in Metropolis GZM, 824 respondents in Gdańsk-Gdynia-Sopot Metropolitan Area (GGS) (*Obszar*

Metropolitalny Gdańsk-Gdynia-Sopot) and 802 respondents form the Ruhr Area in Germany. In GGS research was focused in main cities: Gdańsk, Gdynia, Sopot, Pruszcz Gdański, Reda, Rumnia, Tczew. In the Ruhr Metropolitan Area main cities selected to the research were: Bochum, Bottrop, Dortmund, Duisburg, Essen, Gelsenkirchen, Hagen, Hamm, Herne, Mülheim an der Ruhr, Oberhausen. Data were collected by the Ariadna panel in July and August 2024 and all respondents were adults—18 years old or more. This approach is presented on Fig. 3 below.

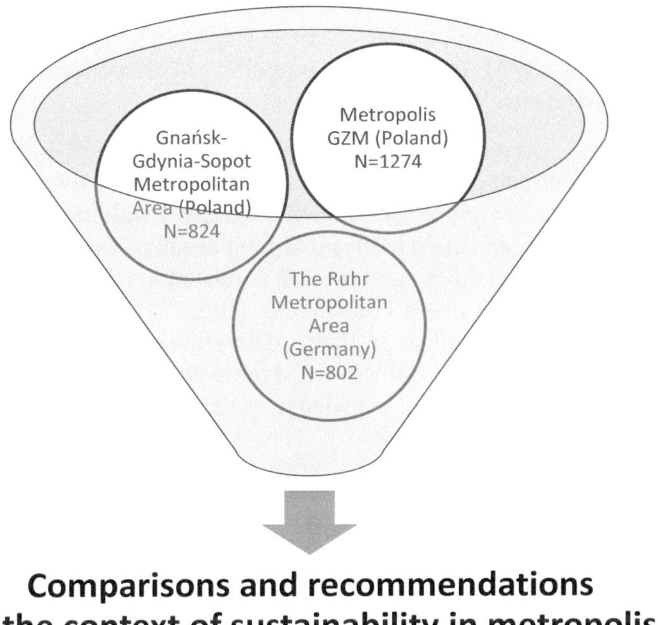

Fig. 3. Metropolitan comparisons in the context of the challenges of sustainable development. Source: authors' own elaboration.

The study followed the ethical requirements of anonymity and voluntary participation. Written informed consent was obtained from each participant before inclusion. The costs of conducting this research were co-financed by two sources: Metropolis GZM under the "Metropolitan Science and Education Support Fund" program in 2022–2024 within granted project "Challenges and recommendations for the management of social inclusion in the context of the internationalization of metropolises—a comparative analysis of GZM with metropolitan areas in Poland and abroad" and Academy of Silesia own founds.

It is also important to explain, that not all answers for all question refer to all 2900 respondents. It is always mentioned about detail respondents, who answered each question. The reason is that questions were asked to employees in companies or organizations in each metropolis, who are only a part of researched adult population, which consist also of people who are retired, unemployed, students or adult pupils.

Results

Table 1 below shows in comparative perspective practical implementation of sustainability activities in company/organization among the employees in metropolitan areas in total, which means:

- in the Ruhr Metropolitan Area (RUHR) 502 out of 802 respondents (62,6%) were employees who answered this question,
- in Gdańsk-Gdynia-Sopot Metropolitan Area (GGS) 674 out of 824 respondents (81,8%) were employees who answered this question,
- in Metropolis GZM (GZM) 928 out of 1274 respondents (72,8%) were employees who answered this question.

There is a big difference between RUHR where almost ¾ of employees observe sustainable activities and polish metropolis, where only 44% in GZM or little more than half in GGS declare implementation of sustainable activities in their company/ organization. In RUHR and in GZM the most popular activities refer to environmental requirements and in GSS the biggest interest is related to training and development programs for employees. In both Polish cases almost 22% of respondents does not declare any sustainable practices in their organisations—in RUHR it is only less than 12% who think so. Additionally in GZM more than 1/3 and GSS almost 30% of respondents also do not have any knowledge in this topic in comparison to RUHR, where only less than 15% declare so.

Table 1. Sustainability implementation in companies and organizations—metropolitan comparative approach.

Implementation of sustainability activities in your company/ organization	**Total employees (%)**		
	The Ruhr Metropolitan Area	**Gdańsk-Gdynia-Sopot Metropolitan Area**	**Metropolis GZM**
YES	**73,5**	**50,9**	**44,4**
environmental requirements	23,5	13,6	15,6
training and development programs for employees	17,1	18,2	13,4
building organizational culture - support inclusivity	13,3	7,0	7,0
of ESG reporting obligations	11,0	6,8	4,4
corporate social responsibility (CSR)	8,6	5,3	4,0
NO, none of the above activities are carried out	**11,6**	**21,8**	**21,9**
I don't know / it's hard to say	**14,9**	**27,3**	**33,7**

Source: own elaboration based on researches results

Moreover Table 2 below shows in comparative perspective practical implementation of sustainability activities in company/organization among the employees in metropolitan areas with division of employees between all types of organizations:

- in the Ruhr Metropolitan Area (RUHR) among all employees who answered this question, 41% work in private sector, 31 % in public sector, 15% in social/non-governmental one and 13% were self-employed,
- in Gdańsk-Gdynia-Sopot Metropolitan Area (GGS) among all employees who answered this question, 59% work in private sector, 30 % in public sector, only 2% in social/non-governmental one and 9% were self-employed,
- in Metropolis GZM (GZM) among all employees who answered this question, 58% work in private sector, 31 % in public sector, only 3% in social/non-governmental one and 8% were self-employed.

This data above also shows structural differences between Polish and German labour market, where employment in RUHR especially social/non-governmental sector is bigger, and the dominance of employees in private sector is not so strong.

Table 2. Sustainability implementation in companies and organizations—metropolitan comparative approach by sectors.

Implementation of sustainability activities in your company/ organization	**Employees in metropolis by sectors (%)**											
	private			**public**			**self-employment**			**social/non-governmental**		
	Ruhr	**GGS**	**GZM**	**Ruhr**	**GGS**	**GZM**	**Ruhr**	**GGS**	**GZM**	**Ruhr**	**GGS**	**GZM**
YES	**71,2**	**48,8**	**40,7**	**75,7**	**56,5**	**50,2**	**75,4**	**44,3**	**41,6**	**73,9**	**60,0**	**64,3**
environmental requirements	22,1	13,4	13,9	21,8	16,7	20,6	29,2	8,2	11,7	26,0	0,0	7,1
training and development programs for employees	17,8	16,2	11,8	15,4	25,1	15,3	18,5	6,6	13,0	17,8	26,7	25,0
building organizational culture - support inclusivity	10,6	6,3	6,7	16,7	6,4	7,7	7,7	9,8	3,9	19,2	20,0	14,3
of ESG reporting obligations	10,6	7,6	5,1	10,3	3,9	2,8	16,9	13,1	6,5	8,2	0,0	3,6
corporate social responsibility (CSR)	10,1	5,3	3,2	11,5	4,4	3,8	3,1	6,6	6,5	2,7	13,3	14,3
NO, none of the above activities are carried out	**13,0**	**22,8**	**24,3**	**7,7**	**17,7**	**16,4**	**18,5**	**29,5**	**29,9**	**9,6**	**20,0**	**10,7**
I don't know/it's hard to say	**15,8**	**28,4**	**35,0**	**16,6**	**25,8**	**33,4**	**6,1**	**26,2**	**28,5**	**16,5**	**20,0**	**25,0**

Source: own elaboration based on researches results

The main results in cross-sectoral comparison of implementation of sustainability activities in company/organization in are as follows:

- public sector is in all metropolis always better than in private one, it means, that the implementation level in public sector is always higher,
- in all sectors the level of implementation is always higher in RUHR, than in Polish metropolis:
    - o social/non-governmental sector is only 9–14% better in RUHR, rest of sectors are much better (20%–30%) in RUHR,
    - o in self-employment sector implementation activities are not observed in 18,5% respondents in RUHR, but in GSS and GZM even in almost 30%,
    - o 6%–16% respondents in RUHR do not have any knowledge in this topic, in polish metropolis this level is higher 20%–35%

Another important issue is incorporation of sustainability in companies' and organizations' strategies and goals. Answers were collected:

- in The Ruhr Metropolitan Area (RUHR) among 372 out of 802 respondents (46%)—employees who answered this question,
- in Gdańsk-Gdynia-Sopot Metropolitan Area (GGS) among 345 out of 824 respondents (42%)—employees who answered this question,
- in Metropolis GZM (GZM) among 413 out of 1274 respondents (32%)—employees who answered this question.

It is presented in Table 3 below in comparative approach.

The answers in all researched cases is similar, and always more than ¾ respondents confirm that company/organization incorporate sustainability to their strategies and goals. In Polish metropolis it is even more than 80%.

These same respondents were also asked to define the biggest challenge in implementing sustainability in their company/organization. Main challenges in metropolitan comparative approach are presented on Graph 1 below.

In all metropolis the biggest challenge in implementing sustainability in company/organization refers to high costs of implementing sustainable development (25,6%–36,8%). Moreover formal and/or organizational difficulties and low measurable benefits for the organisation were also important in all examples (12,7%–18,3%), but in Ruhr Metropolitan Area low sustainability awareness for organizations was

Table 3. Incorporation of sustainability in companies' and organizations' strategies and goals—metropolitan comparative approach.

Incorporation of sustainability in company/organization strategy and goals	Respondents (%)		
	The Ruhr Metropolitan Area	Gdańsk-Gdynia-Sopot Metropolitan Area	Metropolis GZM
YES	76,6%	80,9%	80,6%
NO	23,4%	19,1%	19,4%

Source: own elaboration based on researches results

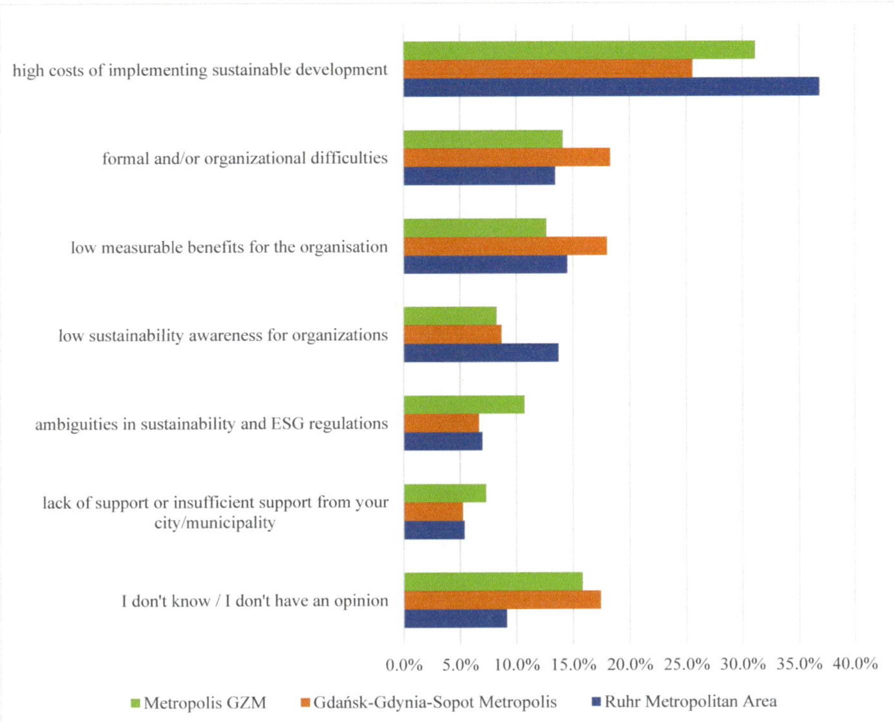

Graph 1. Main challenges in implementation of sustainable development in companies and organizations—metropolitan comparative approach. Source: own elaboration based on researches results.

also important issue (13,7%). Additionally in RUHR 9% of respondents do not have any knowledge or opinion in this topic, but in Polish cases it was 16%–17%.

Last empirical issue is related to another type of challenges, which also refer to sustainability, but in more social approach. Answers were collected among 121 respondents in RUHR, 333 respondents in GGS and 461 respondents in GZM. Main challenges in managing social inclusion in metropolis in comparative approach is presented on Graph 2 below.

Graph 2 presents key challenges based on open question, where respondents' answers were categorised. The challenge "acceptance of others" was the most popular among respondents in Polish cases and second most popular answer refers to communication with environment. In RUHR the most popular one was "acceptance to change" and second most popular was "cultural zone".

Because main categorised challenges might be understood in many ways the most popular interpretation according to researched answers is presented below:

- acceptance of others—counteracting prejudice and xenophobia, tolerance of people with a different religion, nationality, skin colour or sexual orientation, integration processes including also immigrants,
- communication with the community members/stakeholders—effective communication and dialogue with residents, including minority and peripheral

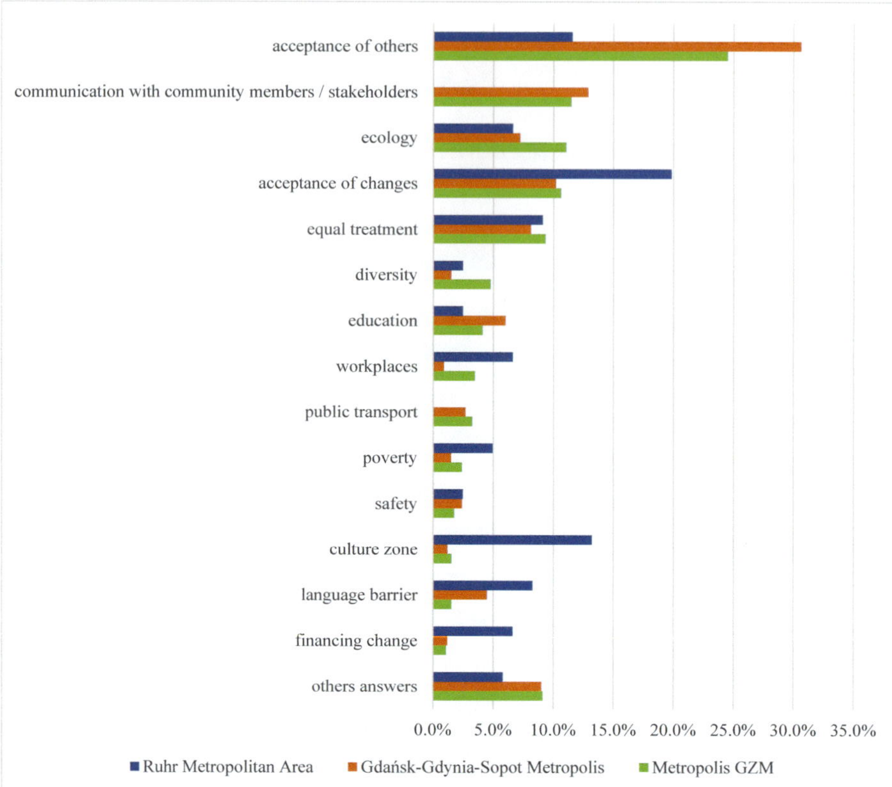

Graph 2. Main challenges in managing social inclusion in metropolis. Source: own elaboration based on researches results.

groups, new ways of reaching residents and various social groups with information, information campaigns and direct meetings,

- ecology—environmental protection and clean air combined with the development of ecological transport and reduction of exhaust and greenhouse gas emissions, counteracting adverse climate change and waste management,
- acceptance of change—the challenge is to change the mentality and awareness of a part of society that still does not want to accept diversity, presents a closed attitude, lack of openness to conversation and arguments,
- equal treatment—equality of society in all areas of functioning, including for every national minority, ensuring equal opportunities for everyone regardless of nationality, accessibility for people with disabilities,
- diversity—respecting the differences and traditions of people from other cultural circles, counteracting stereotypes and fears of other cultures combined with creating common spaces for residents; increasing cultural awareness and equality in rights and duties,

- education—from an early age, equal access to education and social education in the field of inclusivity and tolerance concerning in example, counteracting ethnic, religious or disability prejudices,
- workplaces—decent work that pays well and is combined with more jobs and less unemployment, including jobs regardless of origin and for professionals,
- public transport—accessible, cheap and adapted to the needs of residents, public transport, including collision-free transport and efficient ticketing systems,
- poverty—eliminating poverty, hunger and organic homelessness,
- safety—understood in a multidimensional way, both as security against military, terrorist or criminal threats, but also social and social security and security in virtual space,
- culture zone—understood as physical but also virtual spaces promoting diversity and interculturality,
- language barrier—both in direct communication in everyday matters, as well as in professional or business activity, and the development of systemic mechanisms of language assimilation,
- financing change—concerns, among others, systemic financial solutions for inclusiveness.

Discussion and conclusion

According to the results above answers to all research questions were made. It was also possible to prove or deny each of the hypotheses:

- H1: Sustainability implementation in companies and organizations in German example of Ruhr Metropolitan Area is on much higher level than in Polish cases of Metropolis GZM and Gdańsk-Gdynia-Sopot Metropolis—**was proven**; in all cases in total and in all sector analysis the level of implementation is higher in RUHR, even more than 30%,
- H2: Implementation of sustainability activities in private sector is in all examples on higher level than in the public one—**was denied;** in all cases implementation level in public sector was higher than the private one,
- H3: Environmental requirements are in all examples the most important field of activity in sustainability implementation—**was denied;** in private public and social non-governmental sectors in GGS and in self-employment as well as non-governmental sector in GZM the most important issue was training and development programs for employees,
- H4: High costs are the main challenge in implementation of sustainable development management in companies and organizations in all examples—**was proven,** in all examples it was main challenge,
- H5: Main challenges in managing social inclusion in all examples refer to acceptance of the others and communication with the community members/ stakeholders—was **denied;** the challenge "acceptance of others" was the most

popular only among respondents in Polish cases and second most popular answer refers to communication with environment. In RUHR the most popular one was "acceptance to change" and second most popular was "cultural zone".

All conclusions to be more practical were transformed into recommendations for better development of sustainability in urban and metropolitan areas. It is:

- important to develop professional relations and contacts between Polish and German (and in future from other countries) public and private organizations regarding transfer of good practices in the field of implementing sustainability.
- recommended to develop professional relations and contacts between Polish and German (and in future from other countries) academic, universities to create common in depth projects/research studies regarding sustainability, as a kay issue,
- highly welcomed to create some cross-sectoral and international recommendations regarding sustainability implementation,
- well seen to increase efforts to combine sustainability with companies and organisations strategies and goals,
- expected to prize outstanding leaders in sustainability and spread good examples among others
- necessary to promote among companies and organisations in all sectors activities to increase inclusivity,
- good to increase awareness about popular ways of overcoming main challenges both—in implementing sustainability and managing social inclusion,
- worth to implement sustainability and social inclusion aspects in wider context to university studies, courses and other learning programs.

References

2019 US Cities Sustainable Development Report // Sustainable Development URL: https://www.sdgindex.org/reports/2019-us-cities-sustainable-development-report/ The China Urban Sustainability Index 2013 // McKinsey. URL: http://www.mckinseychina.com/wp-content/uploads/2014/04/china-urban-sustainability-index-2013.pdf.

A guide to assist national and local governments to monitor and report on SDG goal 11+ indicators. P. 3–4 // UN-Habitat). URL: https://unhabitat.org/sdg-goal-11-monitoring-framework.

Akimova, O. E., Volkov, S. K. and Simonov, A. V. 2021. *Transition to the concept of "Smart City" in the regions of the southern federal district: a correlation matrix of indicators of a smart and sustainable city*. Zhurnal Sibirskogo federal'nogo universiteta. Seriya: Gumanitarnyye nauki. 14(12): 1885–1897. DOI: 10.17516/1997-1370-0867.

Alvarez-Risco, A., Rosen, M., Del-Aguila-Arcentales, S. and Marinova, D. (eds.). 2020. *Building Sustainable Cities: Social, Economic and Environmental Factors. Cham: Springer*. Building Sustainable Cities: Social, Economic and Environmental Factors/ed. by A. Alvarez-Risco, M. Rosen,S. Del-Aguila-Arcentales, D. Marinova. Cham: Springer, 2020.

Brandli, L. (eds.). 2020. *Sustainable cities and communities*. Encyclopedia of the UN Sustainable Development Goals.

Budziński, M., Kinelski, G., Raczek, M. and Wrana, K. 2022. Wdrażanie koncepcji Smart City w miastach Górnośląsko-Zagłębiowskiej Metropolii – Identyfikacja przejawów współpracy miast Górnośląsko-Zagłębiowskiej Metropolii w zakresie wdrażania koncepcji Smart City i rozwijania kapitałów

4T, In: Koncepcja Smart City i potencjały 4T. Inteligentne Zarządzanie Miastami Górnośląsko-Zagłębiowskiej Metropolii/Makieła Z. Mucha-Kuś K., Kinelski Gr. (red.), Akademia WSB, p. 189.

Budziński, M., Raczek, M. and Wrana, K. 2022. Koncepcja Smart City i kapitały 4T w politykach rozwoju miast Górnośląsko-Zagłębiowskiej Metropolii, W: Koncepcja Smart City i potencjały 4T. Inteligentne Zarządzanie Miastami Górnośląsko-Zagłębiowskiej Metropolii/Makieła, Z., Mucha-Kuś, K., Kinelski, G. (red.). Akademia WSB, ISBN 978-83-66794-71-9, p. 21-42.

Budziński, M., Vitkovskyi, Y., Ochnik, D., Buława, B., Gachowski, M., Nagel, P. et al. 2024. *Sustainable development management and strategic awareness of the Metropolis GZM inhabitants.* European Research Studies Journal Volume XXVII, Special Issue 3, pp. 17–32.

Calthorpe, P. 1993. *The next american metropolis: ecology, community, and the american dream.* New York: Princeton Architectural Press.

Cervero, R. and Guerra, E., Al S. 2017. *Beyond mobility: Planning cities for people and places.* Washington, DC: Island Press.

Chrysoulakis, N., de Castro, E. A. and Moors, E. J. (eds.). 2014. Understanding Urban Metabolism: A Tool for Urban Planning. New York: Routledge.

Collection Methodology for Key Performance Indicators for Smart Sustainable Cities // ITU URL: https://www.itu.int/dms_pub/itu-t/opb/tut/T-TUT-SMARTCITY-2017-9-PDF-E.pdf.

Conticelli, E. 2019. *Compact city as a model achieving sustainable development.* pp. 1–10. *In*: Leal Filho, W. and Azul, A. (eds.). Sustainable Cities and Communities.

Daly, H. and Farley, J. 2004. *Ecological economics: Principles and applications.* Washington, DC: Island Press.

Daly, H. 2007. *Ecological economics and sustainable development.* Selected Essays of Herman Daly. Cheltenham, UK & Northampton, MA, USA: Edward Elgar Publishing Limited.

Deakin, M. (ed.). 2013. *Smart cities: Governing, modelling and analysing the transition.* London: Routledge.

Dempsey, N. and Jenks, M. 2010. *The future of the compact city.* Built Environment. 36(1): 116–121. DOI: 10.2148/benv.36.1.116.

Denevizyuk, D. A. 2012. *Sustainable development of the city: Questions of the theory and methods of appreciation.* Regional'nyye problemy preobrazovaniya ekonomiki 2(32): 103–112.

Gehl, J. 2010. *Cities for People.* Washington: Island Press.

Geissdoerfer, M., Savageta, P., Bocken, N. M. P. and Hultink, E. J. 2017. *The circular economy—A new sustainability paradigm*? Journal of Cleaner Production. 143: 757–768. DOI: 10.1016/j.jclepro.2016.12.048.

Global Cities Report 2021 // Kearney . URL: https://www.kearney.com/global-cities/2021.

Global Power City Index. 2021 // Institute for Urban Strategies at the Mori Memorial Foundation . URL: https://mori-m-foundation.or.jp/english/ius2/gpci2/index.shtml.

ICLEI in the urban era. Our vision for a sustainable urban world. P. 25–29 // ICLEI URL: https://e-lib.iclei.org/publications/ICLEI_in_the_Urban_Era_2021.pdf.

Kennedy, C., Cuddihy, J. and Engel-Yan, J. 2007. *The changing metabolism of cities.* Journal of Industrial Ecology. 11(2): 43–59. DOI: 10.1162/jie.2007.1107Calthorpe P. The Next American Metropolis: Ecology, Community, and the American Dream. New York: Princeton Architectural Press, 1993.

Landry, C. 2000. *The Creative City: A Toolkit for Urban Innovators.* London: Earthscan Publications, 2000.

Makieła, Z., Stuss, M., Mucha-Kuś, K., Kinelski, G., Budziński, M. and Michałek, J. 2022. *Smart City 4.0: Sustainable Urban Development in the Metropolis GZM.* Sustainability 14(6), 2022, DOI:10.3390/su14063516, p.2.

Recommendation Y.4900/L.1600. 2016. Overview of key performance indicators in smart sustainable cities // International Telecommunication Union. URL: https://www.itu.int/itu-t/recommendations/rec.aspx?rec=12627.

Schiller, P. L. and Kenworthy, J. 2017. An Introduction to Sustainable Transportation: Policy, Planning and Implementation. London: Taylor & Francis Group.

SDG Index and Dashboards Report for European Cities // Sustainable Development URL: https://www.sdgindex.org/reports/sdg-index-and-dashboards-report-for-european-cities/.

Simon, D. (ed.). 2016. Rethinking sustainable cities: Accessible, Green and Fair/ed. by D. Simon. Bristol: Policy Press.

Smart Cities: Governing, Modelling and Analysing the Transition/ed. by M. Deakin. London: Routledge, 2013.

Tanguay, G. A., Rajaonson, J., Lefebvre, J. F. and Lanoie, P. 2010. *Measuring the sustainability of cities: An analysis of the use of local indicators*. Ecological Indicators 10(2): 407–418. DOI: 10.1016/j.ecolind.2009.07.013.

The Global Liveability Index 2021 // Economist Intelligence Unit Foundation URL: https://www.eiu.com/n/campaigns/global-liveability-index-2021/.

The Tenth Session of the World Urban Forum // UN-Habitat. URL: https://unhabitat.org/wuf10.

The Sustainable Cities Index 2018 // Arcadis. URL: https://www.arcadis.com/campaigns/citizencentriccities/index.html.

Transit Oriented Development in America: Experiences, Challenges, and Prospects (Report No. 102). Transit Cooperative Research Program // Valley Metro URL: https://www.valleymetro.org/images/uploads/general_publications/TCRP-Report-102_TOD-in-the-US-Experiences-Challenges-and-Prospects_10-04.pdf.

Understanding Urban Metabolism: A Tool for Urban Planning/ed. by N. Chrysoulakis, E.A. de Castro, E.J. Moors. New York: Routledge, 2014.

United Nations. Sustainable Cities Programme 1990–2000 // UN-Habitat URL: https://unhabitat.org/sites/default/files/download-manager-files/Sustainable%20Cities%20Programme%201990%20-%202000.pdf.

United Nations Conference on Environment & Development. Rio de Janerio, Brazil, 1992 // UN URL: https://sustainabledevelopment.un.org/content/documents/Agenda21.pdf.

Vienna Tops Mercer's 21st Quality of Living Ranking // Mercer . URL: https://www.mercer.com/newsroom/2019-quality-of-living-survey.html.

World's Best Cities to Live in 2021 // Best Cities. URL: https://www.bestcities.org/reports/2021-worlds-best-cities/.

Chapter 12

Towards Sustainable Manufacturing

Implementing Ecological Predictive Maintenance for Enhanced Efficiency and Environmental Stewardship

Marek Jabłoński,[1,*] *Adam Jabłoński,*[1] *Mariusz Bednarek*[2] and *Sławomir Luściński*[3]

Introduction

Ecological and intelligent production poses a significant challenge for modern factories. By implementing innovative and environmentally friendly strategies, manufacturing companies can achieve cost optimisation and enhance the effectiveness and efficiency of their processes, thereby improving the entire value chain. Production processes, equipment operation, and machinery maintenance require optimisation in response to market demands. Generally, consumers—even those not purchasing luxury goods—expect products to meet high-quality standards at the lowest possible prices. In recent years, societal expectations and legal regulations have increasingly focused on encouraging producers to adopt practices that help mitigate climate change, evidenced by the rise in adverse weather events. As customer preferences shift towards sustainable products and legal requirements evolve, companies must consider ecological criteria when evaluating their process sequences (Bergs et al., 2020, pp. 488).

[1] WSB Merito University in Poznań.
Email: adam.jablonski@ottima-plus.com.pl, OCRID: 0000-0003-4008-941X

[2] Institute of Management and Quality, WSB University in Poznan.
Email: mariusz.bednarek@ii4.pl, ORCID: 0000-0002-8402-4370

[3] Kielce University of Technology.
Email: slawomir.luscinski@tu.kielce.pl, OCRID: 0000-0001-7385-6668

* Corresponding author: marek.jablonski@ottima-plus.com.pl, OCRID: 0000-0001-7964-6522

Manufacturing companies should adopt business model configurations that prioritise pro-ecological strategies. They can leverage the principles of a circular economy and seek intelligent solutions through predictive maintenance. This approach aims to generate positive environmental impacts while enhancing product competitiveness, emphasising the synergy between these areas. Green production and maintenance should help reduce product costs without sacrificing quality. The overall configuration of the production system significantly influences ecological factors. The level of mechanisation directly affects the extent of negative impacts on environmental pollution. Clean production relies on optimising the value chain and integrating lean manufacturing principles. Innovations in material science, manufacturing technology, production sequencing, and assembly techniques can produce positive or negative environmental outcomes. Every value-creating activity has implications for these aspects. The production system's structure and the execution of processes reflect ecological considerations, provided conscious management decisions guide these actions.

This chapter aims to illustrate the relationships between the configuration of the production system, the methods used to monitor machines and equipment, and their impacts on the natural environment within the framework of ecological production. It addresses the role of predictive maintenance as a crucial factor in minimising the adverse environmental effects of production. Ecological maintenance based on prediction involves swiftly detecting anomalies—such as potential failures, defects, or irregularities in machinery operation—within the production process. This proactive approach can prevent adverse consequences, such as air and soil pollution or increased energy consumption, which can reduce the overall efficiency of the production system. It also affects cost-related elements of the value chain.

Mitigating climate change can only be achieved if product and process innovations are driven by ideas that promote positive ecological impacts across all production factors. This is possible when the configuration of the production system is optimised, and the manufacturing technologies are focused on minimising environmental impact. Furthermore, products throughout their lifecycle should be designed to serve as potential inputs for future production processes or services. Manufacturers can assess their processes in terms of resource consumption—such as materials and energy—and their outcomes to connect the environmental impact with the produced product. A digital twin can also be utilised in production as a crucial tool for collecting and transforming ecological data into actionable impact variables (Lürken et al., 2023, pp. 62-367). Examples of environmentally conscious manufacturing companies show that their approach can be based on applying the following maintenance management mechanisms. Consideration is given to the characteristics of spare parts (whether used or new) that will be utilised during maintenance operations (corrective or preventive) to reduce management costs, particularly the carbon footprint. The production process examined in this study produces one unique product type to meet random demand. A key aspect is ensuring an optimal production plan that minimises total inventory and production costs within a finite time horizon. The impact of this optimal production plan on system-level degradation is then considered to simultaneously determine the optimal maintenance plan and the optimal order quantity for spare parts (both used and new). This achieves a minimal level of global maintenance costs.

In some companies, environmental monitoring technology uses environmental sensors to conduct real-time monitoring and record ecological data during production. This is followed by correlation analysis with detection results to assess the production process's green performance further. The blue economy, green production, and green maintenance are leading trends in research in production management. However, innovative solutions based on traditional approaches, large datasets, and artificial intelligence within predictive maintenance frameworks require extensive research, conceptual work, and project design. They also require verification and validation of proposed projects based on ongoing research.

Assumptions of ecological production and the development of predictive maintenance concepts

Ecological production is based on minimising the negative environmental impact throughout the entire production process, from resource acquisition to product lifecycle management. The approach to ecological production plays a crucial role in rationalising energy consumption, reducing emissions, promoting a recycling-based economy, and fostering a resource-efficient and environmentally friendly society.

The most crucial leverage for creating the most sustainable production lies in the early stages of technology planning, as selecting sustainable technologies can avoid emissions in the long term. The literature proposes indicators for eco-economic assessment of production process sequences. An evaluation is conducted after quantifying all the necessary material and energy flows. The environmental impact assessment model can be based on material flow cost accounting. This model allows costs and environmental impact to be expressed in a single KPI. The results indicate that more than zero waste emissions alone is needed to provide sufficient resilience, a fundamental ecosystem requirement and a core principle of the blue economy. The blue economy extends the green economy by creating innovative processes that utilise waste as raw materials in multiple cycles, relying on biological processes that naturally occur in nature.

Production processes should align with ecological risk management methods to ensure resilience. This can be achieved by supporting adaptable production systems with flexible product portfolios, allowing companies to adjust production to technological and market changes. To achieve sustainable production, life cycle assessment procedures are proposed between processes to evaluate the various environmental effects of production and remarkably different designs and methods. This environmental assessment is often combined with an economic efficiency evaluation to provide an integrated assessment for designing production process sequences (Kiss et al., 2024, pp. 1).

To achieve sustainable production, life cycle assessment procedures between processes are proposed to evaluate the various environmental effects resulting from production, particularly for different designs and processes. This environmental assessment is often combined with an economic efficiency evaluation to provide an integrated assessment as the foundation for designing production process sequences.

The maintenance process, which must ensure equipment availability, reliability, and safety, is crucial in sustainable operations. However, how maintenance can integrate sustainability goals and contribute to achieving them needs to be clearly defined; there needs to be more research on this topic in the current literature.

Digitalising production process sequences and innovative methods based on big data offers excellent potential for academia and industry, particularly in green predictive maintenance. Developing such solutions contributes to implementing innovative approaches to predictive quality and generating digital twins for individual components, enabling online forecasting regarding quality, economy, and ecology. By applying systems-based analysis of the industrial area, it is possible to model complex systems to design and control mechanisms that create a system that ensures a more efficient flow of materials and energy. Such analyses can modify the structure of production systems by designing systems that more closely resemble a healthy ecosystem.

Extending the lifecycle of machinery and equipment supports blue economy strategies. Monitoring the results of life cycle assessments enables plant operators to select maintenance strategies that consider long-term ecological implications (Burggräf et al., 2020, pp. 320). Improving thermal efficiency in supply chain management within a green production process and assessing its comprehensive environmental impact is crucial in providing manufacturing companies with strategies and methods for optimising supply chain management (Liu and Wen, 2024). Maintenance plays a vital role in the path towards sustainable production. More data-driven predictive maintenance strategies are needed to achieve green production, focusing on reducing energy consumption, maintaining resources such as spare parts, and limiting consumables, such as lubrication. Predictive maintenance strategies aim to enhance equipment availability, reduce the hours spent on reactive maintenance actions, and increase profitability for the manufacturing company. A more integrated application of maintenance-related KPIs is required to pursue more environmentally friendly production (Rødseth and Schjølberg, 2016, pp. 36). The concept of green maintenance is based on the following assumptions (Ajukumar and Gandhi, 2013, pp. 34-46):

- Reduction of issues caused by leaks.
- Reduction of problems related to waste disposal operations.
- Reducing negative environmental impact by adopting effective waste processing principles.
- Encouraging organisations to use environmentally friendly maintenance materials, such as lubricating oils and cleaning agents.
- Maintaining employee health and safety by reducing risks associated with maintenance operations and using non-toxic materials.
- Utilising modern digital technologies in maintenance and moving away from traditional maintenance methods.
- Using energy-efficient materials and maintenance equipment

Sustainable development in maintenance requires a shift from the traditional "failure and repair" approach to a "predict and prevent" approach. In line with this, maintenance management must also focus on condition-based maintenance (CBM) and predictive maintenance (PDM). According to this trend, maintenance actions will only be carried out when a certain level of degradation is reached or when the predicted health condition of the system indicates the appropriate time to perform maintenance.

Management of production system configuration and the design of predictive systems with consideration of ecological factors

Reconfigurable Manufacturing Systems (RMS) represent sophisticated manufacturing paradigms capable of rapidly adapting to fluctuating market demands and production specifications. They encompass flexible components, including reconfigurable machinery and controllers, which allow for prompt modifications in both functionality and capacity. The classification of RMS can be delineated according to their types of flexibility, which encompass machine, routing, process, product, and volume flexibilities (Daniyan et al., 2024). The notion of RMS was conceptualised in the late 20th century, with seminal patents delineating its foundational principles and applications, thereby underscoring the imperative for systems adept at responding promptly to market fluctuations (Kumar et al., 2022). Table 1 presents a taxonomy of RMS.

The current design of manufacturing systems is based on the tenets of Industry 4.0, i.e., the optimisation of business operations through cyber-physical systems communicating with each other in real-time. In this case, analytical tasks are performed by both humans and IT systems. Production systems are often reconfigured for such purposes as, among others (Łukasik, 2020):

- achieving and maintaining a condition that allows the business to respond to predictable and unpredictable changes in the environment,
- achieving customer satisfaction in dynamically changing market conditions,
- running operations lean and innovatively to respond to change without compromising the business's health.

Reconfiguration is a quick change to the system structure (Garbie, 2014, pp. 891-915). The machinery that makes up the internal logistics structure supported by the maintenance systems must provide opportunities for product and volume changes, as this is necessary to achieve the above objectives. The prerequisite for change is compliance with the principles of Group Technology, i.e., similarity of parts, machines, and processes (Bednarek, 2016, pp. 59-81).

The reconfiguration of production systems must take ecological factors into account. According to the author's experience, such a trend is linked to the merging of Industry 4.0 and Industry 5.0, which are beginning to complement each other. Most companies expect the rapid development of digital technologies but must prepare for such a change. Leadership competencies become critical here. The organisation's preparation for such a transformation must be preceded by a reconfiguration of current processes and the preparation of employee teams for change. Otherwise,

Table 1. Taxonomy of Reconfigurable Manufacturing Systems.

Category	Subcategory	Description
Levels of Reconfigurability	System-Level Reconfigurability	It pertains to the comprehensive manufacturing system's capability to undergo reconfiguration. This encompasses alterations to the spatial arrangement, operational processes, and workflows, thereby facilitating the integration of novel products or variations in production volume.
	Machine-Level reconfigurability	It focuses on individual machines within the system. Machines can be adapted or retooled to perform operations and support different products or components.
	Control-Level Reconfigurability	Reprogramming or adapting the control systems allows for changes to operating sequences, process parameters, and coordination between different system components.
	Material Handling Reconfigurability	This is related to the adaptability of material-handling equipment. Conveyors, robots, and other handling equipment can be reconfigured to suit a new system layout or a new flow of products.
Reconfigurable Machines	Modular Machines	Constructed from modular components, these devices can be assembled, disassembled, or reconfigured straightforwardly. Additional modules may be incorporated or extracted to modify the machine's operational capabilities. This flexibility enhances production efficiency and allows manufacturers to respond swiftly to changing market demands or product specifications.
	Convertible Machines	These systems are meticulously designed to facilitate a fluid transition among diverse operational modalities or product categories with negligible physical modifications. Alterations are often implemented by calibrating settings or software configurations rather than requiring changes to the hardware itself.
	Scalable Machines	Facilitate modifications in production capacity. The operational output of the machine can be augmented or diminished through the incorporation or extraction of resources (such as spindles or tooling heads).
Reconfiguration Strategies	Modular Reconfiguration	The process entails modifying the system by incorporating or eliminating modules. This approach underscores the significance of adaptability and facilitates tangible alterations.
	Adjustable Reconfiguration	Modifications are executed without affecting tangible elements. This may encompass modifying machinery configurations, tool alignments, or procedural parameters.
	Adaptive Reconfiguration	The system exhibits autonomous adaptability in response to fluctuations in environmental conditions or shifts in production demands. It employs sensors and control algorithms to recalibrate operational processes in real time.

Table 1 contd. ...

Category	Subcategory	Description
Types of Reconfigurations	Physical Reconfiguration	The process necessitates modifications to the physical hardware components. This may encompass the relocation of machinery, alterations to tooling, or the reconfiguration of material flow.
	Logical Reconfiguration	Modifications are implemented in the control algorithms or software systems without necessitating alterations to the physical components, thereby facilitating the introduction of novel operational sequences or variations in product design.
	Software Reconfiguration	It encompasses enhancing or altering software systems to influence machinery's operational dynamics. This approach is frequently more efficient and economically viable than physical reconfiguration.
Degrees of Reconfigurability	Basic Reconfigurability	The degree of flexibility is constrained, permitting only marginal modifications or alterations. This framework is appropriate for systems characterised by minimal product or process variability.
	High Reconfigurability	Broad adaptability, facilitating substantial modifications in operational capabilities and performance. Particularly suitable for sectors characterised by swiftly evolving product designs.

Source: based on (Mechrabi et al., 2000, pp. 403–419), (Bi, 2008, pp. 967–992), (Koren and Shpitalni, 2010, pp. 130–141), (Koren et al., 2018, pp. 121-136).

digitisation and automation of processes with ecological considerations will fail. This requires the company to implement a new production process strategy (Xu et al., 2021, pp. 530-535). This new manufacturing strategy is to realise a product manufacturing process based on activities involving implementing Industry 4.0 and Industry 5.0 elements. It is preceded by the preparation of the company with the application of Lean Management principles, i.e., building an organisational culture, a company personality, taking care of its internal values and employees' understanding of the company's common goals. We will configure the production systems based on a modern production strategy, and this will be based on Industry 4.5.0. The KPIs of such a formulation will be based on footprint, such as material waste recycling rates and product recycling, for example. The configured production systems will require maintenance according to redesigned predictive maintenance systems.

Taxonomy and ontology of predictive systems—assumptions, differences, similarities, synergies

A taxonomy is the systematic division of a given group of objects into their constituent elements, sets characterised by specific properties (Ogólna Grupa, 1951). The attributes of the systematised objects are used to divide them, assign them to a specific set, and combine them based on individual characteristics. An essential area of taxonomy application is the part related to using quantitative methods. This taxonomy is often used in economics and technical sciences, where the need to categorise sets of variables describing a specific phenomenon is essential. A taxonomy is used as a collection of methods and tools, and its classification in terms of problem, solution and application criteria refers to a taxonomy of diagnostic techniques, simulation models and forecasting methods. A taxonomy including the following meta—characteristics: field of application, orientation as the goal of analysis, origin of data and analysis techniques, taxonomy of anomalies, use of different configurations of taxonomy elements to study their impact on overall performance, use of taxonomy to analyse failure modes in maintenance, taxonomy used to represent critical techniques and concepts, development of a taxonomy to classify predictive maintenance models. It allows comparison and analysis of such models, defined by the type of task, methods used, evaluation metrics, specialised equipment or process. A taxonomy is a way of classifying any objects according to a specific hierarchy.

Regardless of the type of predictive system, the analysis of maintenance process parameters could be more precise in predictive maintenance. Quantitative parameters characterise such a process. A taxonomic method was used to select the most relevant parameters for the predictive process. Heterogeneous variables describe each analysed process. This is because they represent different properties of the processes; hence, they appear in various units of measurement. It is, therefore, necessary to standardise them, and as a starting point for applying the taxonomic method, we will use a matrix /1/, where the variables will be included.

$$X = \begin{bmatrix} x_{11} \cdots\cdots\cdots\cdots\cdots\cdots x_{1n} \\ x_{21} \cdots\cdots\cdots\cdots\cdots\cdots x_{2n} \\ \cdots\cdots\cdots\cdots\cdots\cdots \\ x_{w1} \cdots\cdots\cdots\cdots\cdots\cdots x_{wn} \end{bmatrix} \qquad /1/$$

Standardisation is described by the formula /2/.

$$Z_{ik} = \frac{X_{ik} - \bar{X}_k}{S_k} \qquad /2/$$

where:

- the arithmetic means of the observations /3/:

$$\bar{X}_k = \frac{1}{W}\sum_{i=1}^{W} X_{ik} \qquad /3/$$

- the standard deviation /4/:

$$S_k = \sqrt{\frac{1}{W}\sum_{i=1}^{W} X_{ik} - x_k^2} \qquad /4/$$

Taxonomy organises concepts hierarchically, while ontology defines relationships and properties among those concepts (Fig. 1). Through structured knowledge representation, taxonomy enhances semantic interoperability in predictive

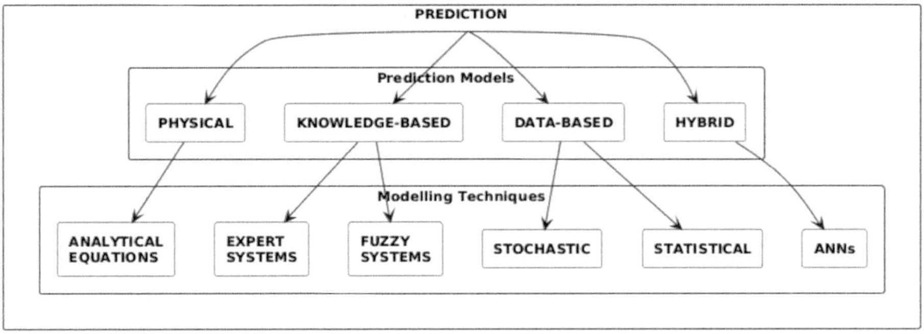

Fig. 1. Taxonomy of Predictive Maintenance System. Source: own study.

maintenance systems (May et al., 2022). The relationship between taxonomy and ontology in predictive maintenance systems is pivotal for improving operational efficiency and decision-making. Taxonomy classifies maintenance tasks, while ontology enriches this framework by defining the relationships and semantics of these tasks. This improves data interoperability and knowledge sharing, crucial for effective predictive maintenance systems (Gispert et al., 2023). Combining taxonomy and ontology fosters a comprehensive understanding of maintenance processes, improving efficiency and reducing costs (Nagy et al., 2023, pp. 1267-1272).

Figure 2 shows an example of the ontology of the predictive maintenance system.

Apart from published literature cases of ontology for PdM, existing public domain ontologies and established standards for condition-based maintenance are as follows:

1. MIMOSA CCOM (OpenO&M Initiative) (Mimosa.org, 2024) establishes a framework for condition-based maintenance and the management of asset lifecycles. It encompasses data models pertinent to asset management, facilitates interoperability across maintenance systems, and incorporates sensors, conditions, alerts, and maintenance intervention principles.
2. ISO 13374 (Condition Monitoring and Diagnostics of Machines) delineates the stipulations for data processing, communication, and presentation within condition monitoring. It provides an overarching framework for data acquisition and analysis and facilitates the advancement of predictive maintenance systems. This standard is crucial for organisations aiming to enhance operational efficiency and reduce downtime through timely interventions based on real-time data insights.
3. OSA—CBM (Open System Architecture for Condition-Based Maintenance) delineates standardised strata for systems operating on condition-based maintenance principles. It encompasses a tiered architectural framework that spans data collection to decision-making support, enhancing interoperability and modularity.

While the synergy between taxonomy and ontology significantly enhances predictive maintenance systems, challenges remain in effectively implementing

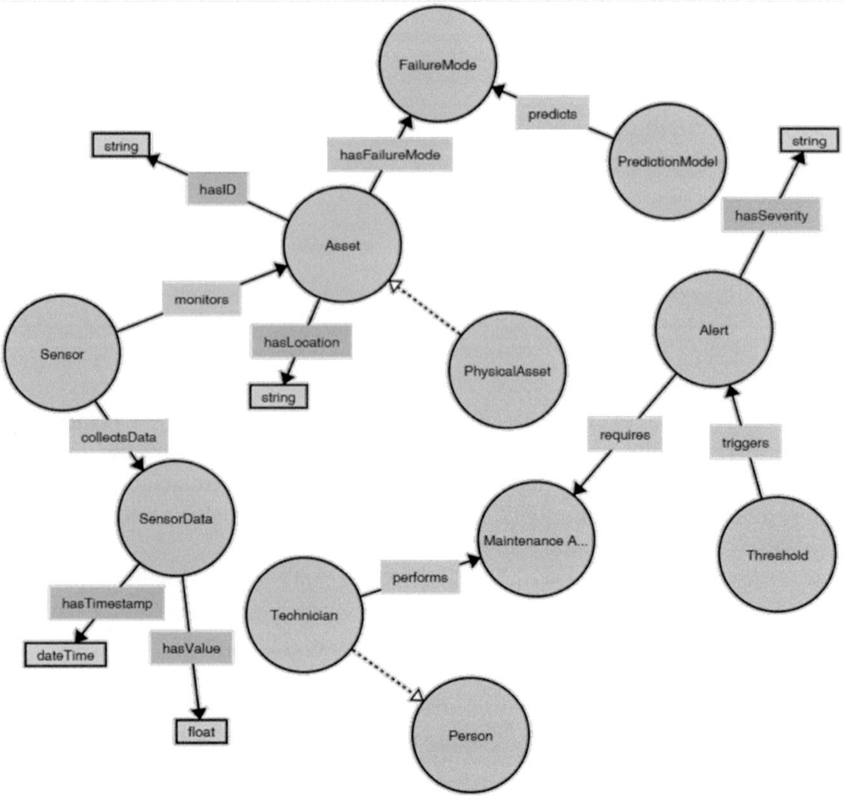

Fig. 2. Example ontology of Predictive Maintenance System. Source: own with using WebVOWL (Lohmann et al., 2015).

these frameworks, particularly in defining comprehensive ontologies that capture all necessary relationships and entities (Gispert et al., 2023).

Theoretical concepts for ecological predictive maintenance for manufacturing companies

Based on a critical literature analysis, a theoretical model of ecological predictive maintenance for manufacturing companies was developed (Fig. 3). It focuses on the dynamic management of production system change in the context of maintenance system determinants and the management of production system change for ecological optimisation.

The model introduces four modules functional modules:

(1) a **data acquisition module** using external sensors as well as sensors directly embedded in machine/process line components,
(2) an **artificial intelligence module** combining physical models, statistical models and machine learning algorithms capable of tracking individual machine health and handling a wide range of resources under dynamic operating conditions,

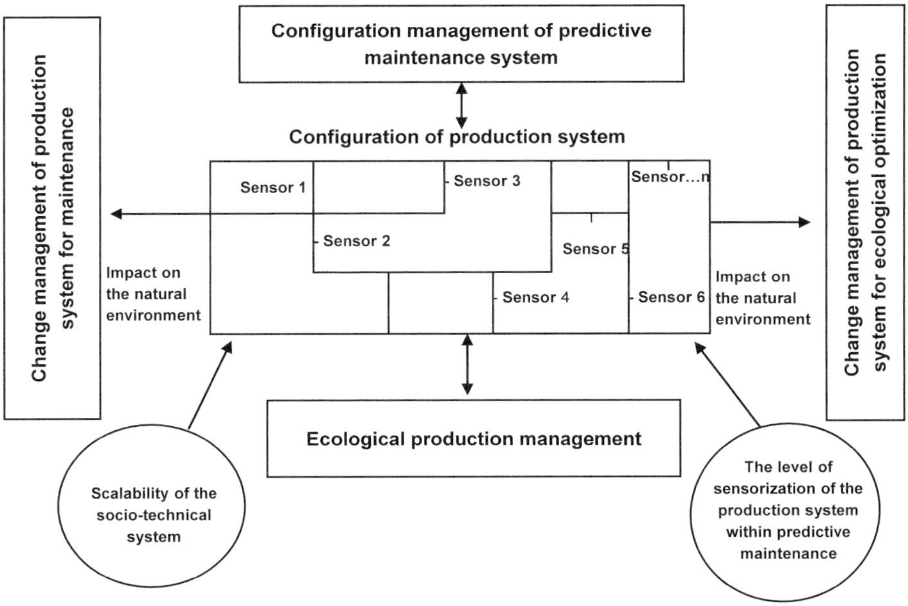

Fig. 3. A theoretical model of predictive ecological maintenance for manufacturing companies. Source: own.

(3) a secure **integration module** linking the platform to production planning and maintenance systems via a private cloud, providing additional security, along with self-diagnostic and self-learning capabilities,

(4) a **human-machine interface module** to support maintenance personnel based on a "virtual twin" and "augmented reality (AR)" model.

The configuration of the production system influences the level of machine sensing. The sensing level is adapted to the designed production system and its reconfiguration. The level of optimal machine sensing should be considered when considering changes in the production system. The sensors used are intended to monitor, in addition to variables directly related to maintaining the performance of machinery and equipment, environmental parameters such as energy consumption, consumption of maintenance resources in spare parts, consumption of consumables in terms of, e.g., lubrication, etc. The production system that influences the environment should not pollute it. Therefore, circular economy solutions replacing the linear traditional value chain with a closed system are recommended. The level of ecological impact is influenced by the effectiveness of the scalability of a socio-technical system such as a production system. This production-specific scalability also includes the predictive maintenance system. Scalability is only achievable when the number of sensors used for predictive maintenance allows effective monitoring of the designed, expected predictive variables. A predictive maintenance system loses the characteristics of scalability when further variables attached to the system adversely affect the system's ability to read and process information. An optimal level of system scalability must be maintained.

Discussion

Integrating ecological considerations into the framework of predictive maintenance methodologies within manufacturing systems signifies a profound transformation in how industries engage with sustainability principles and operational efficacy. As previously articulated, comprehending the interplay between the architecture of production systems and their ecological repercussions is paramount. The ramifications of adopting ecological predictive maintenance, the obstacles encountered, and prospective domains for future inquiry and practical application were delineated as follows.

The proposed ecological predictive maintenance theoretical framework highlights the necessity for adaptive management within manufacturing systems. Producers are positioned to achieve a dual benefit through the amalgamation of environmental surveillance and traditional maintenance indicators: enhanced operational effectiveness in conjunction with reduced environmental impacts. Integrating sensors that evaluate machinery functionality, energy usage, and resource allocation exemplifies a holistic strategy towards maintenance. This transition towards a more comprehensive comprehension of manufacturing processes is congruent with the tenets of the circular economy, wherein waste is mitigated, and the utilisation of resources is optimised more effectively.

Implementing such an extensive system is fraught with complexities. A primary concern lies in the intricacies associated with managing and interpreting the substantial quantities of data produced by a multitude of sensors. Although digital twins and artificial intelligence possess the potential to augment data analytical capabilities significantly, there remains an imperative demand for proficient personnel who can precisely interpret these results. Consequently, developing educational initiatives that prepare the workforce with the requisite competencies to navigate these sophisticated technologies and utilise them effectively for predictive maintenance is vital.

The interplay between taxonomy and ontology within predictive maintenance frameworks reveals potential advantages and inherent difficulties. Taxonomy is essential in the systematic classification of maintenance undertakings and procedures, while ontology enhances this classification by clarifying the interconnections and meanings associated with these undertakings. Formulating comprehensive ontologies that incorporate all pertinent entities, and their interconnections constitutes a formidable challenge that necessitates continuous inquiry and interdisciplinary collaboration. Subsequent research endeavours aim to develop standardised ontologies that facilitate interoperability among diverse predictive maintenance systems, enhancing their overall efficacy.

Scalability is significantly affected by the rigorous observation of particular predictive variables. It is imperative to achieve an optimal equilibrium between the quantity of sensors deployed and the system's ability to process data with efficacy. Excess superfluous information may result in diminished performance, thereby underscoring the necessity of strategic sensor positioning and proficient data administration.

Lastly, ecological predictive maintenance's potential to significantly alleviate climate change's repercussions holds critical significance. Producers are pivotal in advancing a more sustainable future by enhancing production methodologies and minimising waste output. The advantageous environmental repercussions of such systems may also improve corporate reputation and foster increased consumer loyalty, as many consumers prefer enterprises that emphasise sustainability.

Conclusions

Integrating ecological considerations into predictive maintenance represents a significant advancement in manufacturing, underscoring the dual imperatives of sustainability and operational efficacy. Manufacturers can simultaneously elevate their commitment to environmental stewardship and enhance productivity by formulating a framework for ecological predictive maintenance. This innovative strategy leverages sophisticated technologies such as sensors, artificial intelligence, and digital twins to monitor and refine production processes continuously. As industries endeavour to reduce their ecological footprints, comprehending the interplay between production configurations and environmental repercussions becomes increasingly imperative. Adopting predictive maintenance methodologies that prioritise sustainability augments performance metrics and aligns with the tenets of a circular economy, thereby fostering resource efficiency and minimising waste generation. However, obstacles persist, particularly about intricate data management and the necessity for proficient personnel. Ultimately, ecological predictive maintenance possesses considerable potential for addressing climate change challenges. By refining production methodologies and curtailing waste, manufacturers can significantly contribute to advancing a sustainable future while enhancing their corporate image and aligning with consumer inclinations toward sustainable practices. Adopting these innovative solutions is crucial for thriving in an increasingly environmentally conscious marketplace. In conclusion, the shift towards ecological predictive maintenance signifies a noteworthy progression in manufacturing methodologies. Although challenges remain, particularly in data management and the development of comprehensive ontologies, the prospective operational and environmental benefits are substantial. Future inquiries should focus on refining these systems, establishing standardised protocols, and fostering collaboration across diverse sectors to fully capitalise on the advantages of ecological predictive maintenance within the manufacturing domain. Producers can enhance their competitive standing by adopting this progressive methodology while contributing significantly to worldwide sustainability efforts.

References

Ajukumar, V. N. and Gandhi, O. P. 2013. *Evaluation of green maintenance initiatives in design and development of mechanical systems using an integrated approach*. Journal of Cleaner Production 51: 34–46.

Bednarek, M. 2015. *Zastosowanie Lean Manufacturing w Polsce i w Meksyku. Modele-praktyka, doświadczenia, Difin*, pp. 59–81.

Bergs, T., Grünebaum, T., Rey, J., Barth, S. and Goldmanns, M. 2020. *A methodology for the ecological and economic assessment of manufacturing process sequences*. Procedia CIRP 90, pp. 488.

Bi, Z. M. 2008. *Reconfigurable manufacturing systems: The state of the art*. International Journal of Production Research 46(4): 967–992. https://doi.org/10.1080/00207540600905646.

Burggräf, P., Wagner, J., Steinberg, F., Heinbach, B., Wigger, M. and Saßmannshausen, T. 2022. *Life Cycle Assessment for Adaptive Remanufacturing: incorporating ecological considerations into the planning of maintenance activities – a case study in the German heavy machinery industry*. Procedia CIRP 105, 3p. 320.

Daniyan, I., Sibanda, P. S., Adediran, D. A. and Aderoba, O. 2024. *Towards Reconfigurable Production Systems and Technologies in the Manufacturing industries: A Framework* doi: 10.1109/seb4sdg60871.2024.10629808.

Garbie, I. H. 2014. *A methodology for the reconfiguration process in manufacturing systems*. Journal of Manufacturing Technology Management 25.6: 891–915.

Gispert, D. E., Yitmen, I., Sadri, H. and Taheri, A. 2023. *Development of an ontology-based asset information model for predictive maintenance in building facilities*. Smart and Sustainable Built Environment, Vol. ahead-of-print No. ahead-of-print. https://doi.org/10.1108/SASBE-07-2023-0170.

Kiss, T., Hetesi, Z. and Kiss, V. 2024. *Ecological design of a production plant*. Ecological Economics 224: 1.

Koren, Y., Gu, X. and Guo, W. 2018. *Reconfigurable manufacturing systems: Principles, design, and future trends*. Frontiers of Mechanical Engineering 13(2): 121–136. https://doi.org/10.1007/S11465-018-0483-0.

Koren, Y. and Shpitalni, M. M. 2010. *Design of reconfigurable manufacturing systems*. Journal of Manufacturing Systems 29(4): 130–141. https://doi.org/10.1016/J.JMSY.2011.01.001.

Kumar, V., Ramesan, S., Kumar, V. and Madan, A. K. 2022. *Reconfigurable manufacturing system: A review*. International Journal for Science Technology and Engineering, doi: 10.22214/ijraset.2022.40594.

Liu, Y. and Wen, Z. 2024. *Green manufacturing process supply chain management based on thermal efficiency improvement and environmental impact assessment technology*. Thermal Science and Engineering Progress 54, Art. 102847.

Lohmann, S., Link, V., Marbach, E. and Negru, S. 2015. *Online tool for interactive visualisation of ontologies. WebVOWL*. Available at: https://service.tib.eu/webvowl/#file=PM_Semantic.ttl (Accessed: 7 October 2024).

Łukasik, P. 2020. *Rekonfigurowalne systemy produkcyjne–kierunki badań i zastosowania,* Akademia Zarządzania 4.4.

Lürken, C., Grünert, G., Stauder, L., Barth, S. and Bergs, T. 2023. *Concept for life cycle oriented ecological assessment in tooling*, Procedia CIRP 120, 3p. 62–367.

May, G., Cho, S., Majidirad, A. H. and Kiritsis, D. 2022. *A semantic model in the context of maintenance: A predictive maintenance case study*. Applied Sciences 12: 6065–6065. doi: 10.3390/app12126065.

Mehrabi, M. G., Ulsoy, A. G. and Koren, Y. 2000. *Reconfigurable manufacturing systems: Key to future manufacturing*. Journal of Intelligent Manufacturing 11(4): 403–419. https://doi.org/10.1023/A:1008930403506.

Mimosa.org, News (no date) MIMOSA. Available at: https://www.mimosa.org/ (Accessed: 7 October 2024).

Nagy, L., Ruppert, T. and Abonyi, J. 2023. *Towards an Ontology-Based Fault Detection and Diagnosis Framework - A Semantic Approach*. 9th International Conference on Control, Decision and Information Technologies (CoDIT), Rome, Italy, 2023: 1267–1272, doi: 10.1109/CoDIT58514.2023.10284094.

Ogólna Grupa Zastosowań Państwowego Instytutu Matematycznego. „Taksonomia Wrocławska." Prz. Antropol 17(1951): 193–211.

Rødseth, H. and Schjølberg, P. 2016. *Data-driven Predictive Maintenance for Green Manufacturing, International Workshop of Advanced Manufacturing and Automation* (IWAMA 2016), pp. 36.

Xu, X., Lu, Y., Vogel-Heuser, B. and Wang, L. 2021. *Industry 4.0 and Industry 5.0—Inception, conception and perception*. Journal of Manufacturing Systems 61(2021): 530–535.

Index

T

U

V

About the Editors

Adam Jabłoński is Full Professor and Head of Management and Quality Institute of WSB MERITO University in Poznań, Poland, Email: adam.jablonski@ottima-plus.com.pl

Is also Vice-president of the Board of a well reputable management consulting company "OTTIMA plus" Ltd. Katowice and President of the Association "Southern Railway Cluster" Katowice which supports development in railway transport and innovation transfer, also towards cooperation with European railway clusters (European Railway Clusters Initiative member). He holds a Postdoctoral degree in University of Łódź, (Department of Management), POLAND, specializing in Management Science (Business Models, Strategic Management). Working as a management consultant since 1997, his experience and expertise has grown through his contact with a number of leading companies in Poland and abroad. He is the author of a variety of studies and business analyses in the Strategic Performance Management Concept, Value Based Management, and designing of Digital, Social Business Models fields. He has also written and co-written several monographs and over 100 scientific articles in the field of management, published both in Poland and in abroad. The scientific interests of Adam focus on the issues of modern and efficient Strategic Management methods and new approach to the designing of strategic group of key performance indicators and the principles of company value building sustainable strategy. It tries to integrate assumptions strategic management with configuration approach to the shaping business models, and monitor and evaluate their effectiveness. He explore also various features of modern strategic measurement systems and operationalization of strategy and business models oriented for achieving of high performance. Currently, He is also a member of Scientific Boards of International Journals (inter alia Management Decision (Impact Factor – 5.589) and/or he is the Scientific Reviewer in different entities (USA, India, Canada, Switzerland) and in Scientific Boards of National Journals and He is a Scientific Reviewer in many entities. He is also Member of Academy of Management, USA. Author of numerous monographs, publications, articles and scientific concepts published in Poland and internationally in prestigious publishing houses, including Taylor & Francis Group—Routledge, Palgrave Macmillan, Springer Nature, Nova Publishers, IGI Global. Author of many scientific articles published in world-renowned journals. Speaker at many scientific and industry conferences and congresses. Initiator of many scientific and business ventures.

Marek Jabłoński is Associate Professor of Management and Quality Institute of WSB MERITO University in Poznań, Poland, Email: marek.jablonski@ottima-plus.com.pl

Marek Jabłoński—holds Associate Professor, PhD in Economic Sciences, specializing in Management Science, disciplines—Value Based Management and Performance Management Concept, business models of companies in early stage of development, Startup expansion), green strategies of enterprises. He is an Professor in University of WSB University and President of a well reputable management consulting company OTTIMA plus Ltd. in Katowice (Silesia Region—South of Poland).

He is also a Vice-President of Southern Railway Cluster, which supports development in railway transport and innovation transfer, also towards cooperation with European railway clusters (European Railway Clusters Initiative member). Working as a management consultant since 1999. His experience and expertise has grown through his contact with a number of leading companies in Poland and abroad. He is the author of a variety of studies and business analyses in the enterprise value, risk management, balanced scorecard, business models, Startup strategy, entrepreneurships. He has also written and co-written over 10 monographs and over 200 scientific articles in the field of management. The scientific interests of Marek Jabłoński focus on the issues of value based management concept and creating value of companies in early stage of development, climate changing aspects and influences it for industry and business models of companies. He is also expert in management of safety in railway enterprises. Author of numerous monographs, publications, articles and scientific concepts published in Poland and internationally in prestigious publishing houses, including Taylor & Francis Group—Routledge, Palgrave Macmillan, Springer Nature, Nova Publishers, IGI Global. Author of many scientific articles published in world-renowned journals. Speaker at many scientific and industry conferences and congresses. Initiator of many scientific and business ventures.

For Product Safety Concerns and Information please contact our
EU representative GPSR@taylorandfrancis.com Taylor & Francis
Verlag GmbH, Kaufingerstraße 24, 80331 München, Germany